PRAISE FOR THE MODERN FORTUNE TELLER'S FIELD GUIDE

"As a writer, teacher, and tarot reader, Tom Benjamin is the most wonderfully tempered blend of a warm, supportive friend with a sharp, witty, "tell it like it is" provocateur. In *The Modern Fortune-Teller's Field Guide*, he challenges readers to dig deep and discover just what we mean by fortune and fate, truth-telling and empowerment. While poking at our fears, biases, and unconscious loyalties and assumptions, he simultaneously provides a comfortable, conversational container to support our growth. Anyone who strives to be a modern soothsayer (truth-speaker) would do well to immerse themselves in Tom Benjamin's delightfully stimulating Socratic schooling."

– Lane Smith, author of *78 Acts of Liberation: Tarot to Transform Our World*

"In a modern tarot landscape where 'fortune telling' is taboo, *The Modern Fortune Teller's Field Guide* is a searingly insightful, rigorously considered, and delightfully witty love letter to fortune telling as truth-telling. Tom Benjamin reveals the liberatory potential of fortune telling as a practice that inherently resists oppressive power structures and reconnects us with our capacity to interpret the future and contact the Divine. This book will challenge your preconceptions, shore up your foundations, open your mind and heart, and make you a more skilled, courageous, and *truthful* reader. Whether you are a beginner or an expert, *The Modern Fortune Teller's Field Guide* is an absolute necessity for tarot readers and diviners of all levels. People say that about a lot of books, but in this case, it›s true. I wish I›d had this guide at the beginning of my tarot journey, but I›m so grateful to be learning from it now, twenty-something years later. I love this book!"

– Charlie Claire Burgess, author of *Radical Tarot, Fifth Spirit Tarot, The Gay Marseille Tarot*, and *Queer Devotion*

"Tom Benjamin's *The Modern Fortune Teller's Field Guide* dismantles tired stereotypes and reframes fortune telling as an act of truth-telling, resistance, and liberation. This book offers an ethical framework for reading today, while highlighting that modern fortune telling draws on Romani and other often-erased or appropriated BIPOC divination traditions. With humor, humility, and a refreshingly iconoclastic voice, Benjamin invites readers to embrace the discomfort, curiosity, and power of this work with an aim to be a more effective and grounded reader.

– Jezmina Von Thiele, co-author of *Secrets of Romani Fortune-Telling*

"If you're in love with the tarot but find your practice needs some shaking up, *The Modern Fortune Teller's Field Guide* is just the jolt that will wake up your readings. Tom Benajmin's real talk will have you confronting any comfortable notions you have about divination and turn your practice inside out and possibly even upside down (and I don't mean reversals). Like a trickster friend who calls you out to get you thinking, Tom's humorous and engaging writing and the unique exercises he gives throughout will open your eyes to fresh new ways of working with the cards. If you're willing to let go of those pearls you're clutching, you'll find deep wisdom in this book and most assuredly will never see fortune telling the same way again."

– Madame Pamita, author of *Magical Tarot, The Witch's Guide to Animal Familiars, Baba Yaga's Book of Witchcraft,* and *The Book of Candle Magic.*

"If I had to describe *The Modern Fortune Teller's Field Guide* in a single word, that would be "necessary." Tom Benjamin's work touches poignant subjects that most shy away from, in both divination and life, and offers technique, encourages skill development through self-awareness and, above all, gives back legitimacy to prediction in a world in which it's treated like a dirty word."

– María Alviz Hernando, author of *Tarot Tableau Revolution*

"For anyone brave enough to don the mantle of Fortune Teller, Tom Benjamin's book is a candid, thought-provoking guide that strips away the stigma from this often maligned and misunderstood approach to divination."

– Elliot Adam, author of *Fearless Tarot* and *Tarot in Love*

"This is not your grandma's tarot guidebook. It's a bold and much-needed step towards a new era of divination. It shook me up and rewired my brain in the best possible ways. This is a must-read for any cartomancer who is serious about walking a path of authenticity, compassion, and real-world impact."

– Liz Worth, author of *The Power of Tarot* and *Going Beyond the Little White Book*

"This is the book I have been waiting for. It boldly demolishes dogma and fiercely promotes creativity. It's filled with energizing mindset shifts to help you examine your insecurities as a reader, strengthen your practice, and clarify your approach to working with querents. It encourages you to ask deeper and more complex questions about your role as a cardslinger. This book manages to be playful and heartwarming whilst also being deadly serious and -at times- divisive. Tom Benjamin gives Tarot its rightful place in our consciousness, through highlighting its truth-telling potential and honouring its marginalised, political nature. By the time you finish this book, you will be more in love with Tarot and more solid in your foundations as a fortune-teller."

– *Kelly Ann Maddox,* author of *Rebel Witch*

"*The Modern Fortune Teller's Field Guide* pushes past stereotypes of carnivals and con artists to reveal author Tom Benjamin's deep, rich, and insightful reflections on the politics, ethics, and praxis of divination. Tom's philosophy and sense of humour make this an essential guidebook for anyone who divines. Beginner or professional, this book›s engaged approach is guaranteed to amplify every fortune teller's practice."

– Amy Torok, co-author of *Missing Witches* and *New Moon Magic* and co-creator of *Missing Witches Deck of Oracles* and *The Missing Witches*

"*The Modern Fortune Teller's Field Guide* offers nuanced yet practical insights and clear guidance to working as a knowledgeable fortune-telling professional, to being on the ground and in the action of saying *What is and what will be* because that›s the only way to really learn. And I wouldn't expect anything less from a talented reader, teacher, and writer like Tom. But Tom's book isn't just a guide to fortune telling as a craft. It's also the real-life story of becoming and unbecoming and becoming a diviner once more, much bolder and truer as a result. And that's something that will resonate with and give hope to so many readers who have been on that same circuitous path (or who will be at some point). Tom›s done it the hard way so you don›t have to. In *The Modern Fortune Teller's Field Guide.* Tom reminds us that there's always a reason to come back to the questions at hand and many, many ways to do it."

– Thomas Witholt, founder of Hermit's Mirror and author of the *Seaborn Kipper* and *Tarot Tableau: The Fool's Journey*

"This is the book I have been waiting for. [illegible] profound [illegible] our practice [illegible] working with questions [illegible] deep [illegible] complex questions about your role [illegible] this book [illegible] whilst also being [illegible] Tarot a rightful place in our consciousness, through highlighting its multifaceted potential and grounding its [illegible] political nature. By the time you finish this book, you will be more in love with Tarot and more solid in your foundations as a [illegible] reader."

—[illegible], author of *Rebel Witch*

"*The Modern Tarot* [illegible] and [illegible] deep [illegible] of the political, ethics, and practical [illegible] Tarot philosophy [illegible] essential [illegible] book for anyone [illegible]"

—[illegible]

"[illegible] and [illegible] the only way to really learn. And I wouldn't expect anything less from a [illegible]"

"[illegible] we don't have to [illegible] *The Modern Tarot* [illegible] reminds us that there's always [illegible] to come back to the questions at hand and [illegible] many ways to do it."

—[illegible] and *The Tarot's [illegible]*

THE MODERN FORTUNE TELLER'S FIELD GUIDE

ABOUT TOM BENJAMIN

Tom Benjamin is your friendly neighborhood fortune teller. From a childhood terror of tarot, to a reader and teacher with twenty plus years of experience, Tom's aim is to help seekers get the answers they need to all of life's puzzles and to help students find their unique voices as card-slingers. Through a popular YouTube channel, @thefoolsjournal, online courses and workshops, as well as the independently-published *Tarot on Earth* and *Your Tarot Toolkit,* he shares tips, techniques, and even some affectionate slandering of long-beloved dogmas, in the belief that finding your own path is the only way to grow—whether you're a client or a student.

For more, visit:
Instagram: @TomBenjaminTarot
Bluesky: @TomBenjaminTarot
Youtube: TheFoolsJournal
www.TomBenjaminTarot.com

THE MODERN FORTUNE TELLER'S FIELD GUIDE

TOM BENJAMIN

FOREWORD BY MARIA MINNIS

Paperback ISBN: 978-1-964537-45-0

Library of Congress Control Number on file.

Published by:
Crossed Crow Books, LLC
518 Davis St, Suite 205
Evanston, IL 60201
www.crossedcrowbooks.com

Printed in the United States of America.
IBI

TABLE OF CONTENTS

ACKNOWLEDGEMENTS

To say that I'm the king of typos would be an understatement. I also possess the uncanny ability to write a sentence that made sense to me in the moment and that never makes sense to anyone (including me) ever again. This is why editors make my admittedly ornery heart sing. In this case, Lee and Bridget managed to navigate my text and somehow make sense of phrases where each and every word held the gift of an error. Thank God there are meticulous people in the world.

Writers want to feel loved and needed and even fawned over. Blake and Gianluca made me feel like the prettiest dame in the gin joint when I sent this book to Crossed Crow. What more could a Leo need? Thank you, lovely humans. And further thanks to my pal Gianluca for just being among the daupest people in the world and for supporting my work as a reader and teacher.

When I saw the finished product, I said, "Our cover is so fucking metal!" Gabriella rocked this one. I want it on T-shirts. I want to see those T-shirts at merch stands. Where? I don't know. But it deserves it.

I hate having my picture taken. Brittany Taylor made me feel fun, funny, and cute. I told her I wanted people to see the photos and think, "That guy is fun to talk to. I want to hang out with that dude." She served it. I look more welcoming in my photos than I manage to be IRL.

I've never taken a tarot class, but people in the tarot community have given me the gift of their wisdom in ways I probably don't deserve. Those who have had the biggest impact on my worldview in the tarotscape include: Maria Minnis (who wrote the wonderful intro to this, and who was the very first person I asked!), Queen Auset, Aunty K, Lane Smith, Kelly-Ann Maddox, Charlie Claire Burgess, Cassandra Snow, and Havana (Sparkle Divine Tarot); some of whom I have met in real life or have gotten to know rather well, others have never met me. But these and others have helped shape my understanding of the world. Camelia Elias and I are very different readers, but I'm a great admirer of her work and ethos. I've taken lenormand classes with her and admired like hell the precision with which she reads. Her influence is all over my work. As is Robert M. Place's writing—another person I really could not be more different from, but whose techniques have changed the way I read for the better. I also give so much credit to Wald and Ruth Ann Amberstone, both for the work they've given to the tarot world, and also for creating the amazing Reader's

Studio in New York, which remains among the biggest learning experiences of my life—and usually also the most fun. Esther Frankel Tischman and Veronica Jude are two pals from Reader's Studio who I miss and admire. (There are many others. Names are so hard for my poor, addled brain.) I also think it's beyond necessary to thank Kelly Fitzgerald of The Truth in Story, who, it can be fairly said, essentially created and sustained the online tarot community for a big chunk of the 2010s. Without that community, this book would not exist—including the shit that sucked.

I don't always agree with them, but I thank the divinatory ancestors. Among them, Rachel Pollack, Eden Gray, Lady Frieda Harris, Pamela Colman Smith (who, yes, we have some issues with—but let us acknowledge the iconography she created), as well as Etteilla (who I don't really work with, but who I think would have been very into what we're doing today) and even the man who problematically called himself Eliphas Levi (we owe the modern Baphomet to him). I will begrudgingly also include Waite and Crowley—though they know what they did and they are not out of timeout.

Then there are my "students." I adore working with you and I frequently think I learn more from you than the other way around. I include in this those who have been loyal viewers on YouTube for years, even if I don't know you.

Thanks, too; the people who have fucked me over or made my life harder. You don't deserve it, but it made me grow. I'm cooler despite you.

And finally, my peeps: Liz W., Nancy, Derek, Barbara, Holly; my familia, including mom, dad, Lauren, Em, and most importantly Handsome Klaus the Wonderpup; tarot friends who I don't see much, but who I will always be grateful for: Kelly Bear, Gavin, Igor, Gianluca, Lucas, Maria Alvis Hernando, Alana, Jason, Jose, Oliver, all the badass folks from Reader's Studio, and many, many others that I feel bad for not mentioning, but those were the names at the top of my IMs when I wrote this!

Oh, and you—if you're reading this.

It's an honor to be part of this conversation. Thank you.

—TB

PREFACE

Some Important Contexts Before We Start

As a frequent skipper of prefaces and forwards by authors, I hesitated writing one. But I do think it's necessary that I share a few important contexts before we dive in.

This book is about being a reader more than it's a book about how to read. It is a how-to book, but the text that fills these pages explores how to be a really good fortune teller in the world—how to move through life as a reader. Brilliant existing works cover the foundational how-tos of reading tarot, lenormand, and casting (the three methods I use as examples here), along with just about all other open forms of divination. I offer recommendations at the end of the book, but use what you're drawn to.

For the sake of clarity and avoiding awkward sidebars and endless footnotes, this book explains certain social topics as though the reader isn't entirely familiar with them. This is purely to invite those who don't know into the conversation without them having to raise their hand and ask the question. Many of you may already know what I'm saying, in which case simply know you can skim those parts. The aim was as broad an audience as possible, in the hopes that as many folks as want to can come hang out in these pages. (While noting that I'm bringing up topics early on that will turn some folks off, my hope is for curiosity. And I'm inviting the magic of the divinatory ancients to flow through these words—from them through me, to the page, and to you—and in so doing ignite a sense of curiosity and wonder. It'll do you good!)

Speaking of those topics: language changes, as it should. At one point in history the English world *girl* meant a child assigned male at birth. Yes, *girl* once meant *boy*. (You can find valid, trustworthy citations for this all over the web.) We need language to change because we need new ways to talk about our evolving perceptions. These days, language changes faster than ever. What is trendy and appropriate as I write this paragraph was not when I wrote the first draft of this book—and what is trendy and appropriate by the time this lands in your hot little hands will likely be different, too.

This book uses the most inclusive, appropriate language that I understood at the time of writing and editing it. "People of color," for example, is (rightfully) transitioning to "people of global majority," and the book follows suit. "Latinx" is giving way to the more linguistically apt "Latiné" (in my experience, typically pronounced Lateen-ay). These terms and phrases will evolve because they have to. As will other terms I've used. I point this out only to say that the attempt during writing and editing was to use both the most appropriate language, and also to refer to communities by the language they themselves prefer to be used in reference to them. But at the time you're reading this, some of that language may seem fusty, dated, or—potentially—out of touch and problematic. As of June 2025, what's printed here is a record of language today. Please know that if I've used a word or phrase here that in the future is offensive, while intent is less important than impact, the intent was to include rather than exclude—and you belong here, too. If there are ever future editions of the book, I will do my best to update such language because words matter. (This is not the case when referring to groups who use their power to exclude and harm. I talk about them however I want to, and will continue to do so until global atonement is taken on by those groups.)

Throughout the work I try to make the effort to acknowledge that the names we know many countries by today (including the United States) aren't the names given to those lands by the people who rightfully belong here. Thus, these aren't the names of those places; they're colonial titles. As was explained to me (I can no longer recall by who), the "US" is a political entity settling land that "belongs" (that word is tricky) to the indigenous population. That's cumbersome to write each time, as, indeed, are other variations on that theme. After working with my editors, it became clear to me that many of my attempts looked cumbersome at best and performative at worst. Let it be known, then, that I agree with the explanation of the "US" above and that I truly believe there will not be peace on this planet until all the stolen land is given back, reparations are made, and global atonement takes place. In the text, I try to not merely accept the popular names but to, in some way, indicate that these names aren't real. Frequently I'll use quote marks, as I did two sentences ago. Again, I hope you'll pardon the clumsiness and appreciate the reminder that something's ubiquity does not equate with its legitimacy.

With all that said, let's jump in. We have some cool shit to talk about.

—TB, June 2025

FOREWORD

Whenever I pick up a book, I make sure to have a pen and paper nearby. I process through writing, so I take notes to synthesize quotes, capture aha moments, and collect journaling prompts. When I reviewed my notes from *The Modern Fortune Teller's Guide,* it seemed like I'd written and underlined the word "fortune" a million times. I felt perplexed, like this was my first time noticing the word even though I've read, written, and spoken it plenty of times. Staring at a single word long enough can make it appear almost foreign.

The concept of fortune was a familiar one, but I realized that I never once stopped to ask, "What does that even mean?" I would use it casually and monolithically, a term I could interchange with "luck" or "abundance" without thinking twice. But now it didn't even sound like a word when I said it aloud. Confused, I opened my computer and searched "fortune definition."

The first search result was from the Cambridge Dictionary, which described *fortune* as "chance and the way it affects your life." I read it a few times, uttering "hmm" and "huh" as I realized I wasn't any closer to the clarity I'd sought. So, I got curious. It was my first time explicitly considering *chance* as an inherent component of fortune. With this fresh perspective, I returned to my notebook. Everything I wrote meant something different now. I added a new line: "Telling someone a fortune is telling someone about chances."

Fortune telling is an ancient practice and this book expertly illuminates it through the lens of navigating the modern world. My identity exists at many intersections, which often feels like a liability in a structurally and intentionally oppressive society led by absurdly wealthy bigots and their relentless sycophants. They are unapologetic in their racism, misogyny, ableism, classism, and other beliefs that convince them that they are the archetypes of "normal" human beings. Everyone else is an aberration, a deviation.

Even as these voices denigrate and violate, I continue to write about ways that we can individually and collectively get free. Make no mistake, I'm not immune to disillusionment. When your heart breaks, it's hard not to feel hopeless. But I'm ultimately resolute in my belief that a different world is possible. I know a more equitable future exists, even if I can't witness it in my lifetime. I need to believe in order to survive. How could it feel worthwhile to persist in a violently oppressive and manipulative society if I didn't trust in even the slightest potential of a more ideal future for "aberrations" like me?

To get free, we need to believe in chances.

Fortune telling in a modern world involves reminding ourselves and each other that there are many roads to freedom, that there's a chance that something we don't realize—can't even currently perceive—could manifest. To believe in chances is to trust in the reality that our paths are often nonlinear. And this might feel threatening to oppressors who dictate to their subjects that their way is The Only Way™. It's unsurprising they would suggest this—how could one resist a tyrant if they could not perceive a life without tyranny? Modern fortune telling reminds us that there's a chance that all we know isn't all there is.

Or, at least, that's how I feel. One of my favorite parts of *The Modern Fortune Teller's Guide* is when Tom pointedly states, "I don't 'get' to define fortune teller for you. No one does." I agree. Fortune tellers don't dictate how your life should be or will be. Instead, they reveal what might happen if you take a chance in writing your own story, to take a chance in defining how you are affected and what you are affecting. Fortune tellers can help us evolve the way we perceive the past, present, and future. And evolving a more ideal tomorrow starts with evolving our perspectives today.

As you move through this book, I encourage you to consider the context in which you are reading it. Tom writes, "divination is political." How does your practice ripple out into the world? What are the stories you're telling yourself, and how do they play into the greater story of humanity? And what could be the fortune in all of this?

The fortune is ours to tell.

—Maria Minnis
author of *Tarot for the Hard Work*

CHAPTER ONE

THE FORTUNE TELLER TODAY

Who Did What, Now?

Martin Luther King Jr. was a fortune teller. So, too, were Audre Lorde, bell hooks, and Larry Kramer. Marsha P. Johnson and Sylvia Rivera? Fortune tellers, both.

Would any have identified that way? Likely not. None of them slung cards. They didn't *need* them. They saw the world as it was, as it could be, and where it needed to be. None of them mistook the road for an easy one, none of them shied away from that. This didn't stop these folks, whose names ring through time, from saying what they saw—from telling the future, the fortune that could be *if only*....

But, you see, this took doing what others fear so much: seeing the world as it is and then telling that truth regardless of who wants (or wants *not*) to hear it.

That's why they were fortune tellers.

I'm not comparing my work as a card-reader to the life-changing, epoch-changing work of these civil rights icons. This, instead, is an invitation to consider *beyond the stereotype* of the fortune teller so that we can reclaim that term and contextualize it as a role necessary in modern life. I don't know whether these folks would enjoy my classing them with card readers, but they were and are our modern prophets.

It hasn't always been this way, but today, fortune tellers are among the more derisive figures in pop culture—only when they're accepted as having any power, of course. Generally, they're reviled as dangerous and dismissed as frauds. Those who say there's no such thing will also advise you avoid visiting one. Amazing, isn't it, how bias can both negate your existence while also calling you a threat to society?

The popular impression of the fortune teller as a con artist isn't an accident. It is a message carefully crafted by Christian colonial (henceforth *christo-colonial*) power structures to delegitimize practitioners of divinatory arts, happily taken up by our entertainment industrial complex. Conjure a fortune teller in your mind right now and many of you will see a wizened Romani woman in headscarf and colorful raiment, a wicked pack of cards tucked into her skirts. She's wise but dangerous and likely to toy with you as soon as you cross her withered palm with silver. Oh, she'll give you the answers you seek, but there will be a *price*. And why shouldn't you think that? European christo-colonial powers have loathed the Romani since they first "discovered" them and have made it their mission to dehumanize and criminalize this community. After denying them "real" work and relegating them to the margins where things like fortune telling and witch-doctoring were the only options, these powers then set about making fortune telling and healers illegal. Ask any non-traditional healer today the hoops they have to jump through to avoid running afoul of the American Medical Association and you'll see the ways in which this christo-colonial power is alive and well—and dictating the course of our wellness today. (I'm not anti-medicine, before you get anxious. I'm simply anti-bias.)

A fortune teller isn't any better or worse than any other tradesperson, but the societal view of them is deeply impacted by racism, sexism, classism, and often anti-queerness. It has historically been women, people of global majority, queer people, and impoverished people who practice these arts. In some cases, that's because these "survival jobs" were all that was available. In other cases, these communities practiced it because they emerged from a culture in which divination was always part of everyday life. Either way, it is bias and not con artistry that paints the fortune teller with such a negative brush. It went from an intentional attempt to discredit anything considered un-Christian (despite the Bible being *riddled* with fortune tellers—prophets, lot-casters, dreamers, and the like) to a cultural bias that extends today, even into divination communities.

It's also worth mentioning that this has left some descendants of these communities ambivalent and even resentful of fortune telling in particular and divination generally. How could it not? If you are forced to do something and then reviled and criminalized for it, no matter how much you may love it or how talented you might be, there's going to be (to put it mildly) mixed emotions at play. And because of this, some contemporary members of these groups may reasonably say that the term should be retired—or that it belongs only to people whose ancestors suffered with the title in years prior. That's incredibly fair. At the same time, there are also folks in these communities who practice the art of fortune telling and love and appreciate it, despite the realities of history. Both of these can be (and are) true at the same time. No one group is a monolith; no one person can speak for their entire community. And while this book is about the *idea* and even the *reclaiming* of the term and role *fortune teller*, it's ultimately about our worldview and behavior more than what we choose to call ourselves. The main thing in terms of our self-identification as readers is that we don't intentionally commit the sin of rehashing old biases that have existed in the divination world for years.[1]

When I began reading Tarot in the dying embers of the 1990s, the anti-fortune telling view had a powerful hold on the tarot landscape. The American Tarot Association, whose mission was to reclaim tarot *from* fortune tellers, admonished us

---

1 For an exploration of how this history has impacted one community, and for two members' feelings about it, see the wonderful book, *Secrets of Romani Fortune Telling* by Jezmina Von Thiele and Paulina Stevens.

(I think without foreseeing the consequences—ironically) that fortune tellers were frauds, and that "real" tarot readers didn't practice it. They argued that the focus of the cards should be psycho-spiritual self-reflection, not prediction. A "real" reader wouldn't ever do a reading about someone who wasn't present and who hadn't asked for a reading, nor would one read on "serious" topics like health or wealth. And I eagerly ate up these talking points, because fortune telling scared me. Why shouldn't it? I'd seen the movies with the old lady pointing an arthritic finger to the dreaded Death card and watched the look of panic spread across the doomed client's face. I didn't want to do *that*. I certainly didn't want it done to me.... But I did want tarot.

The attempt to rehabilitate the image of tarot wasn't without merit, but the effort focused on a symptom, not the disease. In retrospect, the aim shouldn't have been to rescue tarot from fortune tellers, it should have been to rescue fortune tellers from the pop cultural bias that assumed anyone who picked up a pack of cards for anything other than a game of Old Maid was a con artist out to defraud the public. It is privileged to say, "Oh, I'm not a fortune teller. I use the cards for *good*." And that is what we were doing. I do think this work brought more people into the tarot fold, but I also think it furthered the attitude that fortune tellers are criminals, and that's no good.

As you wander through these pages, let's explore not how to save divination tools from some nefarious stereotype of fortune tellers, but how to reclaim the role—and honor our spiritual ancestors in the process.

What s a Fortune Teller?

It might sound shocking to say at the beginning of a book about it, but I can't define fortune telling for you. No one can. You have to do that for yourself. It's not really my place to do that, for various reasons, not the least of which is none of us gets to speak for the entire divination world. We need a common language to explore together, however, so I'll share my current thinking. But this is the beginning of a conversation, not the end of it. My hope is that more will come—more conversation, more divination, more reclaiming, and more honoring of those who came before—and in all of that, a vision of the fortune teller of the future will emerge and evolve collectively.

When asked, most people that I spoke to in divination circles define fortune tellers as those readers who predict the future. That's for sure part of it, and it's definitely what prompted me to take this journey. I don't think that's all there is to it, though. I do believe predictive reading is essential to the fortune teller's toolkit because it flies in the face of societal norms that deny humans a personal connection with the divine. In fact, I think that's why Christianity hates it so much. Fortune telling is *competition*. Why pay a priest when you can speak to the divine directly? Prediction isn't what makes the fortune teller societally unacceptable, it's the middle finger to convention. But when we look around today, we discover there is a deep craving for liberation from convention, gatekeeping, and biased norms. And so the time of the fortune teller has returned! (Insert deliciously wicked laugh here.)

Fortune telling is a political role simply because fortune tellers thumb our nose at musty power structures. We don't *care* what anyone believes, what anyone thinks about us, or about anyone's NDAs, gag orders, codes of silence, codes of conduct, or limited world view. We use whatever divinatory tools we find effective to reflect the world as it is to clients who want to know about it. And I have no proof, but I think that's because divinity doesn't care about any of those things, either.[2] Dogma is human made. Fortune tellers don't care about dogma—including dogma that tells us what we can and can't do as diviners—which is why it's important that I not be the sole source of your definition of fortune telling. If what I set down here is taken as gospel, it becomes dogma, and thus another way of gatekeeping and limiting—which would be fundamentally against everything I'm saying. This is why it's a *good* thing when you disagree with me, because in the tension between a point of view and a disagreement with that point of view is the opportunity for a perception shift—for both of us.

By taking up the mantle of fortune teller, we are aligning ourselves with a traditionally marginalized group. These truth-tellers throughout history suffered at the hands of christo-colonial invaders and human traffickers, at their inquisitions and revivals. Today, anyone can buy a pack of cards and set themselves up as a reader. More and more diviners, witches, and other alt practitioners are able to "come out of the closet" publicly (depending, of course, on where they live) without much hassle. We aren't, at the moment, the lightning rod for political and religious fundamentalism—not as much as we used to be. We have the luxury of walking into any mass market bookstore in most of the industrialized world and picking up a divination tool of some kind and various books to learn with. But it may not stay that way forever, particularly if the political spectrum keeps moving as it is.

It's disrespectful not to honor those who came before, who suffered for their art so that we could practice it today, and who will be essential guides when/if the fundamentalists come for us again. The aim of this book isn't to sound alarmist, but I do want to ground present-day diviners in the luxury we hold—the privilege we have—and how things *could* change. I hope we never have to face what our predecessors did, but we cannot be divinatory ostriches; we have to understand that tides come and go, and while so-called "Christians" are focused presently on ruining the lives of trans children, that doesn't mean their attention won't spin back to us at some point. Hate works that way.

If one reason for divination is to see our lives and our futures more clearly, then diviners must make sure we remain alert to the realities of life today. We must look

---

2 Author Anne Lamott says, "You know you've successfully created God in your own image when it turns out he hates all the same people you do." So take my impression of the divine with a grain of flavorful, high-end finishing salt.

at the world through un-tinted lenses. We have to. And this will change you. I don't want to scare you, but it will. Or it should. In fact, if you find yourself unchanged during your lifelong journey with divination, that might be a sign you're protecting yourself from discomfort (we'll talk about that more).

It's essential that we not only see the dangers facing fortune tellers, but more importantly and more urgently that we also see the dangers facing humans generally. We need to see the realities of racism, misogyny, queerphobia and anti-queerness, ageism, ableism, and all the biases woven into society so strongly that many of us (especially those of us who are white and male) can't even notice them. This is where I know I start to lose people, but I promise you: if you can't handle what I'm saying right now, then you're simply not up to the challenge of being a diviner. If you refuse to see the world the way it is, then I do believe you are perpetrating a fraud—if for no other reason than that you're giving your clients inaccurate readings because you can't see clearly. If you are someone who doesn't like to be challenged, divination isn't for you. If that sounds a bit like gatekeeping, that's understandable. But we have to recognize that there is a difference between gatekeeping (using influence and power to prevent others from access) and telling tough truths. This is truth-telling, which is what fortune tellers do. It doesn't mean you can't become someone who likes to be challenged. I hope you do. But if you aren't, and you don't get over that, you shouldn't be doing this. Not just because seeing the world is essential, but because you'll also be making your own job harder. Our divination tools can't tell us about things we don't think exist or have no concept of. How can you see in a reading what you don't even think exists? We have to understand life and its nuances in order to read about life and its nuances.

Happily, most people drawn to divination are also rebels, and as soon as we realize something we've held on to is actually manipulative dogma, we can't wait to toss it into the bin. Which is another good thing, because fortune tellers are *iconoclasts.*[3] I love that word. That's *exactly* what we fortune tellers are. Just by existing, just by saying that we do not need the auspices of church leaders or governments to get the answers to life's biggest and smallest questions, is iconoclastic because so many of the power structures that exist in this world are only powerful because we *give* them that power. It is a revolutionary act to take power back. It is iconoclastic, it is subversive, it is everything we know we need. And it's not just fortune tellers who do this: it's witches and activists, and anyone who refuses to hand over their power to systems designed to hurt all of us (even as they benefit some of us).

---

3 Once, when I pitched a breakout session for a tarot conference, the person who managed that part of the event called my idea *iconoclastic.* I didn't know what it meant and I had to go look it up, and I fell in love. If, like me, you didn't know that word, it means "a person who attacks cherished beliefs or institutions." *Isn't that so sexy?* Dear god, if I had a crush on someone and they called me an iconoclast, I'd buy them a *house.*

No, fortune telling does not equate with active resistance. But it contributes to the destabilizing of poisonous systems by thwarting norms that were always problematic.

Divination *is* political—but only if you think that liberation, freedom from oppression, and the massive inequities that keep children starving, men mentally ill and undiagnosed, women without rights, people of global majority oppressed, and Indigenous people off their lands is political. If you accept that all of those are simply truths that need telling, divination isn't political at all, it's simply another thorn in the side of the empire. But if you feel this is all "too political," I invite you to pause and consider why. Why are you interested in divination in the first place, when society says it doesn't exist and it's merely the tool of fraudsters? What is it you're reading about, if not how to get out of the ruts and valleys created by oppressive systems? What are you centering, if not a connection to something bigger than you? Even if your readings are self-centered (not a bad thing), aren't you taking power into your hands, and so don't others deserve to be able to discover they can do the same? Ask yourself those questions honestly and then pick this book up again and keep going. If you're drawn to this work, then you have to recognize that the "normal" methods of getting answers didn't work for you. And if that system is faulty, why can't so many others be faulty, too?

The ability to see and understand the impact of all these issues and more make a fortune teller a *fortune teller.* It's really just *telling the truth.* That's it. Seeing the truth in a reading means seeing the truth in the world around us. That's not political, that's just logic. Whether the truth is about *what is* or about *what is to be* doesn't matter—that's merely timing.

Every time I say something in this book that you feel is "too political," I invite you to come back to the questions I asked above. Attempt to see what I've written through those questions. You don't have to agree with me; again, this isn't dogma, it's seeds. I'm a work in progress, too. I'm not perfect. I don't have it all figured out. But I have lived a little and I know a few things, now. If it still is too much, do a reading about why. Sit with it. I've had to do that and still do. This is a lifelong journey.

Nobody said being a fortune teller was comfortable. Comfort isn't what we're after, because comfort prevents growth. Discomfort is *good.* This book is designed to make you uncomfortable. (It's also designed to amuse, too, so I hope that's clear.) It made me uncomfortable writing it. I set out with a lot of questions I didn't have answers to and had no one to rely on but myself. But that's good. Divination is an act of discomfort. Enjoy it. Fetishize it. Kink it up. Because it's going to be a constant companion.

Disempower to the People?

Modern pop divination is obsessed with empowerment. The argument goes that predictive readings disempower clients by presenting a fatalistic worldview. Nonsense.

The implication seems to be that prediction is bad, but advice is fine.[4] Think of the last time you gave a friend really good advice. Did they take it? No! People don't take advice because we're stubborn and we generally don't learn until we burn our hand on the hot stove we were told not to touch. People hate being told what to do. You know it, I know it. It sucks.

Let's play for a moment. Imagine a mirror—just a normal one, not some fairy tale thing. Assuming you use one (not everyone cares to), consider *why* you use it. When someone looks in a mirror, what are they seeking? This banal non-fairy-tale mirror lacks vocal cords, so it's not saying anything; it's not giving advice. Hell, if you're not an animist, it even lacks life. It's not telling you, "Hey, you gotta pluck that big old nose hair," or "Girl, your roots are showing." It doesn't tell you to change your shirt because it's stained; it doesn't tell you to wipe toothpaste off your face. It can't. So, what does it *do?*

It *reflects*. That's it. Just reflects.

And that's actually kind of magical. Consider:

Even when people want advice, when we ask for it, we listen politely…and then we still go off and do whatever the hell it was we were going do already. Advice is kind of a waste of time. But we *do* react to our reflections, don't we? We pluck the nose hair and change the shirt. We don't get pissed at the mirror or fight with it. It's not the mirror's fault we look stupid in a peacock green satin onesie and Count Orlok mustache. We might get pissed—but only at ourselves. Then, we just make the change. Great readings do this, too! They reflect our clients back to themselves. They can react or not just as they would to looking at their mirror image. And because they figured it out on their own, they're more likely to make the adjustments necessary.

A reflection is more empowering than advice, even though many, many readers make advice their ethical bread-and-butter. If advice is wasting everyone's time, wouldn't it be more empowering to do a reading about something else? Why not find out what the client is thinking about and predict how that will work out for them. Reflect the potential to them. Let them figure out what action to take. *That's* empowering!

Now, look: a lot of readings are advice-based, despite my dissing them just now, and it's fine.[5] This gets us to the main idea, here: painting everything with generalities isn't useful and it isn't what fortune tellers do. The assumption that

4 There's also been a focus on psychology which has placed many readers in the not-very-wise role of unlicensed clinician. This is bad, too. Just because we know therapy words doesn't mean we're therapists. Frankly, a prediction seems more reasonable than anything else!

5 It's just that the person getting the reading probably won't take it. Ya know. No big deal. Wink.

a predictive reading is disempowering when an advice reading isn't is biased. It's also reader-centric, because it centers the reader's ego over the client's agency And, hey: some clients are going to make stupid choices. That's part of being a person![6] Nothing is all one thing and there are no rules in fortune telling. Reflective, predictive, and advice readings are all valid. And even when we try to give "just the facts, ma'am," we sometimes have to give advice—either because it's what the reading is saying or because we can't help ourselves.

A predictive reading can be shockingly empowering when it shows the client something they don't want to see. It's the mirror showing you that puce is not your color, at least not today. It's showing you a thing so you can evaluate whether you'd like to keep it that way. And that's in the cases where the thing is changeable. Not everything is, and that's another thing we need to consider. Sometimes the advice has to be, "You can't change this, you do not have agency right now." That's helpful to know, if only because it can stop someone from fighting a battle they absolutely can't win. Sometimes there's no empowering certain people in specific situations. When we try to empower someone who lacks autonomy, we risk disempowering them. If the reading tells me that you need to go back to school and you're living paycheck to paycheck, trying to care for three kids and work two jobs, my advice ain't remotely empowering. It is a reminder of how unfair the system is.

Later in the book we'll explore the idea of *agency,* meaning those times when the client has power and control and times when they don't. But this is a good time to point out another reason why we need to see the world as it is. Modern divination is super in love with *"manifestation."* And it's exhausting as fuck. With apologies to influencer white ladies in big hats gleefully extolling the power of vision-boarding your way to your very own Becky's Dreamhouse—*no.* You did not manifest that, friend. Look, positive thinking is great if you're disposed to it and it works for you. But you also need to accept that a positive outlook is a privilege many people don't have access to. Either their body chemistry refuses to allow it, their social conditions prevent much optimism, or a host of other nuanced reasons you may or may not believe exist. You cannot positive-think your way out of multiple sclerosis, poverty, the school-to-prison pipeline, abuse, or depression. Full stop. It might help you endure it, but it ain't gonna change it. And any reader who presents that as advice to someone living in one of those conditions is displaying a massive lack of humanity and humility.

Want to talk about *disempowerment?* Tell a struggling single mother of five to go back to school. Tell a Black boy who just got knocked down by the cops to embrace his inner badass. Tell a trans kid to just be themselves when their schoolmates brutally assault them emotionally and physically every single day of the year. That's disempowerment right there. I have zero respect for readers who refuse to see that

6 By the way, it's not our job to judge their choices.

not everyone can "manifest" themselves a better job or a new home. That is more dangerous than a predictive reading presenting to someone that their lover is cheating when they're not. It's more dangerous than nearly anything a diviner can do, except perpetrating a series of scams. It is, to my mind, criminal to present that kind of tone-deaf reading to anyone.

Yes, friends, *sometimes* The Empress is your inner badass. Sometimes, though, she's a woman in power who actively prevents other women from succeeding because she doesn't want the competition. We have to see this, folks, whether we want to take up the title of fortune teller or not, because spiritual bypassing is just *cruel.* Fortune tellers aren't cruel. Even giving bad news can be generous. But pretending the world is nicer, kinder, more equitable than it is? That is just mean and there's no other way to say it.

The point is: question everything. That's what fortune tellers do. We don't just accept what we're told, we hold it to the light and figure out what's true. Hell, maybe we do readings about it. "How bad is it for me to tell clients when their significant other is cheating?" Everything we've learned, even our fondest tactics and techniques, benefit from scrutiny. Because if what we think is empowering turns out not to be, sometimes even the opposite of it, then what other things may be more layered than we thought?

Ethics

A client once sat at my table and I asked what she wanted a reading about. Her face changed and she told me about another reader, one who had given her a horrible prediction that had ruined her quality of life. Privacy prevents elaboration, but sharing even this allows me to point out that fortune tellers cannot behave like free-for-all hacks who shoot indiscriminately. There are consequences.

It's weird to discuss ethics in divination because it risks dealing in dogma. But just so we're all singin' from the same song sheet, let's consider: Traditionally, ethics in the divination landscape have been based on anti-fortune telling nonsense. Predictive readings and readings about health, wealth, and law were also discouraged, as well as third-party readings.[7]

I understand it differently now. Ethics has less to do with what you read about than how you handle yourself and your client. Read about whatever, honestly. I feel that more and more. Who cares? Back in the day, if someone asked about health, I'd say "go see a doctor." It never occurred to me that saying that implied the client had access to a doctor, insurance, the ability to afford treatment, and the

7 Third-party readings are readings about someone who isn't there and hasn't asked for one. Say I'm reading for you about your ex-boyfriend and he doesn't know—that's a third-party reading.

time to take off work.[8] I'm not saying you have to do health readings. I rarely do them because I'm as afraid of the AMA and shady lawyers as anyone else. But if you've got a client you know cannot risk taking too many days off work and they want to know if their condition is serious enough to warrant an expensive trip to the emergency room, there's an earnest argument that it's ethical to *try*. We worry we'll be wrong, I know. We're not doctors. I wouldn't recommend making this your calling card. But if the reading can give the client justification for getting care, that's *good*. People avoid getting help. When they reach out for a reading, they're reaching out for help they view as safe. Sometimes, they need someone safe to give them courage to do the thing they want to avoid. Enabling people to do the right thing for their own health isn't unethical.

It's *unethical* to poison someone's well, like the story fragment I shared earlier. My client had a reader who ruined her sense of wellbeing so badly that anxiety now ruled her life. By predicting a deadly outcome (which turned out to be incorrect), that reader did something profoundly unethical.

Wald and Ruth Ann Amberstone, co-founders of The Tarot School and The Reader's Studio in Queens, New York, have said that readings should be three things: surprising, helpful, and true. They go on to say that if it can only be two of those things, it should be helpful and true. And if it can only be one, it should be true. If you are going to reveal a message that you know, or merely *think*, will terrorize the client, then you better be damn sure that prediction is both *helpful* and *true*—because if it's not, it is simply *fucked*. If you tell someone they're dying—whether it turns out to be true or not—and there's nothing they can do about it, you've robbed them of whatever chance of joy they had in the time they've got left. And I know because someone did that to me. It wasn't until much after the time of my supposed finale—*twenty years later*—that I finally relaxed. You have not become a fortune teller in doing something like that; you have become a cruel egotist and thief of joy.

It's also unethical to say you can do things you can't and taking people's money for services you can't render. Calling yourself a fortune teller and then perpetrating a fraud is gross. You're doing damage not only to the client but to the good work of *actual* fortune tellers. Reading about a pregnancy has nothing to do with ethics and everything to do with boundaries and cosmology.

Now, the sad reality I have to point out is that many states in the political entity known as the "US" have anti-fortune telling laws on the books, usually unenforced but not toothless. Discover, if you can, what is legal and not in your location. That's not always easy. The area now known commonly as the state of Rhode Island, where

8 By the way, for those of you who can't handle hearing about "privilege," I just demonstrated what it is without having a meltdown. Because I had access to a doctor and insurance, I could afford treatment; it didn't occur to me other folks couldn't. It's literally *just that*.

I live, has conditional language and that makes it vague. For example, it requires a license for setting up services as a "fortune teller, palmist or phrenologist." Card reading doesn't factor in. Or *does* it? I call myself a fortune teller, but I don't do any of the things the law explains. So, what's the deal? Of course it's semantic. But protecting yourself from these christo-colonial laws designed to uphold classist, misogynistic, and white supremacist systems and the generally Christian-centric focus of our "justice" system is wise. That's just a matter of practicality. I'd like to see us smite all those laws from every book, but following them doesn't make you "ethical." It makes you safe from *prosecution.* Whether something is legal or not doesn't make it ethical. Capitalism isn't ethical, and it's legal as fuck. Is *fortune telling,* even if it lived up to its vilest stereotypes, really worse than *capitalism?* I'm gonna go out on a limb here and say, "Nah, fam."

What makes you an ethical reader is really all we've talked about so far—being able to see the world as it is, avoiding spiritual bypassing and biased thinking, telling the truth—but doing so with humanity and humility, giving a middle finger to unjust systems, and playing your part in the liberation of anyone experiencing oppression, including those fortune tellers (whether they knew it or not) who came before us.

This isn't ultimately about what you call yourself, though I think there is power to reclaiming, evidenced by the evolution of the word *queer* in modern life. Whatever title you give yourself, what matters more is your worldview. That's the deeper thing we're after here: thinking like a diviner unbound by dogmatic strictures and inequitable, biased thinking. Whatever you call yourself is up to you, but centering this worldview will make you a fortune teller whether you want to call yourself that or not. At least in my view.

The Future

As we work through this book together, we'll explore an array of concepts meant to inspire you on your fortune telling journey. You may even get some insight (I hope!) into your liberation journey. Some of what comes will seem, at first, unrelated to divination, but they're concepts I feel have been absent from divinatory conversations. This includes chapters on the human ego, as well as how to teach and how to learn. I encourage you to take the journey of each chapter even if it doesn't seem relevant at the moment. There will be, I feel strongly, something in even those seemingly off-brand chapters that can inspire a perception shift. (I've also left little gifts at the ends of those chapters to entice you.)[9]

This chapter is in many ways the most forthright, but I'm too old to mince words. I've learned the hard way that being "nice" never gets us anywhere and usually means swallowing bitter pills with zero health value. I want you to understand that

9 Evil laugh, mustache twirl.

though I have strong feelings about aspects of what we do, it is because I believe in the possibility for us all to contribute to a better world, even through spiritual work (but not exclusively).

By taking up divination in a world of not only right-wing religious fundamentalism, but also of fundamentalism from supposedly open-minded scientists who shit on anything they can't immediately explain (which is of course the very *opposite* of the scientific method), you're already making an iconoclastic choice. Why not take it all the way while you're at it?

CHAPTER TWO

GETTING ON THE SAME PAGE

As I said in the last chapter, I can't define fortune telling for you. No one can. But nothing else that follows will make much sense if I don't give you insight into how I've come to think about fortune telling and divination. Because I'm very much a work-in-progress, so are these explanations. As always, this is the beginning of a dialogue. These aren't prescriptions; they're impressions. And though it seems like a one-way experience, you're having reactions to things I've written all the time—so even though I don't know what those are, we are still engaged in a dance, which is nice. You're under zero obligation to agree with anything I say about how I understand things, although I hope it inspires something. And you don't need to agree with me here for the rest of the book to make sense. But when I interpret cards or reference techniques throughout the text, knowing how and why I do what I do will help you understand how and why I arrived at the conclusions I do.

What Is Divination and How Does It Work?

I think of divination as an act of translation. In this case, it's a tool used by a reader to take messages that can't normally be heard from a divinity who sees what we can't. I chose the word *divinity* because I don't have a better word, or one that feels less cringe, and since it's got the same root as "divination," we'll settle on that. Note that I allow it a lower-case "d" because I don't yet know whether it requires proper noun status, and, anyway, grammar is primarily a gatekeeping construct meant to harm people who can't afford college.[10] (So, take that.)

It really doesn't matter what you use to divine. It's helpful if whatever you use can be randomized—so cards, dice, dominos, household curios, and bones make really good choices. There are static divination tools—like divining rods and scrying

10 Alas, this is true. One of the things I learned in school was that the study of English was designed to give the middle class reason to look down on, and then exploit, the poor. Nothing is as innocent as it seems, friends.

mirrors or crystals—too, but like the randomizable ones, they require some sense of how to use them before they can be used.

Finding Foundation

Here's where I might edge close to gatekeeping. Stick with me. Social media has presented to many people the idea that you can be anything you want simply by calling yourself that thing. You want to be a witch, you're a witch! Want to be a tarot reader? Poof, you're a tarot reader. It doesn't matter whether you know what you're doing or not; if you can dream it, you can be it. There's something incredibly inclusive about that. But let's be totally honest: it's also somewhat naïve. Wanting to be something isn't the same thing as being it. I might want to be a surgeon, but that doesn't make me one. And it is difficult, because I strongly believe that gatekeeping is bad. But I also strongly believe that if you're going to present a skill to the world, and in particular ask people to pay you for that skill, you should actually have the experience to back it up. And most people who pick up a pack of cards don't immediately transform into a reader.

When I was starting out as a playwright, I used to hear all these other writers use the word "aspiring" to introduce themselves. "I'm an *aspiring* playwright," they would say, meaning, *I want to be a playwright.* And I'd swing back-and-forth on how I felt about that. On the one hand, if you've written a play, then you're a playwright. Right? You've done the thing that playwrights do. On the other hand, is writing a play *all* that makes you a playwright? Plays aren't novels. They're not meant to be read, they're meant to be produced. Are you really a playwright if you haven't been through the production process in which a play is *really* made? It is in the act of collaborating with actors and directors and designers that the play becomes a play; before that, it's a script. So, isn't it more accurate to say you're a *scriptwriter* rather than a *playwright,* if we're being honest? Or is it being pedantic? I don't know. It often depends on my mood.

Are you a fortune teller just because you call yourself one? Are you a tarot reader if you pick up a deck of cards and call yourself a tarot reader? I mean, *sure.* Why not? And aren't credentials and formal learning just the union of capitalism and gatekeeping? Yes to that, too. Yet, by that logic, anyone who has a medical textbook and a scalpel can call themselves a doctor. And I don't want to go to some rando for my hernia. Know what I mean?

There *are* folks who pick up a divination tool and immediately hear it singing. There *are* geniuses and savants in the world, to be sure. Most of us aren't, though, so—whatever way you choose to do it—if you're starting out in divination, I do feel that *some* kind of foundational learning is important. And, really, that has more to do with the diviner than my feelings about who gets to call themselves what. Frankly, we'd all do well to stop titling ourselves and let our work speak for itself—but here I've written a book about being a fortune teller, so clearly I'm not past my own need to label things, am I?

A foundation is good for you as a reader no matter what system you work with because there are times when the tools stop singing. Not to say you lose your gift, per se. But where readings usually feel like casting your eyes along a supple swath of satin, it suddenly feels like you're rubbing sandpaper into your retinas. The wise, inevitable interpretations that appear for the naturally gifted can suddenly give way to readings that feel like a slog. It is in these moments that having a foundation helps. When the tools ain't singin' as they usually do, you're going to have to start digging into what you know about the "meanings" of the items in front of you. You can still get a good reading, even though it's harder. But if you don't have a system to rely on, you're going to find yourself staring at a lot of meaningless junk—until you eventually give up.

I say this because I've experienced this. Learn from my mistakes. I always do everything the hard way. It's annoying. You don't have to. I beg of you, if you don't have a foundation, build one. When you look back on your life, I promise you will not regret it (and, if you do, well...it's too late at that point, so who cares?)

There's no shame in technique, my friends. There's no embarrassment, either, in being a student. In fact, this book has a whole chapter dedicated to how to be a student because it is *that* important to your career as a fortune teller.

Social media tends to contextualize people as experts, regardless of skill or experience. Confidence stands in for wisdom. The fear and shame that always comes with the discomfort of learning is compounded by the tendency many of us have to think everyone out there is doing better than we are. Look closer, though. Often, the emperor you're so jealous of turns out to be standing there naked, ass hanging out for all to see. There's great honor in being a student. And if you want to be a great diviner, you must remain an even greater student. We never stop learning. Just because we have a system that works for us doesn't mean that we must avoid other systems. No, we go seeking them! We want to know what other people are doing so we can steal (within reason) from them. They may have a technique we've never thought of that completely unlocks our readings.

Robert M. Place's *The Tarot: History, Symbolism, and Divination* offered me that kind of revelation. In his wonderful book, he explains why he doesn't read reversed tarot cards, a tactic some readers use to add more nuance and "vocabulary" (Place's word) to the deck. Instead, he uses three cards per spread position. A tarot deck with reversed cards allows for 156 possible combinations (seventy-eight, doubled). Place explains, "When we use *three cards* as one statement instead of a single card, however, we find that we have 456,456 possible combinations" (emphasis added). Exponentially more nuance! This small adjustment changed the way I read forever—and for the better. In some ways, I owe some of the things I'm most proud of to Place's book, because I never would have unlocked what was blocking me had I not encountered it. But we don't stop there. Place writes a lot about things I'm not that interested in—alchemy, for one—but I eagerly await his new books because there's always something in them that will at least fascinate me, if not change the way I read.

Studying lenormand cards also expanded the way I read. This was a system that I didn't really enjoy at first, but the more I dug into it, the more I found really exciting techniques. I greedily yoinked techniques, applied them to tarot, and found that they revolutionized not only how I read, but what I read about. Initially, I started studying lenormand because I wanted to understand why so many people were leaving tarot behind to focus on it. What I discovered instead: all of the things that made these cards so attractive to modern readers (the lack of dogma, the near-insistence on talking about other people in the client's life, even—yes—the fortune telling vibes) could be applied to tarot, too. I didn't need a new system; I needed to understand the one I knew and loved *better.* I needed to learn how to read tarot without all the psycho-spiritual stuff that kept getting in my damn way. By taking lenormand techniques and applying them to tarot, I evolved closer to the reader I want to be. You wouldn't be reading this without my deep dive into lenormand. We just never know where we're going to find the next, mind-expanding method. Stay alert. It could be waiting for you inside something you don't even like!

I'm a more confident reader *because* I remembered that it's not good to stay stagnant. We, of course, evolve, but so do our clients, and so does society. I mean, if I'd tried to put a book about *fortune telling* out twenty years ago, the community would have reacted with indifference or derision. That was the vibe. And I couldn't have written this book twenty years ago anyway, because my attitudes about fortune telling were in line with that vibe. Now, more and more people are saying "to hell with restrictive and arbitrary rules"—and that's because the divination conversation has changed so much. And that wouldn't have happened unless we were open, which is another thing fortune tellers are: open to possibility.

The first time I went to a tarot conference, and its room full of divination glitterati, I had to sit with someone I didn't know and read for her. The pressure (the imposter syndrome) got to me, and I froze. Instead of giving a reading to my new pal, my brain spiraled to the depths of self-loathing. *"I don't belong here! I'm nobody!"* The rest of the week was skunked. I regretted putting myself into that position and vowed never, ever to go to an event like that again. This is what I mean when I say that having a foundation helps. If, for example, I'd paused long enough to ask myself, "Now, what do you know about the King of Swords?" Something truly magical would have happened: My brain would have stopped focusing on my ineptitude and started regurgitating my foundational meanings for the card. We cannot think about two things at once, though I know my fellow neurodivergent folks feel that we not only *can,* but *have to.* That's simply rapid succession of thoughts, not "multitasking." By returning to my foundation, I would have forced my brain out of the death spiral. My client would have gotten a decent reading and I wouldn't have found another excuse to indulge my inner saboteur. (If you're curious, I did return to that event the next year—and I had a much better time.)

Don't be like me. Have a foundation. Remember your foundation. Don't get so concerned with how you look as a reader that you actually make yourself look inept. You're not inept. You know how to do it. Well, you know how to do it if you have a foundation. When folks work purely from instinct, they run the risk that one day they'll need that instinct and it won't be there. I've met a few mediums who woke up one day and suddenly found themselves deaf to voices that had always spoken. Sometimes they come back in a day or so, sometimes not. I'm not a medium, so I can't say I know what that feels like. To some people, it might be a relief; to others, particularly those who make their living doing that work, it's devastating. A reading I once did for such a person suggested taking up a divination tool as a way of getting back to hearing those messages, even if in a different way. It makes sense. One might look at that as "training wheels," but it's really just another way of translating. Many mediums are *clairsentient* or *clairaudient,* they might *feel, know,* or *hear* a message. But if that stops working, they may just need a different way to channel—to translate—the message. Of course, they need to learn the foundation for that method, but there's no reason why it couldn't be a road back into their inner knowing. And if not, they've got a new skill. Foundations are always helpful!

The Best System for Fortune Telling

The best system for fortune telling is whatever the hell you want it to be. You could use a deck of *Cards Against Humanity* phrases if you wanted to. I don't know why you'd want to, but let's get really saucy and edgy to demonstrate how it can be done. All we need is a system for making it work, and it will work. If you don't have a system, make one up. Why not? I'm about to. Watch:

Let's say any card with a blank spot in the sentence represents "yes" (because it's receptive) and any card that lacks a blank spot means "no." Maybe every card that includes the topic of business or names of people associated with industry represents work; anyone or anything related to political entities represents family; and everything related to dirty jokes and sex represents your love life. The text on the cards, no matter how offensive, represents metaphors of experience that are interpreted in the moment based on context and intuition.

Say we've pulled a card with the admittedly disgusting text *Buffalo Chicken Blowjobs* emblazoned on its noble frontis. Given our system, we know this card speaks to the client's love life because it refers to a sexual act. What does this mean for them? Well, what do I know about Buffalo chicken? Obviously, it's spicy and buttery, it's bright orange, it's deep fried, Buffalo wings are difficult to stop eating, and there's something a little ancient, too, about eating meat off the bone. We also know that Buffalo wings have a pretty well-accepted origin story, at least according to the people of Buffalo, New York. We know people didn't really eat chicken wings prior to Buffalo wings popularity; they were (apparently) mainly used for stock or animal feed.

That's a lot of context, and context is good because that gives us a lot to interpret and connect with. I could pull some details about a client's love life just from what I know so far. I may say, "You need to spice things up (hot sauce), you've let things get too flaccid (how crispy chicken gets after its been sitting in sauce for a while), you need to get wild and crazy (the color and primal nature of the foodstuff), and it might be good to do this in a safe place, like your hometown, so you'll feel safer ('home' coming from knowing the origin of these wings)." That's not a bad answer, given the tool we're working with and the fact that I just did a reading with a card called *Buffalo Chicken Blowjobs*. Point is, it doesn't matter what you use as long as you know how to use it.

Contract with the Divine

If divination is a translation tool used to communicate with something that knows better than we do, then we need that translation tool to work as consistently as possible.[11] This is another reason a foundation can help readers.

For an "intuitive reader" who has no foundation, divination is a lot like going to another country and intuiting the dialogue of others. Context clues will likely give you some information. You'll know, for example, that the French person pointing to the library and using the word *bibliothèque* means that the library is over there. When a waiter hands you *sole meunière* and it's a buttery fish dish, you'll have a sense of what you're about to eat. But there's a lot you'll miss, including nuances (the *poetry!*) that can tell you the difference between someone using the word for kiss literally, or if they're using it to mean "fuck," which (I'm told) can be regional slang.

By having a method of understanding French, you'll have a better sense of what's going on around you and reduce the potential for making an embarrassing mistake. But it's also a nice thing to do for the people you're communicating with who are trying to communicate with you.

If you have a consistent foundational system, structure, or technique (I'll use these all interchangeably), you're telling your messengers how best to work with you. It doesn't mean that things won't get changed up. You absolutely will deviate from your system when necessary, but when you do, you'll feel more confident because this new answer will ring out so loudly you'll know you have to follow where it wants to lead you. When you take chances, there's less risk because you have the foundation to catch you if you realize you've gone off course. You're saying to the divine, "Here is

11 One might ask, given the demo we just finished, if the divine would respond to a reader using *Cards Against Humanity* decks with their profane topics. In my experience, divinity is just as kinky and funny as we are—so, yeah, I think they'd be fine with it. Your mileage may vary.

the basic system we're going to use to talk to one another." Then, the divine can work *with* you rather than making the best guesses and hoping you understand.

You can change your system right up until the moment you start shuffling. Once you start, though, the contract has been signed, and you will want to stay relatively close to your own guidelines. Again, unexpected interpretations will still happen, but you've created a safeguard for yourself and a handrail if you need it.

The system isn't the only way your divinity will communicate with you. They'll also take advantage of your moods, your preferences, sometimes even your peeves. If you can't stand The Lovers card in a particular deck because of its heteronormative and marriage-centric artwork, then that card will likely show up in cases where something cringe is going on rather than when love is in the air or a choice needs to be made. Divinities will use our idiosyncrasies in their choices because they'll start to understand them. You will notice your readings get consistently better as you do this more and more because you and your guides (or whatever language you want to give them; everything always sounds silly to me when put into words) are learning to understand each other better.

Open All Night...

On the other side of the coin, we cannot be so rigid that we get stuck in a systemic rut. This also happened to me. I *had* a system I thought was fine. Suddenly, it wasn't fine anymore, and I needed to re-evaluate. When we get so stiff and so inflexible that we stop being open to possibility, we're also doing ourselves a disservice. We can find our readings getting difficult, stale, fuzzy, and/or unsatisfying. That's no good.

When I say I've been reading since I was in my late teens, I don't deduct the three or so years I spent not looking at the cards. But I did reach a point where I got so burned out from reading that I gave it up entirely. Mostly, I was tired of reading about relationships. Oh, I *hated* doing that. I was such a snob about it. Now, I love doing them; it's my bread and butter. And why shouldn't it be? Relationships impact us more directly than almost anything else. But oh, I just didn't *care* if your boyfriend would propose, or your ex-wife would come back. It was so *lame*. We had the ability to read about *anything*, and you wanted to read about *Chad?* Chad with the bowl cut and the addiction to Taco Bell? Chad who dumped you on Valentine's Day Chad? *That* Chad? You want to know if *he's* coming back? Dear god.

I wasn't open anymore. I was stuck. Part of the reason I was so biased against relationship readings is that I'd been taught, and I'd accepted, they weren't worthwhile. There were some who would argue that doing them is unethical (that word again). And I believed that, because people I respected said so. Why should I disagree? In fact, *who was I* to disagree? Nobody, that's who. Nobody except someone who hadn't yet realized he'd outgrown some outmoded crap.

Having a foundation is important to guide us when we need it, but it's also important that we're open to anything that could happen in a reading. The most amazing things crackle to life when we allow ourselves to *experience* and *receive* the cards before launching into what we think they "mean." Recently, I read for a client who had a lot of plumbing issues in her home, and we were exploring why. Normally, I'm a very earthy reader. I don't get into the metaphysical much, and rarely do I explore the spiritual.[12] Because this client had asked such a compelling question and given me ways in which water issues had been dogging them for a while, we decided to read the cards from two points of view: the practical and the spiritual. In the process of doing that, I discovered that the spread featured a lot of swords and that the swords in this reading represented pipes! *Isn't that cool?*

I think it's cool. And though I may sound like a fogey when I say shit like that, it's still amazing—and is totally impossible if we're not open to it.

Being open is really about curiosity and resisting the temptation of jumping to conclusions too soon. Many readers lay out the cards and jump into, "The High Priestess means this...." Fair. It *might*. But there's a whole world of possibility we can only discover if we stop ourselves from doing that right away.

I've taken a few classes with fortune teller and author Camelia Elias, and she has a practice of saying "no, it doesn't," when facing the meaning of something. For example, "The High Priestess means hidden knowledge—*No, it doesn't.*" As I do, I've taken this and interpreted it in my own way, which is to delay what I think I know about the card generally to see if the reading can offer me something specifically. The High Priestess *doesn't* mean hidden knowledge—*at least not yet*. I might be able to get a good reading if I force the card to mean that, but I'll get a better reading if I don't—if, instead, I listen to what the cards (and, thus, what the divine) is trying to tell me. It is in those moments that the High Priestess suddenly becomes a plumber.

The High Priestess a plumber? Did you sip drain cleaner?

Well, she's associated with water, and she's often got these two wide pillars on either side of her—and what are pillars if not inert pipes? Couldn't they be *actual* pipes? And she's guarding them. Theoretically, a plumber is a "guardian" of pipes, in that they fix them and tell us how to treat them so they don't get clogged. She has knowledge of pipes that we lack; she has abilities we don't. In the case of issues with a home, doesn't that make more sense in a reading than telling the client they

---

12 Note from future me: One of the interesting things about working on a book: things change in the process. At the time I wrote this, none of my clients *wanted* spiritual readings. Suddenly, the spiritual is at the forefront of people's concerns. That means I've got to be ready, willing, and able to address those topics—even if it's not my favorite thing to cover. For what it's worth, my own spiritual journey has grown during this time, too, so it makes sense to me. Trends and themes emerge in readings. I have found that reading at events typically yields several readings on the same topic. But these trends can, and often do, stretch into "eras." We are in a spiritual era and when we look at... *(gestures vaguely)* all this, it does not surprise me at all.

have the power inside them if they can figure out how to use it? And this is another thing fortune tellers do: we give *helpful* answers, *not easy* answers. We try to find the relevant interpretation, not the easy one.

When we let go of our preconceived notions about what things are "supposed" to be, we discover so many potentials beyond that. It is in this way that we discover the surprising, helpful, and true readings that I referenced in Chapter One. So many of us cling to our memorized keywords for the cards, and there's nothing wrong with that—we've already seen the benefit of having them. But when we white-knuckle our meanings, we constrain our ability to listen and learn.

It may sound like I'm asking a lot. This is all easier done than said, to be honest. It's merely the act of laying out the cards and:

1. Knowing you've got a system if and when you need it.
2. Allowing the cards to wash over you and dance together before you start telling them what they mean.

That's it. Yes, it takes practice. Everything does—anything worth doing well, anyway, and I assume you're here because you want to do this well.

This is also a good time to point out that though the focus of this book is tarot, which happens to be my primary system of divination, much of this can be applied to lenormand, bone reading, or any other system. For example, in my bone set (which is called that because there are bones in it, but there's a lot of other stuff, too), I have a nutmeg pod. Nutmegs are traditionally associated with luck. In Hoodoo, nutmegs are often used in gambling mojos, for example. Sometimes luck is contextually relevant, and sometimes gambling can mean more than just playing roulette. But a nutmeg is also a fruit, or in this case the seed of a fruit. Sometimes, then, that item might represent a baby (a fertilized seed) or even a testicle (because it looks like one). Folks who read bones and curios will often switch between the metaphorical and the literal. A pelvis bone might represent the actual pelvis, especially in a health reading; on the other hand, it may stand in for a vagina (as it is bone with an open space in it), or it might signal sexuality or things associated with the sacral chakra. All of these are possibilities, but only if the reader is open to them.

Lenormand is particularly steeped in dogma (from my point of view) because there's such a modern-day desire to keep it from getting "tarot-ized." This betrays not a bias of tarot itself, but of how we've let tarot become a mushy, mealy, imprecise *thing*. Lenormand teachers remind us that the tower in lenormand is *not* The Tower in tarot. Fair. But what *is* The Tower in tarot other than what we've decided it is? In lenormand, the tower can often represent institutions. Why can't The Tower in tarot? Because there's a lightning bolt hitting it? Why isn't the lightning bolt a strike of inspiration for a start-up? Why isn't it the electricity bill in your office? There are many tarots that don't depict a destructive tower, too.

I have a potentially shocking revelation for you: The image on the card isn't the card; it's an *interpretation* of the card. Whether the card shows a tower being blasted or not doesn't mean The Tower *has to mean* something is going to fall apart any more than The Empress means becoming the royal uterus for a titled lord. But it *could* mean that, too.

One of the things that kept me from reading lenormand well for so long was that I simply accepted everything I heard about it as law. But I'm not someone who works particularly well that way and doing so made the lenormand feel limiting. I felt like I was working with an alphabet with no vowels, and I had to somehow find ways to make the hard sounds make sense without soft ones to carry them. It wasn't until I threw out what I was "supposed" to be doing and took Camelia Elias's advice ("no, it doesn't") that I started being able to read those cards well. Context and relevance matter more than dogmatic prescriptions. I still know internally that the tower in that system can represent institutions, but I've also realized that there are other meanings a tower can have that don't fall in any lenormand study guide. Lenormand's tower card can simply be tall things or phallic things; things that you can see from a distance. We might also see jails and isolation and anything related, simply because those are all potential realistic things a tower can be or do. The same goes for The Tower in tarot, not because there's a tradition of doing that, but because it's one of the cards in tarot that nearly always depicts a building.

The Star in tarot is a card that dogged me for years until I discovered a system of reading lenormand in which the star card there represents navigation and direction. Boom! Insight unlocked. That's now how I read The Star in tarot, too.

Allow yourself to experience whatever divination tool you're using by letting it guide you. Don't tell the reading what it's saying, allow the reading to tell you. I used to say, "the reader isn't the oracle." This was a way of de-centering the reader's ego. I will add now, though, that "the reader is *part* of the oracle." We're in dialogue, in dance, with the things that make divination work—and with the client who wants an answer.

Let yourself off the hook. You have a solid foundation, so you know you can reach for that if you need it. But don't worry about being right. Don't worry at all, because worry is a constrictive force—and I'm saying this as someone with chronic anxiety. Just say, "let me listen to the reading." Sit with what you're seeing. Each little thought that pops into your head might be giving you information about the reading; they needn't necessarily be intrusive thoughts. An impulse that might seem odd could be incredibly insightful and unlock the meaning for you.

You don't have to start talking right away, either. Some readers feel that pressure when they have a client sitting across the table, looking at them expectantly, full of hope. Have a pen and paper nearby to make notes as you allow the reading to come together before your eyes. If you're worried about the client getting bored, give them writing materials, too; allow them to do the same. Then start by asking them what *they're* seeing. That could be useful. After all, it's their lived experience. They might see something you never would have thought of.

If you don't want to write notes, make mental ones. This is what I do, because I'm a clumsy scribbler. What strikes you? What surprises you? Which card in the spread seems totally out of place? Start there. Why did *that* card come up among all the others? That sore thumb is calling your attention for a reason. Don't get married to anything right away. Ask questions of the client, if you want. "Do you do any work with social justice?" I find myself asking that any time the Justice card takes a prime spot in a spread. It helps me understand which way to think about that card. "I see The Empress here. Are you involved in any caretaking responsibilities?" Or "I see The Empress here, are you a boss or manager?"

Don't jump to conclusions yet. After a while, you'll start to get a message—or you won't. And if you don't, that's when you can start pulling out your toolkit. "What do I know about Justice? As an idea? As a tarot card? As a perception? What do I know about this person and this question? What connects the card and the client?" Then, you can start building from your foundation, which is equally valuable and may be exactly what's necessary in that moment. But on the chance something else wants to come through, starting by being open will give you the opportunity to discover it.

Divination requires alternating currents of activity and passivity, and that's something readers come to understand innately. You're passive when you're listening to the client, active when interpreting, passive when allowing them space to calibrate with you. It's an exchange. And so is the act of interpreting—alternation between imposing your technique and allowing the reading to speak to you. Sometimes the scales will get tipped in one direction or another. I've had clients come to my table, sit down, pick up my cards, and start shuffling; all before I can introduce myself. I don't particularly love when people touch my cards these days, mostly thanks to global health crises—but, hey, it's not the end of the world, and if they want to pay me to tell me what they think, fine. Not my circus, not my monkeys. I'm open to that, too, while I sit back and sip on my iced coffee. Ethical? Eh. It's what they needed.

Challengers

Another incredible thing readers can do: challenge ourselves constantly. I'll give you an example. Every time I lead workshops, I tell students not to throw out anything they disagree with right away. They might be able to throw it out later, but sitting with *why* they dislike it may lead to a discovery about themselves as a reader. Meanwhile, I'm known to monologue about how much I loathe keywords on tarot cards. I've always found them an imposition because I'm a pretty cerebral person and a writer, and so words—particularly written words—have a big impact on me. It's easier for me to ignore the image on a card than it is to ignore the keyword. Or it was.

Recently, I realized that I was doing the opposite of what I tell my workshop participants to do. I wasn't sitting with why I hated keywords; I was just dismissing them. This is a low-key example of bias, by the way, and is a good example of why constantly challenging ourselves is a good thing. I decided to spend a month working *only* with tarots emblazoned with keywords. Every reading I did, no matter who it was for, was with one of two decks I'd chosen because they had keywords on the minors. The first happened to be one of the first decks I ever owned, the *Voyager Tarot* by James Wanless and Ken Knutson. That was one of the few decks I'd had over the years that I didn't give up on despite keywords. I also picked a deck I'd liked but avoided because of the keywords, the *Sun and Moon Tarot* by Vanessa Decort.

Not only did I do that, but I also did something I've always made fun of: I slept with each of the decks under my pillow for three nights (one at a time, but three each) to see if that had any impact on the readings. I can't tell you whether this impacted my readings or how I feel about those decks, but more than six months later, they are still my primary readers for most clients. Who knew?

What I learned from doing this is that keywords on tarot cards are simply another form of context, much like the image, suit correspondences, and elemental qualities. Sometimes, in some readings, they offer information; sometimes they don't. Sometimes, all the potential interpretive elements (image, keyword, number, element, suit, etc.) will be complimentary and offer the same information; sometimes they'll disagree with each other, and I have to figure out which is speaking the "loudest." But what I've come to see is that the words on the cards are no more important than anything else, and that when I'm really reading, I'll see what's necessary and won't be too influenced by what's not. There are times when I'll consider the keyword and wonder whether it means something and decide it doesn't and throw it out. But I do the same for the common meanings and the images, so it's all one in the end. And now I have two decks that I feel strongly connected to that I would never have added to my rotation otherwise. It was a venture into my bias, and I came out better for it. I'd like to think my clients have, too, because I now have more information to work with and get myself closer to true, useful answers. And that's rather a good thing, no?

I'm going to allow myself a sidebar on consumerism here. For the first time in history, diviners have more decks, books, and tools to choose from than can be imagined—with new ones coming out every week. Many readers have shelves stacked with books they'll never read and cards they'll never use, and many of us bemoan our greed. I've felt it. I know others have, too.

I'm not saying this because I'm writing a book on divination, I really do believe it: there's a lot to be learned from coming into contact with decks, books, and tools that you don't necessarily make part of your practice. An image on a card can stay in your mind and visit at the right time. Something you read in a book you didn't much care for can one day show up and be the answer to a question you're working through. I don't think there's anything wrong with having access to and availing yourself of the options that are out there. In fact, I think it's good to expose ourselves to a lot of different interpretations of the cards and thoughts on how to read. In my opinion, it's not *purely* greed that keeps people buying a lot of decks, books, and other things.

I do think, though, that it's worth tempering our consumerism with alternatives, like trading and bartering. An added benefit of this alternative is that it also makes it possible for folks to get their hands on tools they might not have been able to otherwise, thanks to the cost. We don't have to have clean, new, unopened versions of things. I have plenty of used decks that work just as well as ones I've been the only one to touch—and honestly, I rarely do any kind of "cleansing" on them, though I know I'm in the minority there.[13] Point being, it's okay if you can afford to explore whatever's on the market. It's also good to give up things you know you won't use and someone else will. And being thoughtful about what we consume is always good.

Fatalism

Fortune tellers are frequently accused of fatalism. I don't think it's because we're a particularly fatalistic lot, I think it's because the stereotype of fortune telling as we understand it today formed during a time when people in the Europeanized world experienced death more directly than we do today. This would be roughly the eighteenth century—just about the time tarot was catching the attention of esotericists. They couldn't hide death the way their descendants (we) do. Wakes and funerals were held in the home; the loved ones of the deceased frequently prepared the body, washed it, dressed it, and got it ready for viewing; coffins had slots in the bottom for ice to keep bodies fresh during days-long mourning rituals. Death was more personal before being concealed behind hospital walls. I can't say whether people were less afraid of it, but they couldn't avoid thinking about it in the same way we do. (It is worth pointing out that many cultures in the world today do not "sanitize" death this way, and I'd argue they have a healthier relationship with death and dying as a result of that. I recommend the books and videos of Caitlin Doughty "Ask a Mortician" for more on this topic.)

Not only was death harder to ignore, but your quality of life depended a lot on who you were, what class you were born into, and whether or not you married well. Fortune telling has always been associated with femme people and so it has also been looked on as something silly. "Listen to those women tittering over cards and talking about marriage." Well, if your only hope of a comfortable life is marrying a man who has money and your decision is based more on that than how attracted you are to him, you'd want to know what the hell is going to happen, too. Marriage was a life-or-death prospect for many people—the economic survival of women was based on it. But it wasn't just women whose lives were shaped by who they married.

---

13 When I do cleanse decks, I'll either use some salt or, increasingly, place the deck in a singing bowl and use sound to clear it.

In many European countries, only the eldest son of a family inherited *anything*, because families didn't want giant estates (and fortunes) divvied up. So if you happened to reach adulthood as the spare for an heir, you needed a rich wife as much as your sister needed a rich husband. I point this out to highlight the stupidity of making fun of fortune telling as gendered. People lived and died with their prospects for matrimony. Who *wouldn't* have been fatalistic? Of *course* readings would seem so by today's standards. The cosmology of the time was fatalistic, thanks in part to the fact that *society* was fatalistic.

Modern folks like to think we're superior, but not much has changed. We've hidden death and dying, made it easier to forget about. But all that means is that people don't die in the comfort of home, they die in sterile rooms while being bled financially dry. And I'm not saying that I'm anxious to be waked in someone's living room. Frankly, I find Christo-American funerals to be the *worst*. Point is, just because we're more removed from the experience of death and dying doesn't mean that we're not still impacted by it. In fact, our relationship to those things is worse because we are so separated from them, so we live in fear and hope we'll never have to face death. Our anxiety and sense of identity is poisoned because of this dissociation from a major part of life.

There are still many people whose economic survival depends on marriage, getting out of their neighborhood, or other "escapes" that don't rely entirely on their own force of will. And just because we have a stronger focus on free will today than we have in the past doesn't mean we're always in the driver's seat. The modern divination landscape is loath to talk about it, but there are plenty of times we don't have any influence over what happens to us—whether that's because of health or disease, money, access, family, bias, or hundreds of other conditions that take away our autonomy.

Sometimes we have choice, sometimes we don't; sometimes we have options, sometimes we don't. That means that some readings will be more fatalistic than others, but sometimes they'll show us the way out of a sticky situation.

In many places on this planet, divination isn't separate from medicine, it's a part of treatment. It is divination that diagnoses and that prescribes the cure. It would be bizarre to get a reading and not have some kind of spiritual-medical follow-up. The reading could say you're in grave danger, but it would also show what to do to avoid that danger (assuming it was possible). Again, I'm not advocating for us to take on roles we're not trained to do. But the idea of things being "fatalistic" or grim, or somehow inappropriate or unethical, are really just biased assumptions based on systems we're familiar with. There's a reason notable Hoodoo and Voodoo practitioners in the southern US called themselves "Doctor"; it would have been their role had they or their ancestors not been ripped from their homeland.[14] And since the enslavers didn't believe in providing medical care for their "property,"

14 Please note that "Voodoo" is the American and New Orleanian practice, which is a branch of (but very different from) Haitian Voudou. The spelling isn't the only difference, but it's a useful indication.

these doctors often were *the* option. This is why it's perfectly fine not to do something you don't feel comfortable with as a fortune teller, but it is *not* fine to declare anything you don't do as evil, unethical, or bad—that's bias.

Contextualizing

This is a big chapter! We've explored some of my views, so that the rest of the book will make more sense. We've also challenged some common notions about what fortune tellers do and how we do it. If you found any of this uncomfortable, I applaud you for staying with me. That's big. Many of us live carefully curated lives that prevent us from experiencing discomfort, but discomfort is where growth happens. We love to think of the beautiful transformation of a caterpillar into a butterfly, but we forget what happens in the cocoon. It ain't pretty, friends: caterpillars essentially digest themselves, turn into a goo, and reform. Nobody said magic (and what's more magical than that transformation) was cozy.[15]

This is a good opportunity for you to pause and do a little work around your own feelings about what I've shared with you here. What are your feelings on fatalism? What are your feelings on challenging yourself? Where do you go from here? You may want to do readings on each of these questions, too, and see how the cards you drew to answer them differ from what you've journaled. Where your cards seem to disagree with your perceptions, you're opening yourself up for something really exciting to happen: a perception shift. And, as I'll say time and time again, that's one of the great benefits of being a fortune teller, which I think is exceptionally dope.

15 Thank you to Lane Smith for this metaphor.

CHAPTER THREE

KILL YOUR DARLINGS

Do What, Now?

Imagine you made a movie of your life. You've written it, got it green-lit, got Regina King to star, and it's going through editing. Everything is working individually. Regina is *slaying*. The scenes sparkle and crackle—but the movie as a whole doesn't work. You try everything. And then your editor suggests you cut *the scene*. Your favorite scene. The most beautifully written and astonishingly acted scene in the history of language. You refuse. "That's what the fucking movie is about, Jack," you scream, pretending to do your best Bob Fosse. But nothing else has worked. And when you finally let the editor show you the film with the scene cut, it *works*.

For our purposes, our "darlings" are really things we love about particular cards, interpretations we're proud of that we try to re-use as often as we can, or maybe an over-reliance on one of the tools (the image, the keyword, the elements), or even some dogma we've absorbed about the work we do. It's anything that we think is helpful to us all the time but that may not be in the moment, or even generally; it's anything we don't know that's holding us back until we let it go and discover the freedom therein.

An example from my own experience is the use of Marseille-style tarots. If you're familiar with what those are, feel free to skip to the paragraph beginning with "When I started...." If you're not, hi! Let's talk a little history. In tarot, there are generally three "styles" or types of decks readers use.[16] The most well-known are those inspired by the famous deck by Arthur Edward Waite and Pamela Colman Smith. This deck is justifiably famous because it was the first mass-marketed tarot designed for use in readings. It wasn't the first deck published, nor even the first mass market deck. But it was the first offered to the mass market with an eye toward divination—even though Waite claimed to loathe divination. In this deck, the creators chose to depict scenes from life on each of the minor cards (the fifty-six cards that make up the part of the deck called the *Minor Arcana* [small secrets] by the esotericists). This allowed a reader to read without having to memorize what each card meant, as one typically

16 This is a *massive* oversimplification, but fine for our purposes right now.

does in many kinds of playing card readings. The other deck to emerge from this tradition is the Thoth deck, created by Lady Frieda Harris under the watchful eye of Aleister Crowley, which lacks scenes from life but includes evocative geometric drawings and keywords (or titles) for each of those cards.

Prior to both of these decks, though, were the Marseille-style decks, which were made in and around France and Germany in the seventeen and eighteen hundreds. These decks were designed for playing the game of tarot, and the minors (or *pips*—a word meaning "seed"—which are the spots on dice or the number cards in a playing deck) simply feature repetitions of each of the suit symbols: interlaced swords (curvy scimitars) and wands (straight "batons"), and arrangements of cups and coins. These were not used for divination, *as far as we know,* until an article in the esoteric publication *Le Monde Primitif* in 1781 declared the cards (with no evidence) an Egyptian book of knowledge.[17] Most modern readers discover tarot either through decks inspired by the Waite-Smith or the Thoth, but more and more are discovering the exciting readings that can come from these earlier playing decks. It's worth noting, too, that the Marseille decks weren't the first to exist; they were the first to be mass marketed, at least based on extant copies. That's as much tarot history as you'll get from this guy. Wink.

When I started, I relied heavily on the images of the minors, because that was my *only* foundation. I also found those Marseille decks ugly, because they're usually messy woodcuts painted only in primary colors, a combination of hues I find insanely gross. At a certain point, I found the idea of moving away from those Waite-Smith inspired images really exciting. That meant learning to read all over again in a lot of ways because only the twenty-two majors and sixteen court cards would feature anything "interpretable," which required me to find a method of reading without having images—and that left me with limited choices. For many readers, those choices include the meanings of the suits (what each suit symbol suggests) and numbers. Many folks will often look at the relationship of the suit symbols in each card—how the swords are woven together, or the ways the floral decorations around cups create relationships between the cards.

---

17 It's worth a note: what we know about tarot history is limited, both because nobody thought it was important enough to record, and also because the deck appears to have non-European origins. The man we know today as Etteilla often receives credit for being the first person to divine with tarot, but any critical student of history can tell you that these "firsts" *really* mean "the first white guy to do it." Card divination existed well before tarots were declared magical already, so it's logical to assume that a playing card reader might find the tarot and begin using it, too. The folks most likely to have done this were not wealthy white guys, but the people who needed "survival jobs": women, people of global majority, impoverished people, and often people who happened to be all three. For two really excellent explorations of the non-European history of tarot, see *78 Acts of Liberation: Tarot to Transform Our World* by Lane Smith and *Secrets of Romani Fortune Telling* by Jezmina Von Thiele and Paulina Stevens.

My journey into learning to read this way opened me up and became another formative moment in my journey, much like reading Robert M. Place's three-card method. By removing the images and forcing myself to explore the elements and suits more, I found so many exciting new possibilities to use in readings. And I still retained a mental image of the Waite-Smith cards, too, so if the other methods didn't yield anything, I could always "fall back" on those. Now, no matter what kind of deck I'm reading with, I can use all of these methods—number, suit, element, images in the deck I'm working with, images in other decks I've worked with—to bring the reading to life. This journey made me a much more confident reader, and I think a more accurate one. It also became my first two books: *Tarot on Earth* where I record the methods I used to learn reading with Marseille (or other non-scenic) tarots, and *Your Tarot Toolkit,* which is about using all the tools you have at your disposal to read well.

By "killing" my "darlings"—the images on the cards—I was able to revolutionize how I read and overcome so many of the roadblocks that had dogged me to that point. All I had to do was give up everything I knew. Okay, that's a joke. You don't have to give up anything. You're just adding more to your toolkit.

Ignorance is a Darling, Too

I'm very pushy about the fact that ignorance is a darling because I know first-hand what it's like to have your experience invalidated. As someone who has struggled with various mental health issues for most of my life (depression, anxiety, and the shattered self-image that comes from being emotionally tortured by peers and teachers during impressionable years), I could pay off my student debt if I had a buck for every time someone told me not to worry about something, to cheer up, to forget about it, to rub some dirt on it. It wasn't until I began therapy that I realized these were erasures of something real, and that by having them erased, I was learning that they didn't matter, and that there was something deeply wrong with me and I couldn't tell anyone because there was no way to fix it. It is essential that readers—fortune tellers—don't negate our clients' experiences. That includes our own. Let's explore together.

Say you have an eager young actor sitting at your table, about to finish his BFA in musical theatre from some school no one's ever heard of. For our purposes, we'll name him Oliver, because that's the first musical I fell in love with as a child. Oliver wants to discover the likelihood of him "making it" on Broadway—his great love. You're more than happy to read for this earnest, eager, hopeful star-to-be, and you draw our favorite tarot badass, The Empress. Good news, right?

For those of you who don't know the theatre world, now is a good time to provide you with some relevant context. Talking about how the American commercial theatre industry works in a book about fortune telling may seem out of scope, but see that's just the thing: if you don't care about the world Oliver is trying to move into, how can you give him a decent reading? In the current climate, Oliver—who is a twenty-one-year-old femme queer kid with dreams of playing Hamlet—is more likely to get his dream career by making it big in reality TV first. If you're not familiar with the theatre landscape in this country today, you won't know that Oliver is attempting to break into an industry that advertises itself as progressive and home to freaks but is shockingly conservative and rigid. The people getting cast as Hamlet in commercial theatre today are the Hollywood hotties. Look at who has played Hamlet in New York, and you'll find very few femme boys. Now, the world is changing—but slowly. Oliver isn't likely to be at the top of anyone's casting sheet for that role, not only because he's not the "type" for it (yes, this is a thing you have to know if you're an actor), but because nobody's heard of him. He can't sell any tickets. And the financial risks of the commercial theatre are admittedly huge.

Oliver might get to play Hamlet one day, but the odds of him doing it on Broadway are slim. As I said, our goal isn't to poison Oliver's well, but the answer to his question is not "just be a bad ass." Not, anyway, if we want to give a helpful answer. Do you see what I mean? To tell Oliver that The Empress means being himself is the thing he needs to do to play Hamlet on Broadway would be a lie. The Empress, in this case, is far more likely to suggest creating his own theatre company in the city so that he can play the roles he wants to.

I'm not expecting you to become an expert on the American theatre, that's not the point; the point is that you at least have to ask Oliver some questions about the industry before you jump to conclusions about the cards on the table. Beyond that, though, we need to be curious *about the world at large,* not just the things related to divination. We can easily shut ourselves inside a bubble if we don't have an understanding of "the way things work." I put that in quotes, because there's a lot of things and a lot of ways. This is merely an example. Simply by looking at the world, you can see that talent doesn't equate with success. You can see that Hollywood is a family business, and not a particularly welcoming one. But that's true of corporate landscapes, too, and non-profits. It's not about knowing how to read for someone in the theatre; it's about knowing how to read for anyone who faces long odds. It's knowing life ain't fair and that it takes more than a tug on the ol' bootstraps for most of us to get ahead in life. Be aware. Avoid bypassing. Ask for context. Pay attention.

People of global majority know this already, but for those who don't: The word "woke" has gotten a lot of press in recent years because it's the latest rabid obsession of American right-wing white supremacy. The word may go as far back as Marcus Garvey in the 1920s—or further. Either way, it's a word coined by and for Black Americans, reminding each other to be aware of the dangers of white supremacy. "Stay woke" literally meant "be aware." As always happens to words common in Black Vernacular English (BVE), it got co-opted by white liberals, and then, of course, by white conservatives who are increasingly excited about demonstrating the totality of their racism.[18] It is a mind-bending evolution, and a particularly American one, for a word coined to protect Black people from white supremacy has become a tool of white supremacists to "cancel" anyone they disagree with. But see, knowing that is important as a fortune teller, because it's yet another example of the pervasiveness of discrimination in the world. Beyond that, fortune tellers should be infuriated about the journey of that word, because we too need to stay awake to be able to see not only possibilities but potential dangers in readings.

Challenging ourselves is not merely about card meanings, it's about our understanding of the world. It is choosing to be aware, even of unpleasantness, so that when that unpleasantness shows up in a reading, we can talk about it. Ignorance is bliss, goes the cliche, because not facing the world is easy, particularly if the world is designed to protect you. But ignorance is criminal once you understand that things are bad for others and you refuse to face it. If you can't tell yourself the truth about life, how can you expect to tell the truth in readings?

Try It

If you've got a tarot deck nearby, pull out a card you find beautiful. Doesn't matter why. It might be the card's usual meaning, the artwork, or your feelings at the time you're reading this. You can also do this with an oracle deck or divinatory system where you can choose something based on its ability to please you.

Now, use this card to describe the worst person you know. Don't let yourself off the hook. You can take breaks, but come back to it until you have a logical answer. If this happened easily for you, mix it up—try a card you loathe describing a person you love, or a card you're ambivalent about describing something you're deeply passionate about. It is in these games—these low-stakes experiments—where we begin to see so many possibilities for what the cards *could* mean, because no one is waiting for us to be "right."

Let's Get It On

I'm going to share an example with you that highlights the ways in which we as readers can allow ourselves to be challenged by a reading (in a good way).

I've used The Empress a few times here, so let's move to another card that creates strong feelings when we see it: The Tower. There are readers who'll say this card only appears when something irrevocable and major is about to happen, or is happening. For those readers, their experience guides them, so I'm not here to say otherwise. In my case, the card *rarely* shows up meaning something that huge. That's, I think, partly because most of the folks I read for aren't going through major life events. I

18 Also known as African American Vernacular English (AAVE). I use "BVE" because not all Black Americans identify as African American.

don't tend to get people in the throes of a "Tower moment," so when the card does show up, I need it to do more than that.[19]

A friend once told me that the *tower* (the building itself) isn't the intended focus of the card. The theory is that the *lightning* is actually what we're meant to be focused on, because this card begins a series of lights—The Star, The Moon, and The Sun—each getting progressively larger. The lightning would make sense as the important object, as it's a much smaller light than the others in the deck. In such a case, lightning is a much smaller event than the institutional collapse we frequently associate with tarot's Tower. Obviously, lightning is powerful; we know it is. I used to live across the street from a Catholic church that was constantly getting struck, causing damage and freaking everyone out. But context and scope matter. When you compare lightning to, oh, a major hurricane, lightning can seem much less dramatic. There are layers and levels within a card's potential. If we only have a concept of The Tower as tragic, we might get confused when it shows up in some less dramatic way.

Suppose we had a reading where The Tower was partnered with the Ace of Swords. Let's imagine we have a column of three cards: the Two of Cups on the bottom, above that the Ace of Swords, and above that The Tower. If this were a romance reading, we might actually read the Ace of Swords as a lightning rod, carrying the bolt of attraction from The Tower down into the Two of Cups, activating a new relationship. I don't even need to "know" what any of the cards "mean." The arrangement of them tells me everything I need to know—and this is what I mean about being open and not jumping to conclusions. I for sure could get a reading using the cards' foundational meanings, but—much like a lightning bolt itself—the image of the Ace as a lightning rod became everything I needed to know.

This doesn't mean I couldn't use the cards' foundations for diving deeper into the situation if I needed to, but if the question is whether or not tonight's date will go well, I'd say yes.

A Digression on Comparing Readings and Ourselves

When learning, it's common to share your interpretations of readings with others on social media or in classes. There's nothing wrong with this, per se—but there are risks. Not that other points of view aren't helpful, but everyone is going to see something else and readers can get stuck feeling like they're doing it wrong. Maybe they feel like everyone else's interpretations are better than theirs, or they struggle

---

19 The only time I remember The Tower potentially representing something that large was in the days prior to the attacks on the World Trade Center in September of 2001. But, even then, we could never have imagined that, so I'm not sure the card—which showed up for a lot of us with a lot more frequency—was trying to warn us of that.

to figure out how someone else came up with the answer they did. Either way, they've lost focus on the intent: to get a sense of whether or not they answered the question well.

It's not great to compare ourselves to other readers, even those we want to be like, because—maybe more than any other art—the life experience of the fortune teller is going to completely change what cards come up and how they're read. You can ask clients who have gone to different readers in short spans of time and asked the same question—they're going to keep getting the same answer. They may not get the same cards, though that does happen, but they're going to get the same or a similar answer. The reason different readers can get the same answer using different cards is because we're part of the reading. This is why I say that the person who pulled the cards holds the key to interpretation, not because they're special, but because they're the one who made the agreement with the divine to get the answer. They're a tool in the reading, too, so what they think matters more than someone else.

This is all to say that the sample readings I offer in this book should inspire you but not constrict you. If you don't see how I made the Ace of Swords mean a lightning rod, that's okay. It matters more that you understand the methods I used to read so you can experiment, too. If you saw a column of the Two of Cups, the Ace of Swords, and The Tower and thought that it meant a date was going to go badly, that's fair. You're not wrong. Neither am I. Which is why we get different cards to get to similar answers. The answer is the same; the route to get there differs by reader.

Back to your regularly scheduled programming.

Isn't It Romantic?

One thing that gets in the way of killing our darlings—by which I hope you now know means challenging ourselves and staying open—is romance. Divination is a romantic thing. There's a reason people are drawn to it. And as diviners, we can fall in love with our art. That's lovely. We should love what we do! But there are two ways we can get tripped up by the romance of it all:

We can think too highly of the work.

We can get distracted by attraction.

Let's dig in.

Thinking Too Highly

One reason the anti-fortune telling bias took hold in Tarotland is because the esotericists who declared it magical really didn't like divination. They liked tarot, but it wasn't for anything as icky as telling fortunes. I have to be fully honest here and say I don't really care why, because they mostly annoy me. I tolerate them because we likely wouldn't have the tarot we have today had they not gotten into their costumes and had their little tantrums and tiaras. (No, seriously: these guys were divas.)

There's not only a bias against fortune telling, but there's also a bias against "low magic." We can take this to mean all manner of things, including witchcraft, folk magic, Hoodoo, and candle work—essentially any kind of magic that addresses the actual things actual people deal with while living an actual life on the actual earth. Ew! Using magic to make your quality of life better? Why not try to turn yourself into gold instead?!

Look, I've got a bias of my own—clearly. I can't stand the snobbery of the esotericists, and that carries over into modern-day practitioners who look down on those readers who focus on the kind of nitty-gritty stuff people actually want readings about. We've all heard the cliche: "If you want to know if your partner is cheating, then you already know the answer." Funny in private, but no! Underneath every question people ask is the subtext, "Am I safe?" *Safe* might mean different things to different people. For example, it might mean "worthy" to some, and literally "not in danger" to others. Both are deeply human and deeply humble, even if the overtext doesn't indicate that.[20]

The point is: you don't have to read about anything you don't want to. But to declare "low" readings inappropriate or unethical or beneath you is to betray a lack of humility—and, in my estimation, a lack of understanding about what bugs people as they go about their day. Yes, many humans struggle with the big spiritual questions, but only when we're not working and worrying about making ends meet and getting the kids to practice and trying to find five minutes to eat our lunch in peace. Those daily things, those banalities that are so beneath the great magicians—those are the things that we need to deal with *before* we can sit down and start attempting to find the philosopher's stone. If you can devote your days and nights to high magic, great for you. That's a privilege. Those who lack the time or energy to care about that right now aren't your inferiors; they're probably the people who make it possible for you to sit down and spend time with Aleister Crowley (a person I cannot imagine wanting to spend *any* time with, incidentally).

If you're attracted to high magic and loftier metaphysical goals than fortune telling, fine. But those who aren't interested in that deserve your respect, too. That includes clients who ask questions you don't necessarily find favor with.

We can think too highly of ourselves, too, or at least assume we know more than the client does. There is a tendency for readers to rephrase clients' questions when they fall outside of our bounds or when we don't like how they're worded—or any other impulse a reader finds to do so. Guess who did that all the time? This guy. So, again, please know that my tone might hold some snark, but these are lessons I've learned the hard way. You are under zero obligation to read on topics or questions

---

20 I'll add that my ultimate issue with esotericism is its escapist attitude. I can fully understand wanting to transcend this life, which seems to be the mission of these practices. But I also believe we have a responsibility to each other while embodied on this planet, and so we can't escape from reality. Escaping reality, as you've hopefully seen so far, is not likely to make you a good reader.

you don't feel comfortable with. Saying anything else would be dogmatic gatekeeping, but I also really believe that. You are the arbiter of what your skills can do and what you're comfortable using them for. That said, the client has every right to ask any question they want to, and I fully believe they know what they want to know better than I do, at least in situations where they have a question and aren't asking for me to help them come up with one.

Though I was a big rephraser in my early days, I'm very anti-rephrasing now. It's okay if you do it. I'll present an argument not to—*but it's still okay if you do it.* But *if* you do it, you have to hold the client's ego in your hand. The way you tell someone you're going to rework their questions can open them up or shut them down, and the client needs to be open, too. It helps everyone. If you can't read on a topic, be genuine and offer something like: "Oh, great question! To be honest, that's not in my skill set right now—but if you're up for it, we can come up with a version of that question that fits. Is that okay?" Obviously, this isn't a script, but there is a formula:

1. Hold the value of the client's desire to know the answer.
2. Be honest about your boundaries in a way that doesn't negate the client's question.
3. Offer an alternative that works for you both.

Easy! Humane. *Kind.* This is better than something I've heard many times: "I can't read about that because it's like spying on your ex. Let's look at how you can get over this relationship instead." There's a formula here, too, and it sucks:

1. Negate the client's ego.
2. Accuse them of being a Peeping Tom.
3. Order them to accept what you give them, whether they want it or not.

Annoying. Arrogant. *Cruel.*

I regret that it may sound like I'm scolding. That's the difficulty of the written word: you can't hear my tone. I'm not scolding, I'm *passionate.* If I'm a fundamentalist about anything, it's the great magic and power of the mundane, the necessity of folk magic, and the deeply real, human need to know the answers to the shit that dogs us on the daily. Centering the humanity of our clients is part of the gig, and we cannot do that if we look down on them or don't understand the potential roadblocks that might stand in their way.

Now, I offer an argument for not rephrasing the client's question: *don't.*

Okay, now on to the—

Oh, you'd like me to explain more? Fair. The client knows what they need to know. Now, if you're thinking from a psychological perspective, you might make the argument that clients don't always know what's best for themselves and, in fact, the reason for getting readings is to see what they can't. Okay. But I'm not a psychologist, therapist, or counselor. I'm a card reader. If you're a counselor, great. Remember, you get to draw the lines wherever you want them. But I don't have the ability to psychoanalyze my clients, nor, really, do I have the interest or energy for that. I can intuit a lot about people, but I actually try not to. I don't want to jump to conclusions about the client any more than I do about the cards. So, I take it for granted that the client knows what they want to know better than anyone.

I might, for the sake of clarity, ask if I understand what the client has said. "Just so I make sure I'm on the same page, you're asking...." This might involve a rephrasing to make sure I've interpreted what they said correctly, but I try to get as close to what they asked as possible, and I try to answer the question they asked as closely as possible. For my own benefit, I might give the question different wording in my head to help me read. If the question is, "Is my wife cheating on me?" I might mentally ask, "How likely is it that my client's wife is cheating?" This subtle shift gives me dimension in the spread and allows me to gauge the possibilities I see in the cards, but the answer I'm going to give is the answer to the client's question. It's a small thing, but it allows me to be able to say "there's a good likelihood she is" rather than "yes." The main benefit is that I can explain why I got that answer.

Often, clients will ask if their question is "okay"—which is an indicator to me that clients really care about doing it "right." My aim is to give them all the confidence that they *are* doing it right so they can sit back and experience the reading. Whatever I can do to make the client comfortable before the reading, the better, especially when I'm reading in a less-than-hospitable climate, which often happens at festivals and markets. One of my favorite events is a local witch's market, where a long hallway is reserved for an array of readers and our tables. It's quite cool, and I love overhearing what other readers are doing. But it's also *loud.* And we're moving relatively quickly, especially at Halloween, when there's usually a line. I have twenty minutes to get you comfortable, get you a good answer, and get you gone. But it's not impossible.

Here's a few things I do to make client comfortable: I give all my energy to greeting the client. I'm genuine, I'm smiling, and I'm really happy to see them. I introduce myself and ask their name. A little small talk never hurts, but I keep it brief, and I explain, "This is *your* time. I want you to feel like you're getting what you need from it, so I'll check in with you while we read—but if at any time you have a question or a thought, please let me know. It's your reading, and I'm interested what you think." It's important to remind the client that this is about *them,* not me. It's odd, but sometimes people can be starstruck by readers. We do something many of them don't, so there's a little bit of shyness at play. I want to dispel that as soon as I can. I'm good at what I do, but I'm not "special."

I generally don't take my fee until after the reading, because if they're really unhappy with it, I'm probably going to let it slide. It's a flaw, but I don't want to fight. I will also remember them and not read for them again.

A random anecdote: Once a drunk guy sat down at my table, said some disgusting things, and then demanded I read for him—which I tried to do, while he kept on asking me if I was a "bottom." This self-proclaimed heterosexual man, whose wife was apparently a vendor at the event, was deeply interested in whether I'd let him fuck me. After I finally ended the reading, he tossed a wet five-dollar bill at me and that was—thankfully—that. From then on, I vowed to have better boundaries.[21]

While reading, I check in and see how things are landing. I can usually tell whether or not the client is with me based on body language, and if they're not, I'll ask some questions to understand how the client is feeling about the reading. It's always possible I took a wrong turn somewhere and it's always possible to course correct. There are those stone-faced folks who make it their will to never betray what they're thinking or feeling, but you'd be surprised how much they actually give away in trying not to give anything away. You'll become tuned to little flickers of their face muscles that will tell you you've hit the mark. Usually, they forget to keep being a stonewall and they'll fall into the reading—asking questions or validating what you've said. Sometimes they'll never relax, but I can't recall many.[22]

I've often said to clients, "It's okay to ask whatever you want. I'm not here to judge you, and the more specific you are, the more specific I can be. I'm just a guy in a hallway who you'll probably never see again and who won't be able to remember your name in a few days. I promise, I've heard it all." Again, I do this in a genuine, playful way, in order to help people let their guard down. This is something I do when I can tell they're holding back, but it's not a bad thing to do, generally. Let people know they can ask whatever they want. They'll feel safer and might wind up enjoying the reading more. It's a win-win.

The point of this whole section was exploring the snobbery that can sometimes come from diviners, but the journey it takes us on is really focused on the client. I'm not the judge or jury of anyone who sits across from me—at least, not for the twenty-to-thirty minutes they may spend with me. I'm their employee, and while I'm not going to play yes-man, I'm going to do what they've hired me to do: give them an answer. Whatever it is they want to know, provided it's within my skill set and boundaries, I'll find an answer to. That's the gig.

---

21 I also found an obsidian skull, named Poe, who I've invited into my life and asked to protect me from jerks at events like that.

22 If you're a client, give yourself the gift of relaxing. You're paying for the experience, don't sit there like a statue. I think this comes from old myths that if you show any kind of emotion, the fortune teller will start reading *you*. But why shouldn't they? As we've already seen, your body language will tell me how I'm doing—and if I'm not doing well, I'd like to know so I can do better. Also, who *cares* if the client is reading you as well as the cards? You're part of the reading, too. Are you interested in testing the reader or getting an answer? If it's the former, save your money. Truly. If it's the latter, enjoy the damn session!

Getting Distracted by Attraction

This is a bit more common than the snobbery we just covered, but it can also be more insidious. Many readers fall so in love with their system that they stop doing readings and start doing *classes*. Clients sit down and, instead of an answer to their question, they get a lesson on the symbology of the Kabbalah, the astrological correspondences of an array of cards, or the history of numerology in divination. We forget that what's interesting to us as readers and students isn't what's interesting to clients. I mean, it might be in some other context, but right now they just want to know if they're getting the promotion. This is only bad because we're not giving the client what they need, and it's really just as easy a solve as noticing it and stopping it.

Others of us (It's me, hi, I'm the problem) simply talk too much. I *try* to use as few words as possible, because I want the words I do use to have an impact. This makes it sound like I don't talk much or I'm some kind of disciplined sage who can translate a nine-card reading into a one sentence answer without breaking a sweat. The key word in that phrase is *try*. My aim is to be economical so that what I say is more memorable, but you've been reading me for nearly twenty thousand words and so you're now fully aware that I'm not, by nature, *terse*.

One way to reduce the number of words you use is to leave all the "math" out. The client doesn't need to know that The Emperor is associated with Aries because that may or may not make sense to them. What matters are the *qualities* of Aries that apply to this reading. Right? Don't teach your clients tarot; read for them. That's really it. And this isn't to say you can't explain what you're seeing or why you're saying what you're saying, but they don't need a whole treatise. It can be as simple as, "This is going to be a good thing for you, because sixes usually indicate good things." Simplify, that's all. It takes practice. Sometimes I talk way more than I want to. Sometimes I talk because I *have* to—there's a lot to say. Again, this isn't dogma; it's a practice, and something I've found worthy of working on because clients seem to respond.

Another way we can get distracted by our attraction to the work is when, say, we fall in love with certain cards. They become icons, avatars, something idealized and so very difficult to bring down to earth. I find that this happens with a lot of the majors, even if readers don't particularly like a card. They will raise it up to something so powerful that it becomes nearly unreadable. The *idea* of the card transcends that it's a tool for divination and somehow divorces real life. This is easier to show than to tell, so here's an example:

The first time I saw Pamela Colman Smith's drawing of The Fool, I fell in love. It summed up in an image so much of what I wanted out of life as a nineteen-year-old gay kid struggling with his artistic dreams, undetected and unresolved trauma around his queerness, and still living at home with very Catholic parents. The image felt free! I wanted to *be* that image—so much so that I wore a pendant of it around my neck all the time. I had no idea how far I was from being the kind of person who could have gone on such a journey, and for me, it would have been rather foolish to attempt it. But because I idealized the card so much, when I tried to read it, I couldn't make sense of it. This happened because I could only describe it in terms of what I needed it to be in my own life, not in terms of how people's lives actually work.

Again, this may not be something everyone faces when they're learning, but I've never been the kind of reader where the "right" cards seem to show up at the "right" time—by which I mean I don't get The Tower at moments of destruction, and I don't get The Fool when I expect "freedom." Some readers feel strongly that these cards only show their faces when they mean exactly what the reader thinks they mean and nothing ever deviates from that. I've never been that lucky. The "wrong" cards always seem to show up and I have to make them make sense in the reading. Where I'd expect The Fool, I get The Devil; where I thought I'd see the Two of Cups, I get the Five of Swords. I don't know why, but it forces me to re-contextualize every card every time I see it, because I can't take for granted that it'll mean what it's meant before. I couldn't do that with The Fool, though, because I could only talk in terms of what I wanted to do with my life. It couldn't represent a dumb decision, which is often how I see it these days.

It's not that there's anything wrong with seeing any card this way; you only have an issue when it gets in the way of your ability to interpret the card in other ways. Remember: individual experience isn't common to everyone, our goals aren't the same as other people's, and that we have different worldviews than others. This may seem like a thing that doesn't need to be voiced, but it does—it's surprisingly easy to project our individual desire onto the whole world and assume that everyone views success the same way we do. And honestly, I'm happy my technique forces me to recontextualize the cards every time, because they remain boundlessly fascinating to me! It's exciting, it's sexy, *and* it makes for incredibly useful reading.

In the next chapter, we'll explore seeing the world as a diviner—as a fortune teller—and I think that will help make sense of this.

Who's Your Darling?

It's worth spending some time considering your reading practice. What are things you fundamentally hold to be true about divination? What would happen if you changed them—even just for an experiment? You might find it alarming, but you might find it freeing. Sometimes two things can be true at the same time. It's okay to try things and then go back to what you had been doing, but it's equally okay to try things and then add them to your toolkit.

What things do you have to have for your readings to be successful? A certain crystal? A particular cloth or incense blend? What would happen if you changed it up or tried not using your usual things at all? No one is saying that you have to live without them, but what do you find when you try? Of course you can have them back, but you might discover they're not as necessary as you thought they were. Try a deck you don't vibe with or a system you don't feel you understand intuitively. Read books about divination methods you're not interested in practicing. Just mix things up, try, experiment, and don't rely too much on the things you think you "need." You might find that they're actually holding you back. We never know unless we try, and just because we've killed a darling doesn't mean we can't breathe life back into it later.

Isn't that comforting? Just because you've killed a darling doesn't mean you can't breathe life back into it again. So, what's holding you back?

Only fear!

CHAPTER FOUR

SEEING LIKE A FORTUNE TELLER

I reference Bob Ross a lot because he (along with LeVar Burton and Julia Child) taught me just about everything I needed to learn about life. Bob Ross taught the world to think like a painter, even if we didn't think we could do that. He encouraged us to look at the world around us and see paintings in it, to pay attention to the natural world and our surroundings so that the general became specific. He also taught us how to translate what we see around us into brush techniques that would allow even a first-time painter to achieve results previously only available to people who had studied traditional methods and spent a lifetime working on them. He also did something revolutionary: he made it possible to create an entire landscape painting in thirty minutes. That wasn't possible before he completely rethought how a painter paints.

Bob saw the world like a painter and encouraged us to do the same. If you watch his videos today, after a while you'll find yourself thinking like a painter too, even if you have no intention of putting that to use. It needn't be Bob Ross, either; though I'm a fan of his somnolent vibe, not everyone enjoys that. Any decent painting teacher whose videos you can find online will likely have the same effect, including—and maybe especially—those artists who practice more traditional techniques than Bob Ross. You'll discover how artists see the world in terms of color blocks and shapes, lights and shadows, and other geometries and hues. This is how the artist takes an array of flowers and glassware or a landscape and translates it to a canvas. Art restorer and YouTuber Julien Baumgartner has talked about his work conserving paintings in terms of a dog's ability to both smell a chocolate chip cookie and all the individual ingredients that make up the cookie. Artists do something similar with their eyes.

Learning to see the world as a fortune teller is equally possible, and it allows us to view the world through a few lenses at the same time. It's not quite as logical and natural as a painter because reading fortunes doesn't involve thinking in terms of color blocks and shapes. What it does mean, though, is going into the world and being able to "find" examples of our divination tools. It's easier to describe with tarot, because those cards have a lot of layers, so we'll focus on that. But you can do this kind of activity with anything.

SEEING LIKE A FORTUNE TELLER

Go to a park on a busy Saturday morning, or a mall on a rainy day, or put on a random playlist of social media videos. As you observe people in their natural habitat, saucy creatures that they are, consider which cards in the deck they could be embodying in that moment. This shouldn't be literal. You're not looking for replicas of what is shown on the cards; you don't need to go out and look for three people building a cathedral as seen on the Waite-Smith Three of Pentacles. Rather, it's about seeing people in the act of doing something Three of Pentacles-y. Two kids helping a third up off the ground at the bottom of a slide might do it, or someone studying the *You Are Here* map in a giant shopping plaza. Both of these examples have qualities of that card. Try your best to associate each interaction you see with one of the cards. You don't need to get through the whole deck at once; in fact, you'll likely find yourself seeing similar cards over and over, because familiarity tends to do that.

But you could make a reading of it. If you're out and you keep seeing the same "card," what is that telling you about your day? Your world? Your life? If you see a boss lecturing a cashier at a fast food restaurant and the encounter demonstrates big Hierophant/Pope vibes, and then you see someone stepping onto an escalator while looking at their phone rather than their feet and there's The Fool, imagine you'd just chosen those two cards from a deck and need to find a message about your life in them. "Read" the "cards" you see in the world as though they were cards you drew from the deck, then get an answer that makes sense.

While it's a bit different doing this experiment with other fortune telling tools, it's not impossible. Choose three lenormand or kipper cards, or a small handful of charms and bones, then go off into the world and find situations that remind you of those. Try not to impose what you "know" about the "meanings" of those items; allow the world to present you with information and then see if the array of cards or tools speaks to what you're seeing. I recognize that we're often encouraged *not* to do these kinds of things, particularly in lenormand, but I truly have no interest in operating from that kind of limitation. If the mice card in lenormand doesn't ever make sense in readings, it doesn't matter what it's "supposed" to mean. If it's not working for you, find another meaning for it.

Function Over Form

Something I learned while taking classes with Camelia Elias is to think about the "function" of an item. I learned this in a lenormand class, so when I was faced with the heart card, I had to resist the temptation to say it means "love" and think about what a heart *does*. When I began thinking that way, it reminded me that a heart is a pump. A coffin "means" *endings,* but that's not what a coffin *does*. It's not what it's *for*. It doesn't end anything; it comes after the end. What it does is *contain*. It closes and locks. It protects, seals, and even makes it so that the ground beneath a grave doesn't fall in as the remains inside it decomposes.

This is a technique I have taken and run with in my own special way, which I hope folks do with the things I teach. This way of thinking about divination tools is foundational to how I read not only lenormand but also bones and curios (as well as tarot). I previously explored the potential for the nutmeg in my bone kit, but here are some more examples of items in that kit and what they're "for":

- *Pen:* creating
- *Passport charm:* identity/identifier
- *Beaded bracelet:* "circles" things in a reading I need to pay attention to
- *Doll's head:* for the client's head; "where is your head?"
- *Doll's right arm:* reaches for
- *Doll's left arm:* accepts from
- *Walnut shell:* brain/thinking
- *Snake vertebrae:* flexibility
- *Allen wrench from big box furniture:* fixing, assembling
- *Neck bone (I can't recall what animal):* what's on your shoulders
- *Foot bone (I think it's raccoon):* what grounds you
- *Domino:* chances
- *Old memory card:* memories
- *Dinosaur charm:* things that are extinct
- *Panda bear charm:* things that are in danger
- *Shell:* protects; home
- *Brown chess piece:* the client
- *White chess piece:* the client's adversary

There are many more, but this gives a decent overview. I didn't read how to "do" this in a book, though I did read books about the history and traditions of casting bones or other curios, and I took a class that covered some of the same material. What I did then was to go out into the world and begin gathering things that felt like they had a function that would be useful in readings. It took a while—and I went faster than I should have because I'm monstrously impatient—but I went through my junk drawers, to New Age-y shops, to the grocery store, and I trawled Etsy and eBay. Every time I found something, I took it home and placed it with the others. It's not glamorous, but honestly, I had better luck at craft stores than witchery shops. Look wherever you can find things.

Once I had what I felt was my whole kit, I sat down and "baptized" each piece in the notebook where I record my spiritual work. I don't usually do things like this, but I also smoked them with a "baptismal" incense blend I created along with the basket I hold them in, the cloth I spread them on, and the tray that contains them during readings. From there, I started reading with the kit. I asked a bunch of friends if I could try out my methods on them, they all readily agreed, and I went to work practicing. The results were good! And I think it's because the entire kit *came from me,* in the sense that I chose what was in it and what it would "mean" (while, of course, leaving room for things to occur to me in different contexts). I even created a sigil for my reading cloth designed to ignite my intuition.[23]

You could probably read with my set, but I don't know if you'd find it as exciting, because the experience of gathering the pieces and naming and cleansing them was so personal. I mean, it wasn't like some life changing spiritual revelation, but it was personal, and it was something unique. Even if you modeled your kit on mine, I think you'd get very different readings because what's in my kit comes from the world as I see it. As a writer, a pen in my kit "means" creation. For you, it might mean homework or something you hate doing.

Creating a kit like this is great because it's another way of seeing the world as a fortune teller. Everything you encounter (or at least anything that can fit in the hollow of your hand) becomes a possible tool for reading, and you start to think about everything being a possible divination tool.[24] Your kit can be *anything*. Because of that—even if it's similar to someone else's—your kit will still be entirely your vision, and you will start to see the world differently. And you'll be able to add and subtract from the kit over time. It's a wonderful experience and I encourage you to try something like it, even if you don't enjoy casting. Hell, take pictures of all the items, print them, and make a deck. If you're a tarot reader, go out into the world and make a kit full of seventy-eight items you choose to represent each card, journal why you chose each, and try reading with it. Lenormand is already very much like charm casting, anyway, as it's based on tea leaf reading, which is similar. If you see a bird in the cup, what does that mean?[25]

---

23 This was inspired by Laura Tempest Zakroff's *Sigil Witchery: A Witch's Guide to Crafting Magick Symbols,* which is one of the most accessible and effective books I've ever encountered on spellcraft.

24 Note from future me during the editing of this chapter: I can confirm this is true. This weekend, during my Reiki I and II certifications, I discovered my teacher is a master of acrylic paint pours—and these paintings, which hung triumphantly all over her study, were incredibly readable. In fact, I begged her to make a deck with them! Look and you will find divinatory potential *everywhere.*

25 For my money, the best book on creating a bone reading practice for yourself is *Bones, Shells, and Curios: A Contemporary Method of Casting Bones* by Michele Jackson. It offers a non-culturally specific, open, and easy-to-read approach. And it's nice and short, too! Avoid books that claim to teach "Sangoma-style" reading or "African basket reading." These are culturally specific methods and require not only devoted practice, but a calling from the ancestors to take it up. (Fellow white folks, this is my gentle way of saying, "It's not for us to practice." Let's just let that be something that happens, okay?) You can buy bone and charm casting starter kits, too, but I can tell you they're not helpful. I'll bet you can find at least five things you want from your desk drawer or kitchen.

The Library is Open—Officially

Whatever your method, do readings about *everything*. Every single thing you can think of, do a reading about it—the election, the economy, your neighbor's creepy son, whether or not the Red Sox will win. Read about all the things and do so gleefully, willfully, and with your boldest middle finger to convention. Even if you don't think you'd read about something for clients, play around with readings about it. I give you permission to spy on your loved ones and coworkers, I encourage you to peek into the weirdest corners of humanity, and I demand that you test the limits of what you can read about—if for no other reason than to see what you can do, what you can't do, and what you didn't even know was possible. If you don't do health readings, then do a reading about some famous person's health. Who cares? They're not going to know, and who are you going to tell? If you feel uncouth, then donate to whatever charity they pretend to care about or something. I recognize that I'm being awfully snide here, but when you're alone with your divinatory curiosity, the only thing holding you back is your imagination.

I started my YouTube channel by doing readings for fictional and historical characters, based on the book *Tarot Reading Explained* by James Ricklef, in which he did that very thing. I was shocked how often the readings were *spot on.* I mean, obviously I knew the answers to the questions, but the answers that the cards gave were uncanny in their accuracy. It was as though I were reading for living, breathing folks sitting right next to me. I recall doing a reading for Dracula, and the Five of Cups from the Waite-Smith deck showed up. If you don't know that image, it's a man in a black cape, looking down at a cup spilling red liquid. I also got Strength, with a young woman gently stopping a lion from attacking. If you know the story, Mina does exactly that in destroying my boyfriend—I mean the Count.[26]

Be reckless. I mean, within reason, right? (I guess I should add here that this book is for entertainment purposes only.) But, of course, what I mean is that you're free to do anything and everything you can think of with the cards. In so doing, you will be impacting not only the way you read, but also the way you see the world. And you will find that this opens you up in many ways, including opening you to things you may not have felt comfortable reading about before. You will find things you simply do not enjoy, experiments that show you nothing other than that the experiment didn't work. Think like a scientist—a *real* one, not those jerks who make a name for themselves in pop culture only to go and spew their own fundamentalist dogma about astrology and the like. Approach with curiosity, as a scientist should, and not bias as the more famous ones tend to do. (I dare any of those guys who happen upon this book to practice what I'm preaching: learn to do readings and try not to find yourself delighted by it.)

---

26 It's still up there on my YouTube channel, in all its naïve, low-tech glory. You can find it at www.youtube.com/watch?v=qct6x9x4l60.

SEEING LIKE A FORTUNE TELLER

So often I see students in forums ask about what they can do when they don't have anybody to read for. *Do anything you want!* Really, truly. Many of the most beloved divination tools came to us as games. Why shouldn't we play with divination? I don't believe for a second that the divine doesn't enjoy playing, too. In fact, one thing I think about my early YouTube videos was that the divine *was* playing with me—in a good way, not in a creepy way. I think they said, "You know what, pal? Let's play tennis." And they did. I refuse to operate in a world in which there's no play in the divinatory realm. I think we'd all go nuts, frankly, if there wasn't. I'm so happy when I attend a workshop where the host demands that we play. Oh, is it exciting. But we don't need workshops to do that; we just need to come up with games to play. For example:

- Deal yourself a hand of solitaire with a tarot deck, set a timer for five minutes, and read whatever cards are in front of you when the alarm goes off.
- If you have a deck you haven't looked at in a while, take it out of its home without shuffling it. Place a card here and there, face down, around your living space—maybe one for each day of the week, each in a different location. Each day, turn one of the cards over and let it and the location that it had been stowed tell you about the day to come.
- Pick up the nearest deck to you, count from the top to the seventh card, and let that card tell you how lucky you are today.
- Take a lenormand deck and lay out an entire grand tableau face down. Think of a question. Randomly choose four cards in the tableau to turn over and let them answer the question. Randomly turn over three more cards and let that tell you something you've been missing out on in relation to that question—something you should have seen but haven't. Take the cards you've turned over out of the tableau and put them aside. Gather up the rest of the tableau back into a face-down pile. Take the seven cards you have already looked at and place them in front of you in whatever arrangement makes sense. Then, take the face-down cards and place one face up on top of each of the cards you've already looked at. Read these new cards, using the cards underneath as houses.

Nothing is sacred because everything is! Nothing can't be done. If you're thoughtful and don't ask things you don't want an answer to, you can't go wrong—and you're not going to piss off any divine forces. You might annoy pedants who feel like there's only one right way to do things, but isn't that reason enough to do them? If you feel it's necessary, invite your guides to play the game with you. Why not? I've been lucky as a reader. I've been very dismissive of spirituality (thanks to the religion of my childhood) and whatever works with me to make tarot work has been *exceptionally* patient, because I never invite them to do anything. Luckily, they're there for me, regardless. Perhaps I should give them a little something in thanks. But I also think these divinities know us. They know we're playing when we're playing, and they know we're working when we're working. I think they're a lot kinder than we are—at least they are in my cranky-ass experience embodied on this planet. They have to be, because I can be quite a bitch.

And Then There's Doing Too Much

This is important: *we can get burned out doing things we love.*

The general attitude is that burnout only comes from day jobs and caretaking. It's not that simple, sadly. If we put out more energy than we take in, we're going to burn out. And that can happen with things we really love. In fact, it's *more* likely to happen with things we love because we enjoy it so much that we don't necessarily pay attention when the warning signs start beeping gently in the background. We push through, in part because many of us live in a push-through culture, and in part because we love what we do and want to spend all our time doing it. And when that happens, we can reach a point where we just *can't* anymore.

Can't what? It's different for everybody. In my case, I couldn't read anymore. Just couldn't do it. Couldn't deal with another dumb question, couldn't pretend to care about another ex-boyfriend. I stopped and I fully thought I was done. I'd grown really to dislike tarot and even wondered whether it had ever worked at all. I put all my decks into boxes in the closet, all the books on the shelves reserved for things I didn't look at much, and went about the business of living. I think it was a good two years, at least, before I started feeling the pull again. One of the things that makes me feel like tarot is something I'm "supposed" to be doing is that it *did* call me back—and did so in a big way. I've had other loves (acting, for example) that I burned out with and never went back to, and likely never will, despite the occasional nostalgic desire for applause. Tarot—divination—*made* me come back to it. But I truly believed I was done because I was truly cooked.

How do you know you're getting burned out? The best first indicator is the "I don't feel like doing this" flash that pops into your head when you're about to do the thing. It won't last long, but there will be a moment when your brain will tell you it's tired of something—and it will come and go so fast you might not notice it. But be on the lookout for it, because that's the time when you really want to sit with yourself and examine what might be the root of your impending burnout. There will probably be other signs, too, but in my experience that's the earliest one and it's one we should heed. If we can avoid burning out, much the better. It's a beast to overcome—when we even bother to overcome it.

That flash of "I don't feel like doing this" isn't an indicator that you're too far gone, but it is a sign that your body and mind want to be engaged in something else for a while. There's truth in the cliché that absence makes the heart grow fonder. Taking a little break can do wonders for us. If you're just learning, you *have* to take breaks. Your body needs time to internalize all you're taking in. I know you want to rush to be a "pro," but I promise you that rushing will only make it harder to get where you want to go. (More on this later.) If you've been doing this for a while, you need a vacation. We all do. This is one major reason that I don't try to make my primary income as a fortune teller: I worry that the hustle involved in developing a consistent clientele and then having to do what I do whenever I'm called to do it will send me over the edge. I'm not "there" yet, so I protect myself and my abilities by not asking them to do more than I'm capable of. My thinking is by the time I retire from my corporate gig, maybe I can do this to carry me to the tomb.

Rest is important. Take a week or two and stop doing readings. Get yourself some juicy fiction or tell-alls and do anything and everything unrelated to your lovely divinations. I guarantee that you will be *desperate* to get back to them, refreshed and ready to make it part of your daily life again. We should *want* to practice our art, not be mildly resentful of "having" to do it. If you feel those little resentments, it's rest time. I beg you to. Believe me. Y'all, I've done it with tarot, I've done it with acting, I've done it with my day job multiple times, and I've done it with writing. I never learn. *Don't be like me. Learn.*

I'm Too Far Gone

If, perchance, you're reading the above and feeling a twinge of anxiety that maybe you've gotten to that point and perhaps even beyond it, all is not lost. If you're reading this after a long vacation—of several years—from an art you thought you'd practice forever, there's hope. And I'm quite the pessimist, honestly, so if *I* think there's hope, *there's hope.*

When we have to put something we love away for a while, it does not mean that the magic isn't still working on us. In fact, what's more likely happening is that this too-long break is necessary because your entity needs to absorb and transmogrify everything you've forced into it over however long you've been doing this. Growth is like bread dough. It cannot be rushed, even if it can be encouraged. Bread is one of the most amazing creations of mankind—no matter how we're feeling about gluten—and it is a fascinating machine, particularly yeasted or leavened breads. Living things make this type of bread *bread.* Yeast is alive, and it is the process of those little buggers literally eating the sugars in the dough and burping them up that makes the bread puff. *But wait, there's more!* See, yeast isn't just a fun science experiment in gastro-flatulence; it's also a study in flavor. Allow me to take us further into a not-very-scientific exploration of what bakers call "bulk fermentation" and how this relates to being a person who learns. Yeast makes bread taste like bread (and beer taste like beer, and cider like cider, and so on). And it's true that you can make bread dough rise more quickly if you increase the heat gently, but that doesn't mean it'll be good. In fact, if you let the dough rise slowly in a colder environment, the bread will be much tastier.

We, like bread, benefit from a sort of mental fermentation process. We can force a lot of information into our brains, but we can't make it stick and we can't make it make sense. It is in the between-times where that work happens. If we don't give ourselves breaks, our body will take them—and it will burn us out to make that happen. If you've gotten to the point where you're just "done" with divination, or you feel like you've plateaued, or you're not getting the kinds of results you think you should be, *that's okay.* Just go off and do other things. See other people. Have a fling, if you catch my drift; I'm not suggesting you violate any relationship agreements, I'm talking about fortune telling here. (I will not be responsible for your relationship problems.) But, seriously, do other stuff. Take the pressure off the muscle and let it heal. And don't rush it: you can check in with yourself from time to time and sense whether there's any longing there to return to the work. You might occasionally find yourself wanting to browse the New Age shelves at the bookstore or visit online tarot shops. Okay, good—that's a good sign.

Don't jump right back in! Play hard to get. I know that sounds odd, but trust me. Absence makes the heart grow fonder, baby. It's okay to flirt, but you're not going steady with it again any time soon. If you feel compelled to start paging through an old book you loved on the topic, do so. Watch some old videos you enjoyed. When the time is right, you'll know. I know from experience. And if it's not right, it's not right. But if it's that important to you, it'll be right, and you'll start wanting it again.

The amazing thing is, you'll likely be better than you were before your break, because all of what you couldn't internalize will have processed and sorted, and your worldview will have evolved, and you'll be excited to play and experiment again. You'll be reading better because you took that time, and your enthusiasm will likely quadruple. Just be careful not to burn out again! You don't need to rent the U-Haul quite yet. But it might wind up being sooner than you expect.

Sacre Bleu a Monstre Sacre!

If I had to sum this all up, I'd go back to maybe my favorite point in the whole chapter: *nothing is sacred.* When it comes to the fortune teller, our relationship to the sacred is somewhat different. Being able to see the world involves picking things up and studying them from all directions. We're not going to simply accept something as sacred because we've been told it is; we're going to find out for ourselves. We're also more likely to find sacredness in the mundane than the esoteric. In fact, the word *esoteric* implies secrecy; it suggests something withheld, which is not unlike the tarot's High Priestess. We recognize that there's sacredness in *knowing,* not in withholding. We peek behind the curtains and discover what's inside. In so doing, we eschew dogma and discover unassailable proof (at least for ourselves) that what we ultimately see as sacred truly is and, maybe, that what is sacred is also profane. Nothing, as we know, is all one thing. And when we navigate from that perspective, it's actually difficult to *not* see the world as a fortune teller.

CHAPTER FIVE

GOOD TIMES AND BUM TIMES

No one wants to give bad news. And there are times when, frankly, the "good" news we have to give isn't really that good. It may be what the client wants, but our relationship to that client may make us feel like getting what they want is the worst thing for them. How we handle each situation is a matter of personal preference, but it's a worthy subject to explore. If we accept that one of the essential functions of a fortune teller is to tell the truth, we also have to consider what happens when the truth is hard to hear. And I don't just mean because we're telling someone it's going to be another single season for them—I mean when we have to give good news to someone who doesn't believe that kind of thing can happen for them.

I'm Afraid It's Bad

While writing the chaotic first draft of this book, I happened to pick up Demetra George's *Astrology and the Authentic Self*, which I'd taken off the swap table at a recent tarot event. I'm not an astrologer by any stretch, but I enjoy learning (and stealing) from those who are. This particular book is fascinating, blending traditional (pre-outer planet) astrology with modern. It's a master class in working through a birth chart, though I simply don't have an astrology brain. (This gives me the opportunity to point out that you don't have to be good at every kind of divination. In fact, if you can choose between being fantastic at one kind and being mid at several, be fantastic at one.) In the book, George takes you through the process of doing an astrology consultation, and she talks about using myth as a way of delivering bad news.

Even in the early chapter in which she introduces the idea in passing, my brain was electrified. *Of course!* What a fantastic way of thinking about it. Respectfully borrowing the idea, I offer my own interpretation, but I cannot recommend the book enough. Using myth or story in order to give bad news—or any news you suspect the client may not take well—is an excellent way of making something more palatable. Consider that telling the truth doesn't matter if the person getting it can't *hear* it. It's worthwhile to remember that not every client responds well to the take-no-prisoners approach. Sometimes, we can shut a client down by being too direct. Even when people think they're ready to hear the truth, they may discover they aren't and suddenly swing into protection mode. As a reader, we can use myth to create a version of the answer that lands without shutting down the client's receptors.

In this case, when we talk about myths, we're not necessarily talking about Persephone and Demeter (although you could certainly use them to illustrate a point if you wanted to). It's more about changing the way you explain what you're seeing in a reading. We tend to direct the reading to the client: "You do this, you do that; this happens to you, that doesn't happen to you." But we can also deliver the message in an indirect way that makes its point in the way a myth does. It's easier to demonstrate, so let's work through an example.

For context, it's worth knowing I don't believe there's any negative or positive tarot cards. Context guides me to whether each card is functioning in its light or shadow modes—or, more often, somewhere in between. For the purposes of this example, though, just to make it easier on all of us, I will work with some stereotypically negative cards and automatically assign them their more negative meanings. But again: *there are no positive and negative tarot cards.* (Or there are, who knows? We don't do dogma. We do *italicized, enthusiastic point-making.*)

Say Martini wants to know whether her long-lost lover Rossi will ever come back. When we shuffle, we draw Death, The Tower, and the Ten of Swords—three of the cards everyone looks forward to getting in their romance reading. Frankly, this is one of those spreads I don't even need to "interpret." I've got a ten, which frequently signals conclusions, and Death—which is the ultimate punctuation mark. In this case, The Tower doesn't need to say much because the other cards answered the question without it; maybe The Tower is just there to rub salt in the wound. The answer is *no,* and probably the client would assume that from looking at the depictions of those cards in most decks. But, for the sake of an example, here's how I could use a "myth"—a story to make something understandable—to deliver the news.

Me: I see someone wandering through a barren landscape, looking around at so many things that just don't seem to be thriving right now. Does that suggest anything to you?

Client: Well, I dunno…I mean, I haven't been feeling particularly good about anything since we broke up, so….

Me: Very fair. *(Hands over the Death card for the client to look at it.)* Do you find yourself anywhere in this card?

Client: Definitely not the guy on the horse. I feel more like the kid praying to be saved from the rider.

Me: Right? Okay. So, we've got this kid in a desolate landscape and she's praying to be saved from the rider.[27] Since you identified with her, I'm going to focus on her for a bit, okay? She's the "hero" of our story. You said she's praying that the rider won't get her, but the rider is clearly not interested in the individuals in front of him. He's already got the king, and he's coming for the bishop. Everyone in this landscape knows what's going to happen, but they all react differently. The bishop tries to stop the rider, the maiden looks away, but the kid faces the rider. The kid actually reaches back to the maiden and grabs her arm, as if to say, "It's going to be okay." I think that's the first message of the reading. Whatever happens, it's going to be okay, and you know that inside. But that doesn't mean the reality isn't scary.

Let's look at the next two cards. We've got The Tower and the Ten of Swords. Objectively, those don't look particularly inspiring, do they?

Client: They really don't.

Me: These two cards, The Tower and the Ten of Swords, are where the rider in the Death card is heading. That's where he's moving—into this desolate landscape. Do you want to hop on the horse with him? You could, the kid in the image is small enough that she might be able to hop up on there with him.

Client: I think I'll pass on that.

Me: Heard. So, let's look at what we have right now: there's this rider we're not that into, who freaks us out, and who is basically treading all over everyone in his way. He's heading to this desolate landscape, and we don't want to go with him. Thinking about your question, I see a rider returning from battle (look how the rider is armored) and he's going on to some places we don't want to go. Thinking about your ex, what might this say?

Client: ...I'm not really sure....[28]

Me: Mind if I share what I think?

---

27 I'm calling the kid in the card "she," because my client identifies that way and because she chose this figure, I know the kid represents the client.

28 For context, I will say that most of the time when the client says things like this, I think they actually *do* know—they either don't want to say it or don't want to be wrong. As a reader, you can do two things: tell them what you think or encourage them. "Oh, I know you do. Give it a try! There are no wrong answers." That's the most generous way of doing things, but if the client is especially shy or you've got limited time, it might be easier and safer just to tell them your version of things. Either way, my guess is that they already see where this is going.

Client: Please.

Me: I think your ex, Rossi, will come back. But I think you're going to see him for who he really is and that he's not going anywhere good, and it's not a ride you want to go on. It may be hard, you may want to look away, but I see you like that kid: staring right at him and saying, "I'm gonna pass on this ride, pal."

It's obviously easier to write this imagined scenario than to do a real reading, but instead of coming out and saying "no, he's not coming back," I actually got a completely different answer by not jumping to the conclusion I landed on when I saw the cards. Because I engaged the client and she identified as the child, my perspective changed and I saw Death as being the guy coming back—but bringing nothing but decay with him and heading toward nothing but decay. So, I surprised myself with the answer, but I also avoided a few things. First, when you tell a client they can't have something they want, you often put them on the defensive and their ego will kick in and say, "Oh, you think I can't get him back? I'll show you!" I mean, I don't think the client *knows* they're thinking that, but the response system kicks in and they'll start behaving that way. Another thing I did is offer them some context. "You may *think* you want this guy back, but when you see him again, you're going to see something ugly, armored, and heading in the wrong direction. *You're* not going to want *him.*" We re-center the client and her autonomy, and we appeal to her ego: you're too good for this.

We're also able to spill the tea on this guy. We give advice without giving it: "That rider isn't heading anywhere you want to go." If we were to say, "Girl, you're too good for him, when he comes back, kick him to the curb," that would be a choice, but people don't like that, even if they know they need to do it. On the other hand, just saying, "This dude isn't going anywhere you want to be" could surprise them out of their romantic aspirations.

Or it may not. We can't worry about that too much. But the idea is that if we're somehow oblique in the way we deliver difficult news, we can avoid some of the psychological triggers that get flipped when people's egos are activated—*and,* in Martini's example, we were able to offer a glimpse into what might be in store for her if she gets on the damn horse with her ex. But we didn't give any advice, we simply reflected the situation back (which brings us back to our early chapters). By telling a story *about the cards,* we're able to provide the client with information about themselves that will be likely easier for (some) folks to internalize and come to grips with. We don't present them with scolding or mentor-like guidance. We tell a story about a rider who is going nowhere, and we let Martini paint the picture for herself. This is going to be successful particularly in environments where you lack the luxury of getting deep into the specifics of the relationship's past and anything that may be difficult to talk about, either for you or the client.

There are folks for whom this oblique, mythic approach will not work. These, though, are likely to be folks for whom no reading will work because they simply cannot accept anything other than what they hope will happen. There will be clients who want to negotiate with you. "But you're saying he *could* come back, right?" Or, "It might be good, though, right?" You'll know these folks when you meet them, because no matter what you say, they're going to find something in it that gives them the answer they want—no matter how good or bad it is for them. In such times, frankly, being blunt is your best bet. "No, he's not coming back. At least not in the timespan covered by this reading." You don't owe anyone a negotiation. Say what you see. If you're wrong, you're wrong. These are the kind of people who are going to do what they were always going to do regardless of the reading. In fact, they may leave your table and go text their ex right then and there, feeling fully justified because of your work. You can't give information to people who don't want it.

However you handle bad news, though, I want to focus on two things: first, we don't get to decide what's good or bad to the client; second, humility and humanity are key. Let's talk about the second part first, because I've already done my number on how bad it is to poison people's wells with bad news. (Recall the story of my client who had been told by another reader she'd be dead soon.) Here, I want to talk about things that are less dramatic—*to us*—but that might be dramatic to the client.

While I detest the idea of giving people information that will hurt them without providing anything helpful, I think that there's only a few times where that's possible. Even deaths are worth exploring in a reading. If divination can help someone prepare for an inevitable loss, there's no reason to be pedantic about not reading about death and dying. In fact, we would all do well (at least in the Europeanized world) to develop a closer, deeper, and more positive relationship to death and dying. Someone who comes for a reading about their impending death or the impending death of someone they love could be demonstrating an incredibly mature, healthy reaction. Using a divination session to explore grief, say, or managing loss could be incredibly powerful. And this is another good reason why we as readers would do well to expand our understanding of, well, *everything*. The more nuanced an understanding we have of life (and death), the easier it is to explore such things with nuance in a reading.

There are other forms of bad news that aren't going to be exceptionally welcome, but that the client deserves the answer to. If they're grown up enough to ask the question, they're grown up enough to get the answer. We can't control how they're going to react to the intel, but we can control how we deliver it.

If you're particularly empathic, you may sense how to handle these kinds of things on a client-by-client basis. Not all of us have that gift, so there's a few ways to deal with that. First, you can simply ask the client. "How do you like to get a reading? Do you want it blunt and to-the-point? Are you more interested in puzzling out the details of a metaphor?" Or you can play it by ear and react to the client in real time. However you do it, I think a few things are helpful to consider:

Keep it simple. There's a tendency to want to over-explain or even hedge our bets in an effort to soften the blow. If you don't want to be direct, that's okay; use a method like the one we opened the chapter with, or find something that suits you better. But rip off the Band-Aid and say it as simply as you can: "No, he's not coming back." "Yes, she's cheating." "Yes, they are gossiping about you, and yes, it's hurting your reputation." When you have to give them tough news to face, at least do them the courtesy of being clear. This doesn't mean we can't be humane, but there's nothing gained from obfuscating. If it's bad, it's bad.

Avoid cliches. The worst thing people do in times of loss is bandy cliches back and forth. "She's in a better place." "He had it coming." "There are other fish in the sea." "You're too good for him." None of these help, and no one believes them. When something sucks, it sucks; there's no getting around it. "I'm sorry you're facing this" or something genuinely empathetic is appropriate and enough. If it's a close friend, obviously you're going to do more—but in a "professional" relationship, particularly if you're not a therapist or counselor, it's important not to try to bypass the reality with trite phrases.

Keep yourself out of it. It's okay to use anecdotes about your life to illustrate a point. Sometimes when I'm reading about a work situation, I might say, "I can give you an example from my career: I once had a boss who always threw me under the bus, so I know how this can feel." But a brief example to illustrate a point isn't the same thing as making the whole thing about you: "Oh, I'm so sorry, if there's anything I can do, I hate giving bad news like this...you know, I went through something similar, and I know it doesn't seem like it's possible, but it came out better for me and now I've never been happier." This is cringe, as the youths say. (I think.) See, a thing people tend to do when they're uncomfortable and trying to appear comfortable is reach for what they know: their own experience. And while that *can* be helpful *sometimes,* it's not why fortune tellers are here. It's possible to make space for someone and the reality of their cruddy circumstances without adding a song-and-dance number about our own lives. Be human, sure, but don't make yourself the star of the show.

All this being said, don't hold yourself to impossible standards. I offer guidelines to consider, because we don't really know what we're going to do and how we're going to react until we're in the position of giving *this* bad news to *this* client. Every situation is different. Something you think may be wonderful could send someone running away in tears; something you think will be awful could send someone dancing back into life on winged feet. We just don't know.

This is why I find it helpful to demonstrate a neutral-positive vibe. (That's a sentence I really didn't ever imagine myself typing, but there it is.) I'm upbeat, to the extent that I'm capable of, and I try not to judge anything. I try to mirror the client's attitude about what they're seeing, and if I can't tell, then I simply remain neutral. It's not always easy, and there are times I get excited on behalf of the client. But I'm not an excitable person to begin with, so it's not that often. Again, I need to stress that I'm not asking you to put on your "customer service voice" or affect some kind of AI-generated robot nature. Be genuine above all. Really, truly. If what I'm writing here is freaking you out and making you not want to work with clients, then forget I said anything. In a world of curated social-media inauthenticity, I will take a tarot reader with a heart over another video of a couple "surprising" each other with a "prank" that was *clearly* rehearsed, re-shot, and retouched to within an inch of its damn *life*. Be real. Be you. What I'm sharing is for folks who don't necessarily know how to approach these situations or who have felt like they could have done something "better." But a genuine, humble, kind person—who feels and who reacts—is *much more important than anything else,* good news or bad. I promise. Remember: we don't do dogma.

It's Good!

Okay, so what about when we have good news to deliver? Well, there are two points we'll consider: First, some people can't take good news because they don't believe they're capable of getting it. Second, sometimes what we think is good news isn't, and what we think is bad news is good. Let's start with the first one.

If you're reading for someone you know well, you'll know whether they can hear good things about themselves. You'll have had enough personal experience with them to be prepared for that reality. When you don't know a client, or only know them from limited professional experience, you don't know *how* they'll react. I now return to what I was saying moments ago: it's useful to take your emotional cues from the client. Let them guide you. Err on the side of upbeat, because we don't want to freak them out by downward spiraling with them—but if you sense they're not enthused about what seems like good news, it's okay to not throw a parade. Do check in with the client. "I'm not sure how we're feeling right now," said kindly will often at least cause a reaction from the client that will give you a sense of how they're feeling. Most of the time, though, they'll laugh and say something like, "Oh, I'm just taking it in." Which is also fair and a very real experience.

The point is, it's helpful not to jump to conclusions—about the cards, or whether the news is good or bad. Being open and non-judgmental is key to what we do. There's a kind of receptivity that isn't about taking on other people's energy, but that is about reading the room and reacting to it, that is helpful in our line of work. In fact, that skill tends to come to people who are generally pretty open in life—those who are open to ideas and who are aware of their surroundings and the life people lead. Cultivating one kind of awareness often opens you up to other kinds of awareness, and that can be really helpful in many parts of life. It's for sure going to make you safer, because your intuition will be turned up—and it's going to make you a better reader, because you're going to discover nuances in readings you'd never have discovered before.

Anyway, just as we can't know how clients will react to "bad" news, we can't know how clients will react to "good." It can feel a little weird when you're getting excited for someone but a look of panic slowly spreads across their face.

Then, there are the times when we see what the client wants in the cards and *we're* not pleased. We know that it's not the right thing for them. This tends to not happen much with clients, more with friends, but there have been times when my gut tells me that this isn't quite as ideal as the client would have me believe—or at least as good as they think it is. Here's where we fall down an ethical rabbit hole. Some might say they're obligated to comment on it, the argument being that if we have information that could help the client, we have an ethical responsibility to point it out. (They might be right.) Where I fall down, though, is that message isn't coming from the cards; it's coming from something inside me. The cards are spelling out auspicious messages, but *I'm* feeling ick. I'm not psychic, not in that way. It's hard to tell the difference between my instinct and my bias. And, as someone with chronic anxiety, it's hard to tell the difference between random intuitive hits and intrusive thoughts. So, as a reader, I try really hard to stick to what I see in the cards. That's my guide, and anything else will have to go by the wayside, because I can't trust it like I can trust what's on the table in front of me.

It's hard to differentiate between intrusive thoughts and the flashes of inspiration that come when reading, those intuitive hits that take you in an unexpected direction. Honestly, the intuitive or inspirational hits seem to come from my head—my brain, my eyes; I guess you could argue it's my third eye or pineal gland—and the gut reactions come from, unsurprisingly, my gut. The stuff that I feel in my gut I reserve for readings I do for friends or unhinged social media rants. I just can't trust myself enough to potentially piss on someone's glee. And that gets into a question of judgment for me: I don't get to decide what's good or bad for a client, particularly one I've never met before and will likely not see again, which is the case in many of the public readings I do. Most recurrent clients book me privately, and many of those have been working with me for a while. They're more comfortable giving me context, and I'm more comfortable saying, "I'm getting this sense that something might be off...."

This is another reason why ethics aren't a black-or-white proposition. There are people with whom I have enough of a relationship as a reader to say something like that, but there are many more I don't. I can't do anything that makes them feel like what they want to know is bad, stupid, or wrong. The same goes for their reaction to an answer. There's so much we don't and can't know about individual clients, especially when we're reading for folks in succession at a public event.

Where Am I?

It's worth considering the reading environment, particularly settings that are meant to be informal and fun—for *actual* entertainment purposes. Are there subjects you'd prefer to stay away from when reading at a fair or market, or at a friend's dinner party? There's nothing wrong with keeping it light, particularly during a celebration, and *especially* when there's intoxicants around. I'm not going to shame anyone who likes a tipple or a toke—not remotely—but there are some boundaries that might be worthwhile in environments where some folks are achieving better living through chemicals. I actually don't read in environments where folks are likely to be intoxicated, mostly because I'm in bed by the time people are uncorking bottles. Really, it's because I've never been presented with the opportunity. I don't know that I'd feel comfortable reading in a bar. Not because of the booze—because of the noise. I get easily drained in environments like that.

When I'm reading in public spaces, by which I mean when I'm reading where anyone passing by could sit with me, I don't really put any limits on what I'll read about. The vibes at these kinds of events tend to be relatively upbeat and chill, so most folks aren't sitting down trauma dumping. Although, I've had some astonishingly moving readings in these environments, so that's not to say that heavy things can't come up. You may want to consider whether or not you want to limit certain topics in certain environments. If you do, state it in your bio and promotional materials—give folks a heads up, just so they know what to expect.

A good thing to do if you want to limit the topics is to have something indicating the topics you *will* cover. You could have it on your table with your price list and just say, "These are the topics I can cover today!" However you want to do it, it's never a bad thing to consider the way the environment will play into the reading. Everything can impact it—and if it doesn't impact the reading, it can impact the reader. I will say, though, I hesitated for a long time to offer readings at events like markets and fairs. I thought, as an introvert, that I would get tired too quickly, feel too much pressure, or just generally flame out. I took a leap, and it wound up being an incredible experience—and now it's one of my favorite things to do. I actually find myself not drained but energized after doing it. That's not a feeling I'm used to when being out in public. I'm *really* introverted. Based on my MBTI results (the real ones, not the online freebies), I'm over 75% introverted. There are days when I come home from a perfectly normal day at the office and I'm catatonic until bedtime. But that's not the case when I do readings, which is exciting and strange (but mostly exciting). So, give yourself permission to try things you don't know if you'll enjoy. It could turn out to be your favorite thing. (Another reason to practice this kind of openness, eh?)

Answered Prayers

Noted self-destructive personality and original gay best friend Truman Capote famously used a quote from St. Theresa of Avila as the epigraph of his final, unfinished novel: "More tears are shed over answered prayers than unanswered ones." Capote learned that the hard way when an excerpt from the book appeared in *Vanity Fair,* forcing a wedge between him and the famous women who had been his patronesses and protectors. Of course, it had to; he'd put a thin veil on them, used them all as the source of his scandalous *roman a clef,* and set about his own undoing. It's hard to say whether he thought he could get away with it, or if a life's worth of trauma as a femme, queer, short king left him needing to destroy everything he'd built for himself. Many of his queer peers did the same, including his pal Tennessee Williams. Both got what they wanted—fame, respect, even sex—but both couldn't handle it and self-destructed in their own way.

What we learn from Capote and from St. Theresa is that the perception of an experience is different from its reality, and the things we really want in life can be things we're unable to process having when and if we get them. It's hard to deal with, because we have the talent to back up our desires but not the armor to go into battle for them the way most forms of success require of us. Other, less talented people with more fight will succeed and we'll watch, irritated or horrified, as the bitter pill of life's unfairness festers. I know from personal experience. I've been there a bunch of times.

This isn't to bring down the vibe. It's to say that life is actually far more nuanced than we give it credit for. I reference my life in the theatre a lot as an example, but though I had the gift, I lacked the willingness to subjugate myself, starve myself either for roles or because I couldn't afford to eat, and, in recent years, am no longer willing to accept the poisonous norms that remain in the air long after the lockdown-era reckoning so many arts groups *say* they went through. This is to say that an unwanted answer may not be the news anyone feels like dealing with, but that doesn't mean it's *bad.* Likewise, in a "good" reading, just because the answer is "yes" doesn't mean it's going to be for the best. We well know, and have seen, that the ex could come back and be worse than ever.

This is one reason why I like tarot for yes or no questions, though many folks say it's not a great tool for this type of reading. It's true that a pendulum or a deck of playing cards or a die could get you a yes/no *faster,* but they won't necessarily give you the *why.* And I've found most people want the why—especially when the answer is "no." It usually takes more work to get to a yes or no with tarot cards (or other more interpretive methods) because you have to go through the whole reading in order to get to the answer, and it's usually not what you think when you just spread out the cards and get a first impression. As we saw in the example above, the Death card, which would normally suggest a relationship being over, wound up suggesting a toxic person returning to the client's life. All that said, though, you will feel a lot more confident in your yes-or-no answer when you do all that work. I do, anyway; I'm less likely to chalk the answer up to randomness because I've done the work to justify my thesis. (I'm not going to lie, though; there are times I want a quick answer for myself, and in that case, dice or playing cards are the way to go. Odds are "no"; evens, "yes." Sometimes with playing cards, hearts and diamonds are yes; spades and clubs, no. I tend to adopt the spades/no, hearts/yes, clubs/maybe-no, diamonds/maybe-yes approach. I always pull three cards, so I have layers to justify my answer.)

GOOD TIMES AND BUM TIMES

We live in an age where nuanced issues are regularly, maybe entirely, discussed as completely black-or-white. We react to those discussions with evangelical praise or hellfire's total fury. So, strange as it might seem, it's hard to use nuanced thinking right now. And there are some things where there simply is no room for nuance today. Marginalized people, for example, are being "nuanced" to death—literal death—and then ultimately negated. But fortune tellers benefit from understanding the nuances of a situation and the readings before us. Most things aren't completely good or completely bad; much of the world exists in a space somewhere between that binary. In fact, the good/bad binary appears to be a recent development in human thinking and, as far as I can tell, emerges from the Abrahamic religions—major sects of which have been among the most absolutist faiths in human history. So much of humanity lives in the spaces between. Fortune tellers do well to understand this liminality. It's in the tension between good/bad or yes/no where so many answers live. Let's give ourselves the gift of nuance—so we can give it to our clients, who are likely in deep need of it.

For the First Time in Forever...

A final note before closing this chapter: humans, though we try not to be, are somewhat fatalistic, especially when we get what we want. We have a sense that achieving a certain goal is a "forever" experience. Once we "make it," whatever "it" is, we've gotten where we're going and we can sit back and enjoy it. This might be a relationship or a career milestone, a publishing contract, a good performance review, a validating response from a secret crush. We feel that, having gotten it, it's ours forever. (Though we also weirdly know it's *not* forever, and so many of us also start freaking out that we'll eventually lose it.) There's an absolutism that comes with being alive and causes us trouble.

Most of us understand intellectually that nothing lasts forever, but we have a hard time living with that. I have a tendency, maybe, to overplay my reminders to clients (especially when I'm giving good news) that nothing is forever and that just because something is going well doesn't mean there may not be obstacles and bumps along the way. Of course, I don't want to deflate them; I want people to remember that just because I'm saying they've got something good on the way doesn't mean they can relax. I want them to appreciate that just because the potential for a date looks really good doesn't mean that, even if they get married, it's going to be a completely blissful existence. In fact, I think that good news can sometimes be worse for a client than bad news, because good news can make us lazy. We can stop doing whatever we were doing to make something happen because we now have confirmation it's working. If I tell you you're going to get the promotion, you might stop doing the things that were going to get you that promotion. You might say, "Ah, I've got this on lock," then walk into the office like an arrogant prick and ruin all the good will that got you where you wanted to be. Suddenly, the bosses aren't so sure you're the right person for the job. And this brings us to something that keeps many a reader awake at some point...*consequences.*

Consequences

Good, bad, or indifferent, readings have consequences. We think of this mostly when it comes to things like predictive readings or third-party readings ("Are they cheating?"), because part of the anti-fortune telling bias teaches us that these things are unethical and potentially impossible to do. We already know how I feel about *that* attitude. Readers who subscribe to that anti-fortune telling nonsense sometimes demonstrate an unearned sense of superiority. I know, because I for sure used to do this—and, of course, because I come up against it a lot today. If you avoid doing those kinds of readings, you're fine. You get to do whatever you think is appropriate with your divination. But it's important to recall, especially if we happen to be one of those with the superiority complex, that more "acceptable" types of readings can also have unintended consequences. For example, what happens if a reader gives a client advice that turns out to be terrible? What if a reading suggests that the way a client can keep a partner is to change everything about themselves, a la *My Fair Lady* and *Grease!*, and then it doesn't work? What if, say, I tell you that you'll be coming into to some money, and so you exterminate your rich uncle? There's nothing saying that those things can't happen, and both fit within "traditionally ethical" readings.

We simply can't know the consequences of *any* reading. Full stop. I've joked before that you could do a reading *before* every reading to tell you how the reading is going to turn out—but that's just a little ridiculous. No one is saying we shouldn't consider the consequences of reading; it's just that consequences exist regardless of how "ethical" the reading is. The argument can be made that, like quantum physics, the act of observing something changes it. By doing a reading about *anything*, we're inserting ourselves into the process and that will impact the outcome. Even seeing an outcome can impact that result. There's nothing "wrong" with that, at least I don't think there is. It's inevitable. We *do* become part of the situation merely by commenting on it and, whether we think we do or not, that means we have influence. Any client extends a certain amount of trust to readers, imbuing us with both power and influence. It's hard not to, because we are a society of "influencers." And it's something common across the social landscape. We do this with people who are "famous" in a field. If we've heard of them, they "must" be the real deal. Somehow fame implies ability and wisdom. We may not realize it, but for some clients, we take on that role simply by being someone skilled at reading. They may not even realize they're doing it, but there is a power dynamic at play. We "become" experts in whatever we're talking about, even if we think of ourselves as merely a card reader. And we have to be aware of that, because we don't have the systemic protections that doctors and cops do. We can explain that what we do is for "entertainment purposes only," but that doesn't mean the client stops seeing us as wise and, thus, influential.

That shouldn't stop us from doing readings, though, because the same could be said for taking a friend's advice or an online quiz. As readers, we are not accountable for the actions clients take following a reading. It's good to remind them of that. And, since I referenced it above, I loathe the idea of saying divination is for "entertainment purposes only." Catholics are required to go to unmarried, celibate, inexperienced priests for marriage counseling before their wedding. What the hell do *priests* know about marriage and romantic/sexual relationships? Know what I mean? As spiritual leaders, they're entitled to give advice on something they have no lived experience of. Readers, on the other hand, actually have secular life experience, including (potentially) in long-term relationships. Marriages certainly haven't gotten any *happier* since the church took on this role; in fact, the divorce rate has been ever-growing as the number of couples choosing to marry decreases. Is that the *fault* of priests? As much as I want to say yes, that's probably not so. (In fact, it's probably that the church has less influence on divorce law in many places.) But readers have to couch what we do to protect ourselves. Maybe the real solution is that we all get ordained.

The point is, whatever we read about can have a consequence. So, if that's what's stopping you from doing certain kinds of divinations, recognize that even the most seemingly innocuous reading can and will have unintended consequences. We have to accept our responsibility to our clients when we offer readings, no matter the topic or technique. So, reminding a client that, good or bad, life is activated by *their* choices and *their* actions—and that *they* have the ultimate decision-making responsibility in their life—can go a long way. Remind them that they, in fact, are the subject of the reading, and *they* are the one who *owns the outcome.* Good or bad, the reading is *theirs.* And so is whatever *they choose* to do about it. A reading reflects a potential reality; the client makes or breaks it—at least to the degree they have agency to do so. But readers are not the ones in power, even if the client isn't either. Never be afraid to make that clear. The reading *belongs* to the client, as do the outcomes and the action plan. Fortune tellers, especially those of us who aren't counselors, simply say what we see. And that's another thing I like about being this kind of reader: I'm not interested in living my client's lives for them. And because I'm not, they're the ones in charge. And that is as it should be.

CHAPTER SIX

AGENCY AND AUTONOMY

In the last few years, if you follow anything "New Age-y" (a term I really cannot stand), you'd get the impression that you can have anything you want if you simply "manifest" it. That the folks saying this are usually white, often moneyed, clearly privileged, and full of a special kind of crap doesn't really seem to bother any of their followers. And why should it? We all want to believe that things could be just a little easier. The trouble is, unless you've got the money and the connections, that's usually not possible. We can manifest all we want, but many of us still end up with the shit end of life's stick (as it were). Simply put, the world is designed to make life easier for certain people and harder on others. It's a human-made reality, but it's a reality, nonetheless.

If you grew up in the so-called United States, you learned that all "men" are created equal and have the ability to achieve the goals of life, liberty, and the pursuit of happiness. Most people never get close. The people who do are the obscenely wealthy, who are typically straight, white, cis men with generational or inherited wealth and legacy admissions and spots on boards. There are, of course, a select few who come from "nothing" and achieve "greatness" and influence (in the US, greatness and influence basically means obscene wealth and the microphone and lack of accountability that come with it). Some folks do manage to get through the cracks and achieve upper echelon success. Most don't. It's like Hollywood: it's a company town for a family company. The names you know are the names you know in part because they've been the names in Hollywood since the start. Politics, too. During the 2016 election, generations of voters had never seen anyone who wasn't a Bush or a Clinton on the presidential ballot. Success is a family game in the "developed" (read: colonized) world.

This means that, though we're taught everyone can pick themselves up by their fucking "bootstraps" (who even knows what a bootstrap is anymore?) and succeed, most of us simply will not because the odds are stacked against us. Well, maybe that's a little defeatist. It's somewhat truer to say that the odds are stacked *for* rather than *against* us, but that's semantics. If the odds are in favor of one small group and not in favor of literally everyone else. This is how power works, which is why I'm forcing you to face this grim reality: because influencer culture hinges on a mythological ease that people truly believe exists, even if the reality has more to do with privilege and access than "manifesting." Life does not work that way for most of us. Not because it can't, but because those in power like it that way. After all, who's going to make an influencer's widgets and clean their toilets if not the people yearning to achieve the glory of a consistent paycheck and health insurance? Even tax laws benefit people who sell our labor to corporations over working for ourselves. Despite all the tax contributions I make from my corporate income, I still owe a ton at the end of each year because of whatever money I make from readings, books, and workshops.

This is all to say that there are times when we are the masters of our fate and times when we're not, and those conditions matter in readings, especially because the positive-thinking movement is alive and well and hurting people. It's really just repackaged New Thought, which isn't new anymore—and never really was. It comes from the likes of Napoleon Hill's *Think and Grow Rich* and similar titles that have peddled similar messages over the years. Well, Napoleon Hill was a conman, and while positive thinking seems to be an effective tool for many people, there are limits to its power, especially if you happen to fall into one of the groups that most frequently gets kicked around by the powerful. And the powerful enjoy kicking people around because the sensation of power starts to fade over time, and if you want to feel the dopamine rush, all you need to do is remind yourself of how powerful you are and others aren't.

It's funny, I really didn't want to write a downer of a book, but so much of what we face as readers isn't that sunny. The fact is, most people come for readings when things aren't going well. When things are fine, nobody pauses to question it, and we just hope we can make it last as long as possible. We definitely don't stop in the middle of a good run in order to find out whether it will continue. It's only when we're experiencing loss or frustration that we need to get ourselves read. And that makes sense, right? I would not recommend stopping in the middle of a joyful flow to get a reading about how long it will last. Just take advantage of it as much as you can. Elizabeth Gilbert in *Big Magic* reminds us that "genius" historically wasn't something someone *was*, it was something someone was *visited by*. Nobody is a genius; genius visits us. In those moments, we have to take advantage of our wonderful and powerful visitor! We shouldn't stop to look in the mirror about it! It's when we can't remember how to invite the genius back that we get readings. It's the times when we have feelings of powerlessness and a lack of agency that we want to know how to get it back. In a previous chapter, I said that most readings boil down to the client wanting to know if they're safe. The rest generally fall into, "How do I escape this hell?"

Okay, maybe that's a little over the top—but you get the point.

It's important for readers to be able to see how much power a client (or any subject of a reading, if we're not reading about the client) has to impact change in their situation. This matters because, in order to effectively get out of a situation or change it, we need to understand what obstacles are in our way and what aren't, what things we can do, and what will simply waste our limited reserves of energy. If we have limited power, we should use what we do have wisely. If we have limited influence, we need to know where it's best applied. It's lovely to think that we can all achieve anything we want if only we manifest it, but that's just not a reality for many, many things. So, knowing the degree of power a client has in certain situations can be useful in terms of giving advice, understanding the full measure of their experience, and setting a realistic impression of the likelihood of something becoming achievable or not.

We'll look at two examples to see how this can be done. First, we'll use a quick lenormand spread, just for variety; second, we'll look at a tarot reading. In exploring two methods, you can see that this concept can be applied to other types of divination, too. I built my bone set around this idea, in part by having two chess pieces in the kit: the brown chess piece represents my client; the white, anyone or anything opposing them. Interestingly, I find that many times, the white chess piece (representing opposition) is surrounded by things indicating the client is actually their own opposing force. I find that quite cool. (Though, of course, it's less cool for the client, who now has to deal with themselves. But that's their problem. Wink.)

Say we have a young woman, Liza, who is hoping to get into the MFA acting program at Yale School of Drama. We shuffle a lenormand deck and look for the querent card—in this case, the deck I used has two "gentleman" cards, rather than a lady and a man—and the three cards on either side of her in the deck (assuming there are three on either side), which I'll arrange in a line of seven. In our case, we get:

Tree, Scythe, Ring, Significator (Gentleman #1), Cavalier (Rider), Clover, Ship

I'm not using houses, but you could—that always provides more context. So, the question is whether or not this client will get into Yale School of Drama for her MFA. In lenormand, it's not uncommon to use playing card correspondences to indicate yes/no answers. In this case, we have three hearts, two diamonds, one club, and one spade. If we use hearts as yes, diamonds as maybe yes, clubs as maybe no, and spades as no, this reading gives us a qualified yes. But that's not as interesting to me at the moment, because it doesn't tell me why or how much influence Liza has.

Starting in the middle with the significator, I've got the cavalier (rider), clover, and ship to the right. Since the significator card is facing to the right (thus, facing these three cards), I can read this as where Liza is going. (Not all lenormand readers use where the significator faces, but I do.) That makes the three cards behind her where she's coming from. This is helpful because knowing where the client is coming from helps me understand how much agency she's got in this situation. Let's look at that first: *tree, scythe, ring.* My instinct says she's really committed (ring) to getting away or cutting off (scythe) from her family or some other oppressive obligation (tree). That indicates that she is or feels somewhat helpless. The tree is powerful; a scythe can't fell a tree. She's working with a tool that isn't up to the job. Thinking in terms of her choice of career, this instantly makes me think she's not a very good actor—at least not by the standards of the school she's trying to get into. But she's committed, and sometimes that's all we need in life.[29] Given this particular reading, I'm going to hold on to both ideas for a while.

Now, her significator (in this deck, a man—but I don't consider the gender of the "lady" or "man" cards in lenormand, which is why in this deck I use the two gentleman cards) butts up against the cavalier (rider). The cavalier rides to the clovers. This indicates to me she's got a small amount of ambition that can push her though. The ship, though, presents trouble. It is forward motion, but it's slow motion. Right now, she doesn't have enough motivation to pursue this dream. She's got enough, maybe, to get through the audition—but not through the rejection that follows. (For context, I happen to know that many people who do get into Yale School of Drama only do so after a few attempts.) She may have the raw talent to do it, but she lacks the tenacity. So, she's got *some* agency, but she's also up against the limits of her own ability to care.

If I start mirroring the cards (pairing each duo of cards on either side of her significator), I get the following combos:

Ring/Cavalier (Rider), Scythe/Clover, Tree/Ship

This underscores the message I've already gotten: She's for sure committed to this plan (ring and rider), but hardships (scythe) cut off the little luck/motivation (clover) she's got, because this is a long, long journey (tree/ship).

In this reading, the major obstacle seems to be Liza's sustained interest, rather than any institutional bias against her. She may not have the innate "talent," but they might consider her for her tenacity—except she doesn't have any. So, it looks to me like she's not going to get in. And then she's going to let the rejection stop her from attempting another time, and even another after that. I sense that there's

---

29 Houses would be helpful here, honestly. This is why I really only use lenormand in a grand tableau, including houses—it just shines best there, because I can cross-reference my gut instincts. For example, I also feel like the tree could be her desire to act and the scythe indicating she's not up to that career. Houses would help me contextualize the cards to understand which of those were more likely. If the tree fell, say, in the house of the house, then I'd know it was family; if it fell in the house of the star, then it would make more sense to be acting.

potential if she tries, but it could take as many as five attempts.[30] That is a long haul; you get one chance a year. That means she would have to wait *at least* four years before she gets close to the result she wants, but if she really wants this dream, then she's going to need to figure out a way to work through her own issues. *She's* the obstacle, not the school. The answer is "no, you're not getting in—not this year. You could get in if you don't let defeatism get in the way of trying until you finally get the nod." She's got some agency in this case, although she is up against obstacles, too—because there's a limit to how many students get accepted, and there's no way of knowing who she'll be up against from year to year.

This reading makes me think this goal isn't quite as important to her as she thinks it is. The ring is a commitment, but it's not forever. She'll likely have to go through a lot before she knows what she really needs or wants out of life, which is common for most people thinking about school. But that's not really relevant here, and if I told her that, she wouldn't believe me. The salient point here is that she's got some agency, but not enough to carry her through; on the other hand, if she finds some motivation to sustain interest, she *might* get what she wants after a journey. Remember that this reading is based on the likely events right now, so the answer is about *now.* The reality, though, is that sustaining her tenacity *could* get her what she wants, but it doesn't guarantee it. We're simply reading about the likelihood as it stands in this moment. We'd have to read again down the line to see if her chances have improved. (A final note on this reading: my lenormand interpretations are decidedly non-traditional, so if you think I'm wrong, that's fine. I'm not, but that's fine. If you read more traditionally, you may have gotten a different answer and that's A-okay with me.) Next, let's try the same reading using tarot cards.

A Brief Digression on the Rider-Waite-Smith Tarot

I'm working with the Waite-Smith cards in this book, mostly because they're so familiar to so many people that folks can conjure the image of each card just by hearing its name. It's not a deck I really read with these days, though it is what I learned with. I will confess, laying out cards for this exercise, I had a strong emotional reaction to them because it's been *ages* since I've looked at them. They were once my daily companion, and over time, other decks that are more in line with my methods and thinking (and that have far less Christian imagery) have come to be my main tools. It's funny, because I'm so hard on A. E. Waite, the Golden Dawn, and this deck. Even Smith gets a little derision, because she liked to cosplay as a Jamaican woman while being a whiter shade of pale herself. It's a problematic deck. It's got zero diversity and represents an idealized never-time that even features some

30 This is because the ship is the third card and the tree is the fifth card, which suggests that it could take between three and five tries. There's nothing in lenormand saying that's how things go, but it's an intuitive hit that comes both from the vibe of the reading and also my experience with graduate programs.

colonizer realness (the Two and Three of Wands). Yes, it's a product of its time, but we ain't in that time anymore. Many of its iterations have been ugly to boot, so it's not even that attractive in many common editions.

And yet.

There's an emotional impact that's (in my case) unavoidable. It's like coming back to family, with all its problems. And the cleverness of the deck, the wit of the minors—I really do think it's iconic. It's also one of the most plagiarized works of art in history. A lot of artists have benefited more than Pamela Colman Smith ever could have from both her work and the freedom that exists to take it and adapt it—sometimes changing or adding nearly nothing. Problematic though it is, and though Smith clearly could have made less appropriative wardrobe choices in her life, the Waite-Smith cards made tarot *accessible*. That's why I can't dismiss it, and why I can't say it's not a valuable part of tarot's legacy. It may well have *saved* tarot—or even re-invented it, if we're generous. There's nothing particularly interesting about the mass-market playing tarots made in the Marseille style, even though I find them quite beautiful. The works of esotericists before Waite weren't always available or of interest to the general public, and had no designs made for normies. Had this tarot deck not been published, interest in tarot would never have achieved the levels it has. I don't doubt that eventually someone would have come along and done what Waite and Smith did. But they didn't get to, because these two weirdos got there first and they did so in a way that has spoken so deeply to so many people *despite* all of its problems—and the relatively crap job many early publishers have done putting it into the world.

This deck has survived the bombings of world wars *and* tacky print jobs—sometimes reducing it to nothing more than a McDonaldsian red and yellow that just makes me want to shove pencils in my eyes. It has survived the pretenses of Waite's often-inscrutable *The Pictorial Key to the Tarot* (what he surely would have viewed as the more valuable part of the package). It has survived being an esoteric curiosity and even the onslaught of new decks in the last thirty years. It remains as popular as ever, and even in new iterations, it stirs up controversy. Every time I attend a tarot event, I'm always amazed by how many folks default to this deck. It is debated, pissed on, adored, dismissed, scoffed, re-colored, rectified, restored, and even its ugliest iterations have gone for thousands at auctions. It is the Motha' of the House of Golden, children, and no one can take that away. It has shaped every single modern reader, whether they like it or not, and as a result, I think it's one of the most important pieces of spiritual literature and pieces of art in history.

When I interviewed Maria Minnis, author of *Tarot for the Hard Work* (for my money, one of the best books on modern tarot currently in or out of print), she said of her work, "This book is a spell!" I loved that. And I think, like it or not, the Waite-Smith deck is a spell, too. Luckily, it's a more productive, positive, and accessible spell than what the Golden Dawn typically seemed to like. But it really *is* tarot in a lot of ways, purely because it made reading possible for people who don't have an esoteric background. What is amazing to me—and I really do wonder if there was some part of Waite that knew he was doing this—is that this deck really made it possible to practice divination without having to learn a complicated system. Waite seemed so fascinated with secrecy and his writing is so tedious. But he made this deck, and though he said it wasn't for fortune telling, what else *could* it be for? Sometimes I wonder if his posturing was all for show, and deep down the dude was a true-blue fortune teller. How subversive would that be? I don't really think it's that likely, but it's hard not to look at this—the only thing he's known for by the general population—and think he didn't know *exactly* what he was doing.

There's always a possibility. Nothing is all one thing, after all.

Back to Liza's case, I'll draw five cards in an arc. This is something I commonly do for follow-ups to larger readings, to cover a second topic for a client when we have additional time, or quick readings for myself. I lay out the first card in the middle, and then alternate left and right for the remaining. Similar to lenormand, I will often use mirroring and pairings with tarot, depending on whether or not they add more context. We'll use the same question and client just so you can see the ways I work through the same reading with two systems. Obviously, the answers may be different.

In a line, I've drawn:

Seven of Pentacles (4), King of Wands (2), Six of Swords (1),
Five of Swords (3), The Hanged Man (5)

The number in parentheses indicates the order in which that card was drawn and laid out.

Interestingly, this set of cards is insisting I do something similar to what I did with the lenormand: read what's to the right of the central card as where the client is going, and what's to the left as where she's coming from. In this case, it's because the Six of Swords is a "travel" card (indicating a forward motion), and it's "facing" the right. Actually, a quick scan of these cards suggests rather a similar overall flow to the lenormand spread. The Seven of Pentacles has a tree vibe, the Five of Swords a scythe-iness, and The Hanged Man a ship quality. This, incidentally, is one of many examples of why I love doing what I do. I love divination. The older I get and more willing I've been to experiment, the more I find these delightful little connections. I've allowed myself to open up to the cards, rather than getting closed and constricted.

It's tempting when I see a court card to assume that this is the main actor in the reading. That's not always the case, though, so I don't want to jump to any conclusions just yet. I want to start by thinking about the Six of Swords.

The Six of Swords at the heart of our spread always creates a moody, mournful atmosphere. That's one reason I don't really like working with Waite-Smith decks that much. I prefer a more neutral image if there's an image on the card. Sixes are not particularly negative cards (though, like all cards, they can be). They rebalance after the upheaval of fives and, in many traditions, they're associated with beauty. They can be somewhat vain, however, with an over-reliance on beauty. They're three plus three, so there's an expansive nature to sixes, too. The darker tones we find in many versions of this card likely derive from the fact that it's a sword. In playing card divination, this suit is spades and it is typically the most negative suit. It's also because the Golden Dawn titles for the minors influenced Pamela Colman Smith, and so everyone that followed. The titles of the Golden Dawn wands and swords are pretty negative, which is why Smith's images are.

This is why I always say "the image is not the card." The card is the Six of Swords, *not* the image of a boatman sailing two veiled figures in a small craft. There is more than just the image, including the function of swords, the element, and the number—in this case, a generally positive number. What do I mean about the function of swords? Much! We've talked about function already, and I like to think about the function of the suit object when reading. Swords are status symbols, frequently having no actual function beyond that; they're used to bludgeon or slice; they're forged from metal, so they're strong; they're emblematic of folkloric heroes, like King Arthur; and they're weapons, so they wound. I'll also think about more practical tools that could be replaced by swords: knives, say, or even pens (the pen is mightier than the sword). Knives slice and pare, making surgery possible; pens make communication possible. All of these can add interest and context to a reading.

Then there's the element of Air, at least in my system. (Some readers associate swords with Fire, and you are welcome to do the same! It's also common to associate wands with Earth, because sticks grow from the Earth. If it works for you, do it.) Air has similar attributes to the function of swords, and it's also associated with communication. Air is intellectual, mercurial, flighty, expansive, and *necessary*. We can't live without it, Fire can't burn without it, and Water is made of it. Life on Earth just isn't possible without it. It's common to think in terms of the elements' adversarial and complimentary relationships with each other. Borrowed from astrology, these are known as elemental dignities. Air and Fire, being active, aggressive elements are complimentary; Earth and Water, being receptive and regressive, are also complimentary. Water and Fire are adversarial; Air and Earth, the same. Fire and Earth are neutral-to-adversarial; Water and Air, the same. These used to be a big part of how I read, but no longer. There's nothing wrong with it. I just outgrew it. It wasn't even a conscious choice; I noticed one day that I'd changed my method. Now, as we've explored elsewhere, I tend to think of the element in terms of its function: what is it for, what does it do? I'll cover this more in Chapter Fourteen, where I do something I thought I'd never do—share written meanings for each of the cards. But we'll come back to that. You've got a decent sense of my Air qualities for the time being.

Another thing I do before I start reading individual cards in a spread is look at the elemental makeup of the array. Here, we've got two swords (making it the dominant suit, although its dominance is relatively weak), one pentacle, one wand, and one major. There are no Water cards (cups), so there's an elemental deficit. This could tell me something, but it might not be that important. Sometimes the absence of an element in a reading can indicate that it's needed; other times, that it's not necessary. Sometimes, it's both. (We'll explore more as we go on.) I'll also look at the mix of numbers. We've got a seven, a six, and a five, along with the twelve of The Hanged Man. These are all mid-journey, in terms of their respective suits: five, six, and seven fall in the middle, edging toward the higher end of the range; The Hanged Man's twelve is also about in the middle of the majors. This can be useful from a timing perspective. It can indicate that the client is in the middle of a journey, or it can indicate that there is a lot of distance between them and their goal. Context will clue us in if it becomes relevant.

In this case, I'm trying not to be too influenced by the reading I've already done on this because they're theoretically unrelated. I don't do a lenormand reading before a tarot reading; it's one or the other. So, I'm trying not to jump to any conclusions about what the numbers mean for Liza. Right now, I'm getting an overall perspective of what I'm seeing. The final thing I note is the King of Wands. We've got a court card, which *can* represent the client, but it can also represent someone in the client's life, as well as a state of being. As the only court card, it's tempting to assume it's Liza, but I can't jump to conclusions yet. It's the only wands card in the reading, though, and it's a king, so it's got some potency. It also happens to have its back turned to the cards that follow.

When reading tarot, the amount of information in a single card can overwhelm. There's a tendency, especially for those who come from esoteric-minded traditions, to assume that all cards and all symbols within the card have equal weight. That's not helpful. It's accepted among astrologers that not all planets have equal weight in a natal or transit chart. Planets will be stronger or weaker, astrologically, based on where they fall, what house they're in, and the aspects (or angular relationships) between the planets, asteroids, and other objects considered in a reading. This is also true of any card reading. Some cards will have stronger, more powerful influences on a reading; others may serve more like vowel sounds, carrying information from one card to the next. Same for all the images and associations we have for cards. We don't need all of them. Attempting to make all of them make sense in a reading will frustrate you. And there's a lot to draw on: astrological correspondences, elemental and numerological correspondences, Kabbalistic correspondences, and all of the various pieces of the image that make up a card. You only need the ones that are relevant for *this* reading, meaning the reading you're doing. Don't get bogged down in all the potential connections. You don't need them all and they can get distracting. How do you know which to go with? Context will guide you. The first context that will be helpful is the question.

Writing out a reading while explaining what I'm doing is time consuming. You've got a sense of my preliminary scan, but really that happens incredibly quickly—a matter of seconds. I'm not putting any pressure on myself or the cards; I'm simply noting what jumps out at me, looking for themes, seeing if there is any weighting toward one suit or element, one number, or a preponderance of majors. I don't really read the majors as "major," which sets me apart from a lot of readers—but I don't mean that my tendency is good or bad. I just mean that I see them on par with the minors and the courts. For me, the "bigness" of a card has more to do with the bigness of the question. I call this *size* and *scope:* what is the relative size of the question, in terms of its heaviness in life? To clients, all questions are big. To me as a reader, I need to consider whether it's big in terms of bringing a baby into the world, or if it's less dramatic, like wondering if we'll get into grad school. I don't discuss size with clients; I just know that my interpretation of the cards has to match the size of the reading. Scope refers to what potential card meanings are relevant to this question. Anything that isn't relevant is out of scope and I don't worry about it for this reading.

The Hanged Man is a great card to talk these concepts through, because it's collected a big array of meanings over the years: perspective shifts is common, but it can also suggest consequences (that guy isn't hanging there because he wants to be; he's being punished, whether he's guilty or not), as well as a traitor—which is the original name of the card. Finally, it can simply suggest arrested development or being stuck in a rut. For our purposes, consequences and being a traitor are simply out of scope. They don't make sense for this situation. Perspective shifts might be relevant, but honestly, it's rare that I read the card that way because it's just not that common in my experience. Actually, I tend to see The Tower as perspective shifts, because that's what a shift in viewpoint feels like, more than the idealized Hanged Man presented in many decks. These are all things I consider as I'm laying out the cards.

Now, I read—and at long last, we return to the first card I put down, the Six of Swords, and consider the reading. This is a motion card in many decks, and sixes are beautiful and rebalancing; these are good signs, though the mood of the image is, as we said, mournful. The Five of Swords, which follows it in the spread indicates disruptive forces, challenges—particularly mental and communicative—and then the reading resolves in The Hanged Man. Stasis. So, I could say that this client is going to get close to the goal. Liza is making strides on getting into Yale. But when she encounters a snag in the Five, she'll let herself get stuck. This is more or less exactly what the last reading said, although in a different way.

Here I have more context than I did with the lenormand reading, because there's more information in the cards. The Five and Six of Swords have an interesting relationship: the reading starts with the six and then goes *backward.* She will view this audition as a step back. Also, because the swords deal with language and learning, it ties both to the art of acting and the institution of higher learning. I'm compelled to say that the auditors may dislike Liza's choice of audition material—the words (swords/Air) she uses make them unhappy (five). This could also be about her interview, if she gets one, so there are two ways I could read this. Typically, only finalists are given interviews. She should be thoughtful about her choices, maybe get some good advice, and practice her answers if she is invited to interview.

This set of three also tells me that the answer is no: there's some progress (six), a snafu or challenge (five), and the progress stops (Hanged Man). I still do have the two other cards that sit to the left of the Six of Swords, though. The King of Wands is a fascinating card here, sitting as it does with his back to the answer and eyes on the Seven of Pentacles. This suggests to me an ego at play. The client thinks they've already earned their place (the seven indicating that they've done work toward this goal; the king giving ego, thanks in part to Fire's association with Leo). In fact, the King of Wands mirrors with the Five of Swords, so that arrogance may be the source of the school's disinterest. The Hanged Man and the Seven of Pentacles mirror as well, suggesting that Liza thinks she's grown enough and doesn't have more to do.

This essentially gives me the same answer: no, you're not going to get in, and your defeatism will stop you from trying again. This time, I also get the added nuance of the arrogance at play and the reason why the school may not be attracted to her as a candidate. This is not meant to compare lenormand and tarot. The main goal was to show that you can use any system to answer any question. But this example delights me because, even though this is a fake reading for a fake client with a fake goal, all of which I made up, we got the same exact answer every time. *It's so cool!* This is why, incidentally, I think doing these kinds of fake readings is so useful for folks when they're learning.

As a reader, I've spent my life with tarot in a way I haven't with lenormand, so it's "home" for me. I find that I get better, more nuanced answers with tarot than other card systems. But that's just me.

To return to the central point of this chapter, though, we're looking at whether or not Liza has any agency. This reading does suggest she has more agency than the lenormand one does, because if she can deal with her ego and her audition material, then she might change the outcome. That doesn't mean it's *certain.* There may be other issues at play—in fact, there are almost certainly going to be other issues at play. When we apply for jobs or school programs or audition for the local community choir or try out for the adult baseball league, we're not just up against our own gifts and limitations; we're up against the other candidates. You may be a great shortstop, but if there's an even better shortstop, they may get the opportunity over you. That's another thing we can look for in readings, and, honestly, you don't even need to pull another spread if you want to extrapolate.

If you know that there are other conditions at play, look at the spread you already have to see if they're contextually visible in the cards. You would have to know, more or less, what the other factors might be, but that's not necessarily a difficult thing to do. Even if we know nothing about graduate acting programs, it's not a bad assumption that most schools don't audition only one candidate for any spot. So there have to be other applicants, and the Five of Swords in this reading suggests that the competition will be stiff—and, mirroring the King with the Five, there may be more people with more justification for their arrogance to compete against. The Five of Swords in this particular reading speaks *directly* to the experience of competing, because that's what's pictured on this card. (Some readers may take issue with my interpretation, particularly if they're reading my client as the large figure in the Five. That's fair, for sure. As I will say over and over, there is no right way. In this case, reading the Five that way doesn't make contextual sense for me, because the final card in the spread, The Hanged Man, is not a progress-oriented card; in fact, it's the opposite. Liza does not win here.)

Liza lacks agency, too, because she can't control who else auditions and how good (or not) they will be. This adds another layer to the reading and doesn't negate what we got from my first pass at the cards. They can both be real obstacles, impacting her ability to move forward in the cycle. I could go further: the King of Wands staring away from the Six of Swords reminds me of the audition panel who will be watching Liza perform. Their focus isn't her journey, it's the financial sustainability of their program (the King looks at the Seven of Pentacles, who is doing just that—considering the longevity of their project). Liza's hopes and dreams aren't a factor in the selection process; the continued viability (read: money-making) of the program is. They want students who are going to go off and become famous so that more students will want to compete for a slot there. It's a business, after all, not a life-coaching organization (at least from their theoretical point of view). Liza is at the mercy of not only the tastes of the audition panel, but also a host of other unknown factors that will impact the mood of the auditors. I've seen actors dismissed from consideration because they glued their resume to their headshot instead of stapling it, or because they forgot to mention the name of the playwright they're performing when they introduce themselves before their piece.

It's common to draw new cards to look at a situation from different angles, but you don't have to. If you're open, you can read the same cards in different ways just by thinking about the different connections the cards have to the question and the different ways they dance with one another. This is more common in methods like lenormand, but tarot can do it, too—only if we're open to it and ask it to.

Motivation

The prospect of telling a client they lack agency in a situation may sound defeatist and demotivating. There's a fine line between exploring the degrees of control a client has in a situation and turning the client into a victim. That's not the aim. This approach is about estimating the degree of control a client has in a situation. Many folks are motivated by obstacles and will use a reading to fuel their push toward what they want to do. "Oh, you think I can't get into Yale? Watch me." Doesn't mean it'll work, but now they're more motivated! It's also a question of whether it's better to know about life's disappointments or not. The very practice of divination by nature assumes that it's better to know.[31]

We're very concerned with empowerment these days, and I think part of the reason is that many of us are feeling incredibly disempowered. We want to believe that overcoming obstacles is possible, that we can achieve goals easily, and that anybody can be anything they want. This chapter isn't to say they can't; it's to explore in a reading how likely it is they'll be able to *in the span of time set for the reading*. That's important, too, because when we say, "you don't have much agency here," it doesn't mean it's forever. It *might* be, but it's not necessarily the case. It's also not to say that people can't find ways of exerting influence they (and we) didn't know they had. They might be able to find a workaround. And they wouldn't have known they needed to unless they got a reading saying there was an obstacle in the way.

The degree to which we have free will and control over our destiny isn't dependent only on our desires. There are people who, for whatever reason, seem to have good things fall into their lap no matter the conditions; others seem to suffer no matter what they do. Some of us are more motivated than others, some more given to networking and self-promotion, and some are granted unearned self-confidence and a willingness to try things. Others aren't and don't. One of the benefits of any form of divination, be it a reading or a natal chart, is that we can see the obstacles we face and go about the business of trying to overcome them. But we can't do that unless we know they're there.

I've already talked about the ways in which it's potentially harmful to tell someone they just need to think positively. It can dismiss very real circumstances the client has no control over. But this also negates their power to overcome obstacles that they could influence. If we just say "dream it and be it," we're not preparing them to deal with the obstacles that will inevitably come their way—even lucky people still have to deal with crap situations from time to time. By being able to see the degree to which a client can influence the outcome, we also provide them with the chance

31 Allow me to add, too, that white people in particular (but anyone of privilege) can fall into the trap of explaining oppression to oppressed people. Cringe though it sounds, and *is*, it's *shockingly* easy to do this—particularly when we're trying to show how much we know about systems of bias. "Look, I'm an ally! I'm one of the *good* ones!" I'm not going to pretend I haven't done that. Instead, we report what we see as much as possible and attempt to avoid assigning motive where we don't have evidence for it. "Ah," we might say to a queer femme man attempting to climb the corporate ladder in a masc man environment, "it looks like there's a lot of energy behind the other candidate. I see a pack mentality. Ring a bell?" Oppressed people know what oppression looks like. It's not necessary to whitesplain racism, straightsplain queerness, etc. Avoid editorializing. Describe the situation.

to get crafty and creative in overcoming even things the reading suggests are out of their control. Clever people can solve problems that otherwise seem impossible. By dismissing the reality of obstacles and pretending they don't exist, we deny the client the chance to face them. And I don't think there could be anything more disempowering or demotivating than that.

CHAPTER SEVEN

EGO TRIP

We're going to spend three chapters now talking about things that don't seem directly connected to divination but are foundational to the fortune teller's life. We're going to talk about the ego, and we're going to talk about how to be both a student and a teacher. These are all things a good fortune teller—a good *anything*, really—needs to consider. Even if we have no desire to teach classes, a reading is an act of teaching. We need to understand the ways in which people process and remember information. And we need to talk about one of the greatest obstacles that life presents us with: our own egos. This is true for clients as much as it is for readers, and it doesn't get the attention it deserves.

The Red Soles of Your Louboutins

Before we get into the topic fully, let's talk about what "ego" is in this context. Following the lead of Ryan Holiday, author of *Ego is the Enemy*, we're not talking about the Freudian concept of ego. In this case, we mean the more banal use of the term equating with arrogance or vanity. These are things we're all capable of at different times and in different parts of our lives. But while we tend to experience ego as arrogance in others, it's really a more complicated notion than that. And it is a big, bad wolf that can get us at the worst possible times—even after we think we've conquered its worst tendencies.

The ego is a protective mechanism. It doesn't want us feeling stupid or uncomfortable. We need a bit of ego to do anything; we need to believe in our ability. The problem is that the ego seems to overreact to everything. It views any challenge to its comfort in about the same way our brains react to a herd of bison running directly at us: as a major threat to life and limb. When the ego feels threatened, it appears to activate our fight, flight, or freeze response system. At this point, we're faced with a choice: do we fight? If so, that's where we get arrogance and vanity. "How *dare* you give me this feedback?!" If we choose flight, we run away from a potentially valuable learning experience. And if we freeze, we wind up stuck much like The Hanged Man—unable to move or grow, creating an arrested development scenario. Whatever path we choose, though, we wind up "protecting" ourselves from growth. This is no bueno. Growth is central to what we as diviners do—and it's essential to our lifelong journey to improve our skills and be even more useful to those we read for. Even if we read just for ourselves, we deserve to keep growing.

Tennessee Williams, known for writing *Cat on a Hot Tin Roof* and *A Streetcar Named Desire,* famously talked about the three phases of a writer's life. These are the three phases of any experience doing anything we care about. The first phase is when we're new and we don't know anything; we feel insecure and that everyone knows better than we do. Today, we call this *imposter syndrome*—but it's always been a thing, and most people who are new to something experience it. We loathe being students these days, so we disdain anyone in this position. We shouldn't. It's natural. Here, we defer to others who know more than we do, we might take a natural step back and try to de-center ourselves. Nothing wrong with any of that, although something I've learned the hard way is that we can also come off as particularly fragile during this phase. This is the danger of phase one, that we'll somehow come off as so insecure that others will think they need to baby us. As a fortune teller, we don't want our clients thinking they need to take care of us.

I've discovered that insecurity can make us selfish. Looking back on my life, there have been many times I've projected my insecurity in such a way that it *did* force people to baby me. I used to be in a writing group where four of five of us would meet every week or so and share pages we'd been working on. I always put my friends into the position of playing defense attorney for what I'd written. Rather than letting them give me notes, I'd start pointing out all the crap in the work and how bad it was, and they would have to buck me up and show me it was better. This was selfish in two ways: First, I was protecting myself from getting their notes, which was the whole point of being there. I was, in essence, negating their perspectives by forcing them to tell me what was good about my work rather than what needed improvement. Second, I was making them deal with my ego. Rather than sitting there like a grownup and listening to what they had to say, I made them stroke my hair and sing me a lullaby (metaphorically). Insecurity makes us self-centered. Not in the way we usually think of that term, which is mostly thoughtlessness, but in the sense of putting ourselves in the literal center and asking others to care for us.

Look, we all need to be cared for from time to time, but when it becomes ritualized, then we're really taking advantage of people. It's not our loved ones' jobs to prove our worth to us; we have to find it in ourselves. Relationships are at their best when they're in balance generally, and are able to adapt the scales as each person needs something. Insecurity can create an imbalance where one person is constantly nursing the other. And that's selfish.

In the second phase, we have more confidence. The skills are there but there's always more to learn. At this point, the hunger for learning doesn't decrease, but it's matched by a strong foundation that stabilizes us while we're working. Readers in this phase tend to demonstrate that all-important openness and receptivity explored in prior chapters. Here, there's less insecurity. Other people's differing methods and opinions don't serve as examples of our own ineptitude, but as interesting (or not) methods that we can try out (or not) and adapt (or not—we get to decide). We're inspired by our peers, which is as it should be. This is when we do go from that page-like role to *reader.* We're equal to others, but not above anyone. In essence, this is a lovely, balanced place and when you're in this phase you should find your confidence increasing regularly.

This is the best phase to be in and really should be our aim for the entirety of our careers—whatever is we're doing. It is in this phase, this balanced phase, where confidence meets humility and where we're at our best. Everything we can do to stay in phase two we should do, because it is the very definition of the "happy medium."

The final phase, phase three, need not ever be experienced. But many of us feel it, nonetheless. This is when we're old pros, and we don't feel the need to be students anymore. This is where arrogance creeps in—the other side of the insecurity coin. Having achieved success and prestige, we're desperate to keep it. We cannot face the idea of losing it, because it becomes our identity. We begin to *identify* as our reputation, our persona, or our brand, and we cannot function when that isn't recognized. This is a major danger zone.

The writer Anne Lamott, author of *Bird by Bird,* maybe the best book on writing ever written, has said that some of the most unhealthy people she's ever met are those who have what we all want: fame and fortune. They discover there is no amount of success, no tonnage of praise, that will ever make them feel like they've truly "made it." There will always been someone more successful, someone richer, someone whose work sells more, someone hotter, someone whose reviews are more glittering. We cannot reach the pinnacle of success because it doesn't exist. But trying to get there becomes an addiction and sustaining the feeling of being successful and special becomes the main focus of life—not doing the work that got us there. No one can love you enough to make yourself feel lovable; no one can be impressed with you enough for you to feel impressive; no one can praise you enough that you feel worthy of praise. You might start to surround yourself with people who remind you of your success. These will often be people who haven't achieved the things you have and who envy you—who think that you can be a route to their success. These folks are generally going to be yes-people who care more about staying in your good graces than about what's good for you. They will protect you from critics to a sometimes rabid degree, and they will attempt to destroy anyone who dares make you feel less-than. Would that we all had such an army. They will feel special because *you like them,* and they will make your praise their personality. So they might lie to you, they might keep things from you, they might even say shit behind your back—but they will make sure you believe they're loyal. At least until someone better comes along, or they realize you can't help them.

This may sound like a movie star, diva-level plot device. It isn't *remotely*. Look around your workplace or your social circles. Who is the "star" in your spaces? Their own little Regina George? The ones who everyone gags over, who have the most social media followers, who everyone wants to fuck or at least hang out with, the ones who have a natural charisma that seemingly draws everyone to them. Try giving them some corrective feedback or advice. See what happens when you suggest they do something differently or that their behavior may have been inappropriate. See how they react. See if you remain on the guest list or its equivalent. No, this isn't the stuff of Bette Davis and Joan Crawford, kids. This is real life and it's happening in your book club, your PTA, your baseball team, or your family. It's *definitely* happening in your office or community theatre or Ponzi scheme collective. It's happening right now in divination circles. There are a lot of people who are in a cult and don't realize it—and other people who have no idea they're leading one! I've experienced both sides of that equation myself, both the cult leader and the banished acolyte who dared point out the king's nudism. Social media almost demands it, almost insists that we sort ourselves into factions—sometimes gentle, overlapping ones; other times, dangerous sects on the way to forming gangs.

Ego is the battery that powers social media. And I'm not a social media absolutist. I rely on it for many reasons, not the least of which is the divination community. But because social media is so powerful, it means that ego is powerful too—potentially in ways it never has been, because most of us previously lacked the ability to indulge our egos to such a deep degree. There's never been a way of comparing ourselves to each other so relentlessly. We're in a new gilded age, but instead of huge houses on the cliffs of Newport, we signal wealth through the brands we buy and post on the socials. The Stanley cup, the iPad Pro, the red soles of your Louboutins.[32] We join factions by drinking at Starbucks instead of Dunkin' Donuts; we are Team Android or iOS; we like that particular influencer and we will go to *war* on his behalf, because he might see us and bring us into the dazzlingly warm glow of his presence. Humans are naturally tribal—societies seem to function best in small clusters. But we've taken that to whole new levels of devotion. I saw a YouTuber get attacked by fans of the band BTS because they thought he was trying to get likes and subs by using the band's name in his video titles. They didn't know he was using the much older BTS, short for "behind the scenes." This is *all* ego. We're *surrounded* by it today and it's *not healthy*. Especially when we're taking on someone else's ego and fighting on their behalf and they don't even know or care we're doing it.

This is real and happens in micro- and macrocosms. Social media companies and their advertisers have learned that they can make money off of our need to fit in, feel part of the correct demographic, and to signal our values to as broad an audience as we can. So I don't anticipate the ego relaxing any time soon. Most

32 Note from future me: I originally subtitled this section "The Red Soles of Your Manolos" and felt so proud of the rhyme...until I realized I had the wrong brand. Sometimes, and I mean this from the bottom of my heart, writing can be *devastating*. Ah, well.

of media is designed to trigger it so that we spend money on shit we don't need, but think we do. And I'm not acting superior, here; I'm thirsty for certain brands and I will hand over entire paychecks so people know I have the coolest version of whatever gadget I'm in love with this week. I'm not immune. Most of us aren't.

Which is why we have to be vigilant about our own egos—and our clients'.

The Well-Tempered Fortune Teller

Okay, you stuck with me long enough and now we can connect all of this to divination. The risk in our profession is that we'll start to believe our own press. If we're good, and probably we are, people will tell us so. If we're not careful, that can go to our head. There's nothing wrong with celebrating a job well done, nothing at all. But if we lose touch with the earth, we'll float away. We need to be grounded. The reading isn't about us and, honestly, neither is the client's feedback. The notes we get from clients are really about their own perceptions—what they wanted to get out the reading and whether or not you said things that surprised or impressed them. You can give a bad reading that made a client feel good, and they'll tell you it was amazing. It *feels* good to them, so it *is* good. Great! But we have to remember that humility is part of the fortune teller's toolkit.

If a reader loses their earthly tether and starts floating away on the breeze of their own coolness, they will be drifting from the clients and potentially their guides. The reader who is focused on their own brilliance isn't focused on the client, the question, or the cards. The reader who begins to imagine themselves somehow unique or special can begin centering themselves above the art form. The acting teacher Stanislavsky once said, "Love the art in yourself, not yourself in the art." The reader isn't the oracle, the reader isn't the reading, and the reader certainly isn't the star of the show. The reader is for sure *part* of the oracle, *part* of the reading, and a supporting cast member. But the star is the client, and the oracle is the tools being used and whatever divinity makes them work. We need to love the divination in ourselves, but not ourselves in the divination.

Also dangerous is the reader who believes there's nothing more to learn. They stop experimenting, stop exploring new methods and techniques, stop growing. They may lock their card meanings, refusing to see anything other than what they "know" the cards mean, they may start giving stale readings as a result. The meanings of the cards have to reflect the life we're living today, not the life we were living two, three, ten years ago. And life moves faster than ever, these days. We're not living the life we were living six months ago. Our card meanings need to reflect today if we're reading about today and tomorrow. They can't stay locked in yesterday. Nor can our worldviews and cosmologies. We must evolve and we can't do that if we think we've reached the apex of our abilities—or of everyone else's.

There's a tendency for this kind of reader to dismiss any negative feedback from a client. This reader is never wrong, and if the client felt the reading didn't connect, then it's because the client wasn't listening. This reader may default to giving advice, and may even make up their minds about what should be done and what's best for the client before they even shuffle the cards or shake the bones. The client goes from the reason we're all here to a nuisance who would be better served shutting up and obeying. This reader looks down on certain kinds of questions—and on readers who read about those things. They look down on clients who focus on banalities and trivialities. Where most readers exist because people want readings, this reader believes that people want readings because this reader exists. They are the sun and the rest of us merely revolve around them. They cannot take feedback, they cannot consider that they may have taken a wrong turn, they cannot be questioned or asked to explain anything. They become deified. And that's a real snooze fest, to be honest. For the reader and for anyone who comes into contact with them. No one wants to put up with that kind of arrogance. Actually, that's not entirely true. But the people who do want to put up with that kind of arrogance are not really the healthiest folks to keep around. In fact, they sustain the cycle of arrogance by constantly centering the lofty ego of the object of their affections.

Again, this may sound dramatic but if you've spent any appreciable time in just about any field, you'll encounter these folks. They're everywhere and they're definitely in divinatory spaces, because it's a niche space so it's easier to become a big fish in our small pond. I'm not dismissing the pond, I love this pond. I'm just saying, niche spaces attract egos because there's more opportunity to shine. I'm not saying I've never fallen victim to my ego. I've got a big ego. It's sensitive. I'm majorly insecure. I'm as guilty of these things as anyone. That's how I know so much about it. And that's how I know we have to be vigilant. I've let my guard down on both sides of this equation and got burned by people who I thought were the real deal. It happens. Sometimes we can't know the stove is ripping hot until we touch it, ya know? That's life, that's growth, and the one thing I'll pat myself on the back for is that I've come out the other side knowing this—rather than protecting myself from it, as my ego would prefer I'd do. My ego and I tussle, actually.

My ego tried to protect me from exploring my privilege, the ways in which I've internalized white supremacy, the ways in which I've internalized classist ideas about language, the ways in which I get in my own way thanks to my temper or sense of superiority. I have to engage my ego a lot, and more frequently the older I get. But only in doing it am I able to grow. I've really had to come to understand the world in a majorly different way from how I grew up thinking of it. I was raised not to "see" color, while also receiving avalanches of micro-messages about the life choices and even wardrobe choices of people of global majority. I was raised to believe that everyone was "equal," while also learning that only people who thought like "us" were going to heaven. We all get these micro-messages that inform our view of the world; this is where our unconscious biases come from. And untangling them becomes a lifelong journey—but only when we start to do that do we really kick our life's journey into gear. We cannot do that if our ego gets the way. And it's not one-and-done. I constantly have to reevaluate what I understand to be true and I constantly have to wrestle with my ego when I discover that something I thought was fundamentally true turns out to be fully false.

Not every interaction with the ego is a battle. Sometimes a little self-celebration is all it needs. But the times where it rears its head in the ugliest ways are the times when we really need to take it on. The times when we feel the most resistance to ideas—such as facing the reality of white supremacy—are the times we have to recognize we're being "protected" from growing and becoming a better person, a better friend, and—yes—a better fortune teller. It is when we tell our egos to unclench and we face the thing we're resistant to that we come closer to seeing the world as it is. And, as we now know, seeing the world as it is becomes an essential part of the fortune teller's skillset. We simply cannot see reality if we're wearing blinders, and the ego wants us wearing them so that we don't have to experience discomfort. Listen, sometimes we resist shit because it's, well...*shit.* But we can't know that for sure until we sit with it and figure out why. Sitting and figuring things out is part of the fortune teller's gig, anyway, so why not do it when we come up against something that triggers resistance?

Say for example you see a political post on social media that upsets you. Except that you're seeing it being posted from a ton of people you always agree with and you've always respected. Your reaction to the post is your reaction to it, but people you're always aligned with are now sharing this thing you don't like. Why? Rather than thinking they've all gone round the bend, ask yourself what they might know that you don't. Go explore the issue and figure out what your sources have been on it, whose voice you've heard speak to it, and whether or not you've truly encountered all sides of the issue. Likely, you haven't, and your feelings—though real and valid—are coming from a lack of understanding of the issue. When you dig deeper, you might see that these other folks are right. Again, it doesn't mean they *are.* I'm not advocating groupthink. I'm saying that if people you always agree with start saying things that make you uncomfortable, it's worth figuring out whether that discomfort is your ego protecting you from learning—or whether it's simply your bullshit detector going off and everyone has actually gone round the bend.

Question everything. Really. Be curious.

As readers, we like to think of ourselves as The Magician or The Hermit or one of the royalty. No, friends: we are the pages, the squires, the curious ones, the seekers of knowledge! We don't take anything for granted, including our own superiority or inferiority. Pages are curious, and so are fortune tellers. Curiosity is *everything.*

It's cruel that we discourage curiosity in children. First, because curiosity is the antidote to ego. When we're curious, we don't get defensive; when we're curious, we don't avoid feedback. We want to know and consider everything from every angle. We should be encouraging kids to be curious—and maybe modern parents are. But for those of us who are long past childhood, we need to actively cultivate curiosity because it is the main way of avoiding getting bored, stale, and stuck in our arrogance or vanity. There's always another thing to try, another experiment to make. Nothing is ever settled. One way to know we're not being curious is when we get defensive and resistant; one way to stop being defensive and resistant is to be curious. It's rather a magical experience, and though it takes practice, it's not impossible. If more people operated from curiosity before judgement, then the world would be a dramatically different place. Curiosity might just be one of the ways we save this planet and each other. It is *that* important, which means that fortune tellers prize it highly.

I Was Right!

Now, a word on being "right." I remember a reader telling me once that they're never wrong. It made me uncomfortable. The law of averages suggests that we can't *always* be right—nothing and no one can be. Perfection is a statistical and literal impossibility. I don't trust folks who tell me they never experience doubt and have never been wrong. We're not born knowing everything, we have to learn, and the only way we can learn is if we doubt and question and make mistakes. Hell, maybe there are some perfect people out there, but I sure ain't one of them, and I don't know anyone who is.

Readers spend a lot of time worrying about whether or not we're correct. It's a good thing, because otherwise that would be arrogant. We want to do a good job and we want to know we're doing a good job and we want to feel valuable and worthy. All natural things. There's an added thing here, too, because—unlike, say, a math problem or most of what we do in "normal" day jobs—we don't have as sure a barometer of our quality of work. When we're making dinner, we know we're doing okay if it tastes good and if the people we're feeding don't get sick. In my day job, I know I've led a meeting well or built an effective learning intervention because I have the results of that meeting or training event to look at and quantify. With a tarot reading, there's basically whether or not the client thinks it's right and, where there's a prediction, that the prediction came true. That's the only objective feedback we get.

Whether or not a prediction comes true depends on a lot of factors, including the agency of the reading's subject. It also comes down to other people and the hundreds of choices that everyone makes over the course of a day. It comes down to what's possible in given contexts. We can't be the weightlifting champion of the world if we struggle to pick up a gallon of milk. It's not to say we can't get there, but it's going to be a journey. Some situations are more predictable than others, given things like science and human behavior. A pregnancy is a more predictable thing to read on than a job offer, because a pregnancy is based on scientific processes and a job interview is based on personality, moods, bias, and chemistry. On the other hand, I don't get asked about pregnancy because it *is* so predictable, and I do get asked about job stuff all the time precisely because it's a crap shoot in many ways.

There's also the fact that many predictions are things we want to *avoid.* If I predict something unpleasant, we *want* me to be wrong—and the reading could help us see if there's a way to avoid it.

Readers have to develop a method of measuring the quality of their readings without relying on whether or not predictions came true or the client liked it. In *Your Tarot Toolkit,* I offer readers a checklist that we can use to reflect on each reading and judge its effectiveness. I'll share it again, here. This isn't the kind of thing we want to print off and fill out every time we finish with a client; really, it's a mental checklist that I'm constantly referring to, at this point without thinking much about it, as I read and definitely while I'm summing up. It's meant to be as objective a method of judging a reading as can be had from the inside.

Self-Assessment

- ☐ I developed a clear answer.
- ☐ The answer was logical, given the context.
- ☐ I'm able to justify the answer based on the cards on the table.
- ☐ The size and scope of the answer match the size and scope of the question/theme.
- ☐ If I got this answer from a reader, I would feel like I now had one or more of these:
  - Clarity about a situation that once felt cloudy
  - Clear next steps to take
  - Insight into someone or something I lacked before
  - A point of view I hadn't considered
  - A stronger picture of what the outcome might be

Feel free to modify this in whatever way makes more sense for you. The main point is, of course, to take ourselves out of the work and observe how close we came to these relatively objective concepts. If I can give myself a check in these five boxes, I deem the reading a success—even if the client wasn't happy. Is that arrogance? I can't control how the client feels and if I tell them something they don't want to hear, then they're potentially not going to like it or me. That's tough luck for them, but I can't base my self-perception on that. It's not helpful and it's way more subjective than the list I created above. If I can say that I've done these things, I can go on with my life feeling like I'm still doing my job as a reader.

If, however, I experience a situation where a succession of clients tells me I'm off, then I really have some work to do to figure out why. Thankfully that's never happened to me or any other reader I know. But to be honest, the main reason I can see that happening is when the reader gets into their ego and starts moving through the world in prima donna fashion. In such times, they may have divorced themselves from their skill because they're stagnant and too busy being impressed with themselves to actually get the job done as it's supposed to be. Happily, I've never met anyone that far gone.

What if I Might Be an Ego Monster?

If you're asking that question, there's hope. It means, if nothing else, you're not a sociopath. But my guess is that if you truly are an ego maniac, you wouldn't have reached this far into this book. If you are an ego maniac and you're just here to hate-read, hi there! This might help! If you're an ego monster but you've been letting yourself go for the ride anyway, I salute you. Either way, the answer is curiosity. It's a matter of training yourself, in a somewhat Pavlovian way, to equate the impulse to defend yourself or get hurt or insulted or defensive when facing negative feedback or the like with the reminder to get curious. It's the matter of swapping *"I don't like that"* for *"help me understand that."* It's asking a question where a shut-down would normally go, allowing for the possibility that there may be a point of view you haven't considered, and the acceptance that encountering something you haven't thought of before doesn't indicate that you were a failure all along. It is simply the need to build a curious habit in response to ego reactions. That's it. Of course, that's easier said than done—*but* it's also not as hard as it may seem. It's doable and not at all dramatic, and it actually lets you off the hook in so many ways that you may fall in love with this art again. Because you don't *have* to *know.* You get to *not* know, you get to be *curious,* you get to be like the page—even though you may have the exterior of a monarch. That's freeing, truly. And there's so much to encounter and learn that once you whet your curiosity's appetite, you're likely going to find yourself on a learning binge that extends the rest of your life. What could be cooler?

Luckily, most divination-minded folks are curious. It was curiosity that called us to the cards, or whatever tool we use. And because it's so innate, it's always there when we need it. We just have to call on it, over the loud, braying belt of our ego's Broadway best.

In Balance

To return to Tennessee Williams and his three phases, I remind you that phase two is the ideal place. In that space, we find a mix of humility and confidence that allows us to do what we do well, assuredly, and with style—while recognizing we're in a service industry, we always have more to learn, and the clients may be able to tell us as much about a reading as we can tell them. It's a balancing act, and it's very possible. Of course, there are times when we're more tilted in one direction than another, but that's okay. With experience, we learn how to course correct—because, of course, we're curious about ourselves as much as the world, and so we're given to reflection on how we're doing both in our work and in our worldview.

Listen to Me!

Now, the client's ego. This we have no control over, and really this short section is meant to remind you that you cannot live a client's life for them. Just as we can't know the outcome of a reading, we can't know whether or not a client's ego will allow them to hear anything the reading is telling them. It's tempting to get caught up in that, but honestly it's none of our business. I've said it before and I'll say it again, unless we actually are a therapist with the training and paperwork to prove it, it's best to stay away from psychoanalyzing our clients. That's a fancy way of saying, "don't judge them." There are plenty of gifted people who will never believe in themselves enough to achieve the dazzling career we know they could. Maybe they're not worried about it. There are plenty of people with potential who won't live up to it, and plenty of people who are stuck in ruts they could easily get out of but won't because they feel safer that way.

This is another reason why it's difficult to gauge our effectiveness as a reader based on a client's reaction. There is so much going on for the client, it's impossible to know what's a direct reaction to the reading rather than some memory from twenty years ago that we somehow triggered. The client isn't really concerned about you, or they shouldn't be. If they are, that's a bit of a red flag, honestly. If you sense that a client is starting to become concerned with your thoughts about them and their situation, a boundary has been crossed and it's wise to re-set it. Unless I'm reading for a friend, I try to leave anything that sounds like my own opinion out of the conversation. Again, that doesn't mean I always succeed—but it's something I aim to do, and I'm fairly successful. Honestly, I don't want the client thinking about me at all. And the older I get, the more of a mystery I prefer to be. You know. When I'm not in attention-hungry mode.

We can't make our clients listen, take our advice, change their behavior, or even extract themselves from dangerous situations. We can only say what we see and offer the basic human level support afforded to people with whom we are in a business relationship. One of the difficulties is that people can't face their real situations until they're ready to. Someone living with an addiction can't be told, they have to realize it—and, for some folks, even hinting that they have an addiction may send them further into denial. We tell ourselves protective stories about ourselves that make life more bearable. Sometimes they're as harmless as, "Oh, I'll start going for daily walks once I finish this leftover birthday cake." Sometimes they're more dramatic, "This time he's *really* changed."

Again, we're faced with an ethical dilemma. If we see potential danger in a reading and the client dismisses it, are we obligated to expand on the topic? If we see that the client needs to get out of a dangerous situation, are we obligated to insist? It's likely that ego is going to "protect" them, and if we tell someone they're in danger they might shut down or freak out. These are tricky questions and why there's some worth to the "for entertainment only" slogan. But a slogan is just a slogan. It's not action and it's not telling us what to do when we face a situation like that. As we've explored, it's almost impossible to know what to do in that situation until we're in it—and then we have only our intuition to rely on.

You have to decide for yourself, and one way to do that is to read as many opinions on this as possible. I've been lucky not to have seen any major horrors in my twenty-five years of reading, though I've definitely seen some danger signs. I once read for a friend and as soon as I looked at the cards, I blurted, "Did you go off your birth control?" All the cards spelled *motherhood* with a capital *I'm Not Ready*. My friend dismissed me, but because we're pals, I was able to say, "You better be safe, gurl, 'cuz I'm not ready to be an aunty." Happily, she was safe and I remain un-auntified. Other times, where I've seen a potential health hiccup, I've said, "Ooh, I don't know what this is here, but there's something physical that could be an issue. Be on the lookout." This was in the case of a recorded reading when I didn't have the client there to ask questions of.

It's common for readers to have a list of resources available for clients who need it. This could include shelters for people experiencing an abusive relationship, twelve-step programs, organizations that offer pro bono legal or financial counseling. I've never needed it, to be honest, and because so many people are holding their cell phones during the entire reading, I can nod to it and say, "You know, we can always find support for things, too." This being my gentle way of indicating, "Hey, if you need help, get it," without sounding like a scold. Were I in a position of seeing real danger, I believe I would calmly explain to my client what I see, as neutrally as possible. "So, I'm concerned about this area here and I see that a relationship may be creating some really deep pain. Can you think of any part of your life where that might be true?" You'll note my oblique language here, too, which is purposeful. The aim is not to trigger the defenses. If I imply that a client is *allowing* themselves to be hurt, that could shut them down. "A relationship may be creating some really deep pain" offsets accusation and blame. This statement could be referencing anything in the client's life, which means that the client doesn't need to defend themselves. All they need to say is, "I think so...." This more general approach frequently takes the pressure off them to explain or expand. By implying that I don't know the specifics, which I usually don't, I'm avoiding any implication or trigger words that could amp the client's anxiety. The aim is also to respect them enough to believe they can handle whatever it is. From there, I take my cues from them. I'm not going to insist that they share anything they don't want to. I'll just do my best to underscore, "This is an area we really want to take care of, because we want you to be and feel safe, right?" Again, I can't make them do anything, but I can let them know that they should consider their safety.

It's important not to jump to conclusions. Too many of us, including me, watch too many true crime documentaries and listen to too many murder podcasts for our own good. We can easily start seeing threats everywhere. Problem is, there are many people for whom threats *are* everywhere and it's very difficult to know the difference in most readings—unless you happen to experience clairsentience or similar events, which could clue you in to more details. I don't want to freak them out if they know exactly what the pain is and they're, like, *into* it, you know what I mean? Which is why I'm such a devotee of context. If I don't have context for something, I don't say it. If a reading seems to be pulling me in a certain direction that seems out of context, I check with the client to see if that's a valid path to take. And if I'm still worried, I just remind the client to do the things that are best for their wellbeing. I can't remediate. I'm not trained to. That's not avoidance of accountability, it's the recognition that I'm a fortune teller, not a counselor. I'm not Superman.

It's a Bird, It's a Plane...Actually, Yeah. It's Just a Bird. Or a Plane.

A final note on the reader's ego: *We are not saviors, guides, or idols; we are not mentors or even coaches.* There are some (not many, but some) readers who begin to believe they are more than "just" a reader. Of course, I'm speaking to people who aren't trained in areas of mental healthcare or healing/medicine. If you're qualified to do those things and you want to integrate them into your divination practice and vice versa, go for it. As we've already seen, a lot of divination in the world involves remediation. Because the secular and spiritual are so divorced in all the wrong ways of modern life (and welded together in all the wrong ways, too), most of us come to divination *without* a healing art to go along with it. That's a shame, really, because one of the great benefits of divination is integrated remediation. I'm not a person who believes that physical problems are only ever the direct result of spiritual problems, but I do know that they *can* be related, for sure. It would be nice to be able to offer people assistance aligned with the reading—but I don't have that particular skill.

Some may take issue with my insistence that we aren't coaches. I say this in part because too many people today call themselves that without really knowing what it is they're doing or what it means to be a coach. It's an actual job with actual training that requires more than simply going on social media and calling yourself one. Some of the worst interactions I've had on social media are with people who call themselves coaches and have no clue what they're doing. A coach/protégé relationship is formal and requires more than a fifteen-minute reading. Same with a mentor. There is a formal set of things that should be agreed to when mentoring someone, boundaries should be set, and there should be specific goals that are being worked toward. If you actually *are* a real coach, this section doesn't apply to you. I'm talking to folks who think that simply calling themselves something means they have the ability to do it.

This is important because what *real* coaches and mentors know is that a danger of dependence arises with certain clients and we don't know it will happen until it does. For people who are insecure or seek validation, having a client depend on you can feel fulfilling and a sign of your worth. It's neither. It's a sign of a needy client who really should be working with an *actual* coach or therapist. Readers who allow these kinds of dependencies to grow *will* face consequences—usually in the form of a dependent client growing angry and resentful when you can't fix their life for them. These are often not people who are truly after coaching; they're after a lightning rod on whom they can blame their problems, and they will eventually blame you. I've never seen that grow into actual legal issues, but these days anything is possible. There are communities of privileged people who have learned how rigged the system is and are actively weaponizing it. Do not allow a client's appeals to vanity put you in the position of becoming parent, guardian, or guide. You will not like what happens when it turns sour, and it almost always does, because it is not a relationship founded on equality or mutual aid; it is a hero/supplicant dynamic and these often get complicated, to say the least.

There's an egotism to the idea that fortune tellers have the power to change the path of a client's life with a reading. If things are pre-ordained in some way, then we were always going to say what we said to them—and so there's nothing special about having done that. What's more likely, though, is that the life of the client has lined up in such a way that they're receiving this message right now from you, but that they could have gotten from somewhere else, too. In fact, what's also likely is that clients *are* getting the same messages our readings deliver in various parts of their life, and it's simply a matter of whichever one gets their attention that gets the credit. Clients constantly say, "Oh, I just got that same message when I read about this," or "Oh, my partner said the same thing." Life being life, if a message is important, it's going to get through to the client *some*how.

There are readers who have stressed themselves out about whether or not saying something different during a reading may have saved a client some heartache—or even the client's life. "Oh, I thought maybe there was a chance that could have meant something dangerous...." Anything is possible, obviously. But Yoav Ben-Dov, author of *Tarot: The Open Reading,* explains that everything happening in a reading is, in a way, a part of that reading. Nothing is accidental. If that is so, and why shouldn't it be, then there must be a reason the reader didn't say anything. Potentially, it's simply that the news wouldn't have helped and may, in fact, have hurt. The client may have been on a path there was no stepping off, and so the reader ultimately wasn't moved to say anything.

It's easy to dismiss this as passing the buck, but really, it's a reminder that we are mere mortals. Yes, even fortune tellers. There is much we simply cannot know, even the most talented of us. To think otherwise is ego. This isn't to wash our hands of responsibility. I think we need to take our role as readers seriously and recognize that doing a reading about anything can have unintended consequences.

We shouldn't be flip and we shouldn't say anything we can't point to the cards and prove. But we also need to recognize that we're cogs in a larger cosmic machine and, as messengers, we don't make the future, we just report it.

Parasocial Network

This is as good a time as any to talk about parasocial relationships. We think of these, when we think of them, relating to celebrities and their fans. The thing is, these days anyone can become a celebrity to someone else. Anyone we admire might become a celebrity to us, anyone we want to be like, anyone we're attracted to, anyone who has what we want—these can all be the basis of parasocial relationships. To define that term for our purposes, these are sort-of-relationships between people where Person A may not even know they're *in* the relationship with Person B, and Person B may know *everything* about Person A. If I obsessively follow your content and I like and share your posts and maybe even interact with you from time to time, I might be in a parasocial relationship—particularly if I think that you think I'm unique or different from other of your fans or followers. I may imagine a whole relationship in my mind that you know nothing about.

Now, because I'm fairly averse to joining and trusting people, I'm not prone to these. But I've for sure experienced the consequences of them when I forget that, by nature of having a small social media following, people *think* they know me. I don't think of myself as particularly interesting or special, and I'm really not. But folks who only know me through YouTube may have an impression of me that is cooler than the reality. And when I disobey their unspoken rules or expectations, that can bite me in the ass. Although it really only happens when I let my guard down. There have been times when I've met people in this community and assumed that they actually liked *me*—the version of me that I am when I'm not online. Then I discover that they have invented a version of me that isn't real—usually it's one that's much better than I really am. But it's one I can't live up to. So, of course, I fell. I used to be so open a book on social media that I found myself robbed of my own personhood a few times. I've learned.

It's not that any relationship that exists principally online is parasocial or even that all parasocial relationships are problematic. But it is wise for those of us who put ourselves into public view—whether through social media, teaching, workshops, books, or doing readings at public events—to be careful about the relationships we build with folks. A measure of caution is important in any new relationships; we shouldn't ever give ourselves entirely away to anyone, at least not in a few days or a few conversations. (As always, I've learned this the hard way.) And as someone who is insecure by nature and who needs validation and praise, those have been access points to me that I've sometimes forgotten to protect. We're social creatures, we want to be liked. And many of us, when people indicate that they like us, can throw ourselves out the window in order to sustain that validation. It can get really messy and has been for me. In the middle of a really low moment in my life, a very human moment in my life, I remember someone saying to me, "You're not the first mentor to disappoint me." I was aghast. Then devastated. I thought we were friends. I didn't realize that I was just some kind of non-human Gandalf. Live and learn. And boy, have I learned.

If you've been in the online divination landscape, it's possible you've seen the impact of parasocial relationships in the divination community many times. We see it in the larger world, too. It's not just famous people who get celebritized and deified. The way that social media personalities can blow up overnight means that really anyone could be the next big thing, assuming you manage to get into the zeitgeist at the most advantageous time. Reader, you could be the object of a parasocial relationship right now and not know. *Oh my god, it's with me! The call is coming from inside the book!* I'm kidding (obviously). Alas, though, this isn't entirely a joking matter. I've been deeply hurt by people with whom I thought I had a real connection only to discover that those relationships were *fully* conditional and never anything more than a transaction. It was my ego that led me there.

It was my ego that made me think, "Ah, this well-known person thinks of me as an equal." And then I discover, when I happen to disagree with such a person, that, in fact, I was tolerated because I validated them. Once I no longer served that purpose, I was blackballed. In at least one case, quite literally. I'll say it again: Live and learn. And *boy,* have I *learned.*

I don't want to freak you out. But it is worth recognizing that a power dynamic exists in parasocial relationships and we as the object of that relationship may not realize we have that power. A lot of people in the world are looking for someone to hand their power to, sometimes because they don't know what to do with it, sometimes because they want actual help, and sometimes because they're looking for someone to live their life for them. Pay close attention to the behavior of the people you interact with in your "professional" capacity. Are they revealing shockingly personal information quickly after a first encounter? Are they potentially love-bombing you? Do you detect an incongruent level of hurt or attitude when you fail to respond to them right away? Are they sending you a lot of gifts and adoration? These are all signs you may have someone who thinks of you as more than just a normal person they enjoy talking with. You don't have to cut them out, but you do have to set boundaries. Do not lower them for anyone; you need to center yourself in this particular way.

It's important to note that I'm not necessarily talking about stalkers here. A parasocial relationship *could* lead to that behavior, but it's far less likely in a divination space than, say, Hollywood. You can have friendships with clients and students, just be wise about the amount of ourselves you give away to people you don't know that well—especially in a space where people may be awed by your work, because then it becomes really easy to deify someone. If you sense a client is getting dependent, don't ignore it and don't let your ego cloud your judgement. Be safe, be cautious, and be kind. And, as we've already said, don't believe your own press. I love effusive praise as the next Leo, but my scars remind me to be careful. It's much better if you can avoid those scars altogether and be cautious from the get-go. Learn from my mistakes, my friends, *please.* That will at least make them more useful.

Something to Think About

Before we close this chapter on ego, I want to share a quote from Ira Glass. When I wrote the first draft of this chapter, it was far messier and much more personal—and this quote managed to play a more central role. But I think it's one of the smartest things that's ever been said about anything, especially ego and learning. It's a nice finale to this chapter and an equally nice set up for the next two. This comes from Ira Glass, NPR personality and creator/host of *This American Life.* Though it's directed at people new to something, there's much to be gained for all of us here in any phase of our journey. He says:

> *Nobody tells this to people who are beginners, I wish someone told me. All of us who do creative work, we get into it because we have good taste. But there is this gap. For the first couple years you make stuff, it's just not that good. It's trying to be good, it has potential, but it's not. But your taste, the thing that got you into the game, is still killer. And your taste is why your work disappoints you. A lot of people never get past this phase, they quit. Most people I know who do interesting, creative work went through years of this. We know our work doesn't have this special thing that we want it to have. We all go through this. If you are just starting out or you are still in this phase, you gotta know it's normal and the most important thing you can do is do a lot of work. ...It is only by going through a volume of work that you will close that gap, and your work will be as good as your ambitions. And I took longer to figure out how to do that than anyone I've ever met. It's gonna take a while. It's normal to take a while. You've just gotta fight your way through.*[33]

I like this quote in part because it's *not* just beginners who experience a gap between where we are and where we want to be. We can experience this after fifteen years of doing something. We can plateau, we can get stale, we can go off the rails—but coming back to what we do, and doing it for the love of doing it without worrying about its quality, is often a way of getting through the ego and back to a place of joy. And, really, being a diviner is a privilege, even when we have to give bad news, so a core or foundation of joy is wonderful. Experiment, as we've already said. You'll see.

---

 33 "Ira Glass on Storytelling 3," *YouTube,* uploaded by warphotography, 11 July 2009, www.youtube.com/watch?v=X2wLP0izeJE.

CHAPTER EIGHT

LEARN ME SOMETHIN'

Teaser

At the end of this chapter, I create an entirely from-scratch and yet quite effective method of reading playing cards to demonstrate that you are capable of doing the same thing! Stay tuned!

With Many a Winding Turn...

Learning is directly connected to ego because it is the ego that stops us from learning. Typically, the biggest gap between where a person is in their skill and where they want to be is the ego. In the Ira Glass quote from the end of the last chapter, it is the ego that stops people from continuing to do things even when our first attempts suck. The ego says, "Okay, I guess this isn't for me. I don't look good doing this. Time to throw in the towel." But that's not a natural state of existence. Children don't feel that way because *everything* is something they don't know how to do. They just assume not knowing is the default state and because they're curious, they're eager to find out. Adults, not so much. As adults, we assume that we should know better and that it's far better to pretend to know than to admit that we don't, or far better not to grow than to experience the discomfort of learning. If you can't teach an old dog new tricks, it's not because the old dog can't learn them; it's because the old dog's ego is getting in the way.

We revile the student in modern life. This is a direct result of ego, too, because we all want to be among the pantheon of greats in whatever fields we're in. Or maybe only Leos feel that way, but judging by what I see across the limited social media apps I use, I see a lot of folks pretending to know more about shit than they do—frequently betraying their ineptitude more fully than if they'd not announced themselves as skillful. The thing is that truly skillful people don't need to prove it, they just go about their work. Insecure people, beginners, frequently want to avoid the cringe feelings of newness and so aim to position themselves higher than they really are. I remember hearing the cliche, "There's no expert like a novice," and getting really pissed about it. I, of course, was very much a beginner in many things at the time, so of course this sozzled me. My ego was wounded.

This always reminds me of a trend I've noticed among people who move to New York City from elsewhere: They cannot *wait* to tell you how to get places on the subway. They love showing off how good they are at getting around, because that's, in their mind, the mark of a *real* New Yorker. Real New Yorkers aren't that interested in showing you how good they are at getting around because they're, ya know, trying to get there themselves. This newbie trend is cute. It's an attempt to say "I belong here!" But when we're so focused on showing how good we are at something, we often betray the reality because we're not paying attention to where we're going; we're paying attention to showing off. I'm sure people end up in the wrong location all the time because the new New Yorker couldn't say, "Let's use the maps app." De-center the ego and the desire to prove how much you know, and you'll end up getting where you want to go faster and more accurately.

I truly wish we celebrated students in modern life, because learning is a vulnerable thing—particularly for adults. We have all this baggage, all this ego that gets in the way. I'm sometimes amazed that I ever learned to do anything, because I do have a fairly big ego. Most of what I've tried to do in life I've given up on before I even started for fear of failing. I don't know how I managed to learn to read cards. Sometimes my ego allows me to think that it must be a calling because I've been so tenacious not only in learning my foundations when I started, but also in shoring up that foundation when I realized I needed to. There have been times when I really did have to go back to the drawing board in order to get through a slump. Again, I've managed that *despite* my ego.

If your ego prevents you from learning, take heart. It may not be your fault. In my case, I was treated abysmally by teachers and classmates throughout my formative school years. The biggest lesson I took away from grade school and high school was that I'm stupid. And by the time I reached college—which I barely did, not only because I only applied to one school I was neither qualified for nor could I have afforded, but also because I failed a lot of classes in high school—I'd given up and managed to get through classes that interested me (theatre and writing) but nothing else. I dropped out after a few years with very few credits and wound up getting a full-time job taking hotel reservations in a call center. Eventually, because I had a theatre background, I was put in a training role. It was through training others that I learned both the power of being a student and the shocking ways in which education demotivates kids and teaches them their own worthlessness. It's criminal, frankly, but not unsurprising in the country I live in.

We should be proud of being students and we should enjoy learning. And if we can do that, we can make it a lifelong goal. We may have to unpack some major baggage, though. Sad to say, there are a lot of folks out there teaching who should never have been allowed around students of any age, let alone impressionable kids.

And I do include college-age kids, here. A bad teacher can do more damage than poor technique. My high school voice teacher pushed one student into material she wasn't vocally mature enough for and she wound up having to have surgery to deal with vocal nodes at around seventeen years old. That's something only pro singers experience, and only after years and years of constant performances with no rest. He also ruined my self-confidence, not teaching me much about singing or music, but telling me what parts I'd never get to play and punishing me for not taking his advice. One more bad experience with a vocal director, and by twenty years old, I'd given it up completely—something I *adored* and did naturally before I had a "teacher" show me "how" to do it "correctly." Many of us have stories like this and it's not considered appropriate to talk about bad teachers because teachers are so poorly treated, especially in the US. But that doesn't mean they're not out there, ruining people's self-confidence and destroying potential.

This is why adults learn differently than children do. We understand shame and kids don't. We know what it's like to have parents tell us to shush when we sing around the house, we know what it's like to have our drawings laughed at, or our tender little hearts wounded by getting cutting feedback on something that wasn't ready for it. Or *we* weren't ready for it. If you are verbal, think about how you learned to speak. You just picked up the words, using them weirdly and wonkily, and over time you learned how to make them make more sense. Nobody sits you down as a child and says, "Okay, I'm going to teach you your native language." Not until we've already learned it does modern education come along and tell us what we're doing wrong. But we absorb an *entire* native language just by listening and repeating and making associations. Compare that to trying to learn a language as an adult. There's a whole set of companies dedicated to helping adults learn a language *because learning a language is hard as an adult.* And while there's a slew of new gamification apps meant to help people learn, research is starting to show they don't work. This is because nothing is as effective as immersion. If you really want to learn a new language, have yourself airdropped into a place where *only* that language is spoken. You'll learn to communicate quickly if your needs are dependent on it.

Kids *can* immerse themselves in learning in part because their needs do depend on it, but also because no one is shaming them for doing things wrong—or they damn well shouldn't be. We know that the only way kids learn is to try. This can be frustrating, as when my parents found me drawing all over the wallpaper in our apartment. But it's the deal. Adults can't immerse ourselves in things in part because we have too many things to do, but also because our egos won't let us sink fully into the unknown and uncomfortable. On top of that, many of us are worried about how we'll look if we do it wrong or if anyone sees us looking weird. If we do give ourselves the luxury of learning something new, many of us tend to race through that process. We attempt to absorb as much as we can as quickly as possible and reduce what we in the learning and development biz call "time to proficiency."

God, there's a term I hate—and yet in corporate L&D, we're not hiring scholars, we're hiring performers (people who produce results)—we need them to get from zero to sixty. Know what? It never works. People learn at the pace they learn, and that includes when we're hyper motivated to get through it.

People who rush through learning usually cut out the most important part of the process: safe failure. Fucking up in safe ways, in low-risk situations? That's super helpful. Part of the reason for this *is* ego. If we do something badly, we're more likely to remember a better way because we don't want to feel crappy by doing it wrong again. It is a truly bizarre thing about being human, but if we trick our egos, we can actually make them useful. Making a mess is a good way to ignite the ego, who never makes a mess. If we can connect what went wrong to our ego's desire to never feel bad, we make things more memorable. They become important to us, suddenly, because in a strange way our very survival depends on it. I mean, not really—but we *feel* that way. Practice, which is another term for safe failure, is essential when we're learning to do anything. If we don't have safe failure, then the ego really will flare up in all its negating glory and convince you never to do this again. I've been working in corporate learning for as long as I've been reading tarot (in fact, I got my first training job by doing a lesson on how to read!) and a lot of that time has been spent in and around new hire training. That's exactly what it sounds like. You get hired for a job and we teach you how to do it. In call centers, new hire training is usually long and complex because of both company and skill requirements, along with a proprietary computer software that has to be learned from the ground up. People gleefully make it through the training assuming they've "got it," then they get on the phone for the first time and freeze—and it's not uncommon to lose between two and three new people within a day or so of starting to take calls. This usually happens to people who don't like practicing and who assume they can do it without needing to get in the sandbox first.

Most of my adult life, I've been a bad student—not because I can't learn, but because of my ego. I'd gotten so insecure that I needed to show that I didn't need to learn. This was especially true in areas I really cared about. I would take an acting class and instead of allowing it to be what it is, a lab to play and experiment in, I treated it like an audition. I had zero fun. My main aim was to impress the teacher who, I hoped, might refer me for jobs. I was awful to myself until I got the result I wanted, berating myself the entire drive home, say, or staying up late lecturing myself for not being better. I could only relax once I felt I'd delivered a grand slam performance. But the pressure I put on myself was so great that I completely flamed out. I couldn't do it anymore. The last acting class I did, I was working on a scene and I could not find what the teacher was looking for. I didn't know what to do. And by the time of the performance (these classes always had a showcase for an audience), I'd melted down. I actually gave a great performance, mostly because I was in the middle of having an actual breakdown. I was sobbing. It was great theatre. The teacher said to me later, "You're the only person I know who gets *better* when there's people to impress." I laughed, but knew that wasn't acting—that was me realizing I couldn't do it anymore. That's why I stopped. I didn't remotely enjoy it. In this case, it wasn't a teacher who took away something I loved; it was my own ego, the thing that's supposed to "protect" me. Well, it did. It protected me right out of the performing arts.

I wound up doing something similar when I went to grad school, but luckily, I had *really good* teachers there who made me forget to be obsessed with myself and to focus instead on their experience. I wound up *loving* grad school, more than any other learning experience in my life—and that was in part because it was designed to be a lab. In fact, the word "lab" was in the name of the program. So, because we were constantly being forced to write so much, I rarely had time to worry about whether or not it was impressive. Mostly I was worried about it being done. And that freed me up a lot, and it made me a better writer. After finishing that program, and after global health crises, I've noticed my writing getting even freer still. It feels great, and that's because I've gotten out of my own way. I've calmed my ego enough to do it

Don't make my mistakes, though. Don't worry about being impressive, don't approach learning like an interview or an audition, and don't think of your teachers as key holders to success. Speaking as a teacher, I can tell you the folks who impress me most are the ones who are open and curious and want to explore. For a teacher, a good one, that's the most exciting thing. I've been really lucky as a teacher; most of my students have that attitude and it makes the workshops just as fun for me. If you have all the answers when you take a workshop with me, why are you wasting your money? I'm not famous and I don't have connections. I can't grant you access to the divinatory glitterati because I'm not part of it. Who cares what I think? No one. I mean, that's maybe a little brusque, but truly. I'm just me. I'm just a person. You don't need my permission or validation. And even if you did, I can't grant it. No one can. We don't have that power. You have to find it in yourself, Wizard-of-Oz-like. You don't need anyone's—including the glitterati, whoever they are—because every person whose work you admire and career you envy is *just a person,* too. Don't elevate them above that for your sake *and* theirs. They have their biases and triggers and tastes and peeves, and they still have to eat and poop and they still screw up. You don't need them to like you or be impressed by you. Be impressed by yourself, as a wise one once said to me.

Let go of all the pressure you put on yourself, all the posturing and posing you think you need to do. You don't need it. It's not impressing anyone and it's not helping you. I'm not saying people aren't impressed with you; I'd be willing to bet a lot of people are. I'm saying, let go of the need to "be impressive."[34] We've already seen what can happen when folks prioritize their impressiveness over openness and curiosity—they're miserable. Don't deny yourself the joy of discovery because we live in an ego-centric society. And don't feel like you need to go from zero to

34 Note: At the end of the prior paragraph, I told you to be impressed with yourself. When I say "be impressive" here, I mean the performance of being impressive, and/or the need to have other people find you impressive. Find the validation within, not without.

hero because everyone around you seems to be so much farther on their journey. They're not. We live very curated personas these days, but those aren't our lives. That's our brand. Don't be distracted by other people's branding. They're sitting there terrified someone's going to find out they're a fraud—and, you know what? Someone probably will, because they're not devoting themselves to improving whatever craft they practice; they're devoted to showing off. To borrow from the theme some of *Reading Rainbow,* you could go anywhere, do anything—friends to know, ways to grow! But only if you let go of the ego!

This is the single, solitary way to get good at *everything,* at least in adulthood. And if you're trying to learn something new, chances are it interests you and you enjoy doing it. Why not enjoy the learning, then? Don't race to the finish line, because there is no finish line.

I so regret the time I spent operating from a validation-centric place. Now, lots of inner work tells me that this tendency was the result of trauma and other unfortunate events. I couldn't have helped being that way and I'm lucky I've become aware of it so that I can keep an eye on things. I'm also hopeful that this discussion will help someone out there avoid having the same experiences I had. But, like success, there's never enough validation in the world to sustain us. That's actually the business model social media is based on. We're addicted to the dopamine hits that come from likes, subs, and comments; even when those comments are nasty and the likes are bots. We stay looking and posting because we know we're going to get a hit, and that's good for the business model because that means we're seeing ads. And as we see other people getting more likes than we are and living their fabulous lives, we get depressed—so we start to buy all the shit being advertised to us and the cycle continues. We post the cool shit we got, other people envy it, and *they* go on their own dopamine hunt. It's insidious.

I'm about to reference Bob Ross again here and in the next chapter, he of the happy trees and happy accidents. He said on several of his episodes that, "Talent is nothing more than pursued interest." Bob Ross and Julia Child both understood how people learn innately. They didn't go through any fancy learning and development certifications to do what they did, they simply figured out a way to make their topic accessible to the home viewer. What they understood is that fear of failure keeps people from trying new things, and they both in their way made it safe for someone at home to try something. They could paint an entire landscape or make a three-course French feast and not have to sweat the consequences. Julia Child did this by learning everything she could about French cooking and finding ways of making somewhat arcane techniques and ingredients understandable to the home cook. Bob Ross knew that what he called "traditional" (or classical) oil painting techniques not only required years of practice with expensive equipment to master, but even once you got through that long apprenticeship, an actual painting could take ages to achieve. He simplified ways of achieving painterly techniques by using old tools in new ways—literally taking paint brushes and canvass knives and using them in ways they weren't intended to be. In doing so, he sped up the process of making a painting, so that you could see results in thirty minutes or an hour rather than months or a year. And, like Julia Child, he also made it safe to screw up. "There are no mistakes," he intoned gently several times an episode, "only happy accidents."

These concepts have become a cliche by now, mostly because they've been parodied so much. Ask someone if they know who Julia Child was and they'll likely do an impression of her ebullient voice. Ask about Bob Ross, and you'll get happy trees. But what they did was revolutionary and we should embrace their view of learning with our entire being.

Their view was open, experimental, and not results-focused. Neither of them guaranteed you a magazine-worthy spread. What they did guarantee you was a process that, if you followed it, would deliver results you could be proud of. That's not nothing. Think of how many times in your life you've heard someone say, "I've always wanted to..." and trail off wistfully. No, no, no! *Try* it. Just try. What have you got to lose? Not something you're already good at. So, what's the big deal? You don't have to stick with it if you don't like it; you're not tattooing it on your face or quitting your job for it. You're giving it a go. If you fail, no bigs. And if you fail and have fun? You're going to want to do it again, and if you keep wanting to do it again, you will *inevitably* improve.

This openness and freeness becomes *especially* important the longer we do things, especially if we want to stay in that second phase Tennessee Williams told us about. Because no matter how long we do this, we need to retain some semblance of the beginner. This is essential, unless we want to get stale or musty or fusty or pedantic and then turn into one of those cranks who think there's only one right way to do things—*their* way. That's the opposite of what we do as fortune tellers, because we're not fusty or conservative or stuck; we're open and curious! We are—wait for it—*try curious*. Get it? (Anybody?) No, but seriously, folks. We must frequently challenge ourselves in order to stay fresh. We never want to become one of those people bemoaning the fact that we don't know what "the kids" are saying "these days." Right? Of course, right.

All that's required of us is that we keep trying new things. Experiment with an old spread you used to use as your go-to. What happens if you mix it up a little? Or return to a deck that you once *loved* but have long since moved on from. What happens if you return to the very first divination book you ever read and see if there are any lessons you learned a hundred years ago that you've forgotten and that could help your practice? Read books on other forms of divination and see what you could adapt to your primary method. If you read tarot, read about casting; if you read lenormand, read about dominos. What can you borrow from casting in your tarot practice?

What happens if you had a deck that you could throw around like a set of bones? What if you did a grand tableau but with a feel-good, mass-market oracle deck?[35] What if you made grand tableau houses out of the weirdest oracle deck you have and then put your most conservative tarot deck into those houses and read that way?[36] What if you reached out and grabbed the closest divination tool to you and picked a card or a rune or a bone and let it tell you a lesson you could insert into your practice to shake things up for the better?

Reader, I beg you: *Play.*

Play, play, play, play, play, goddammit!

Tarot was a game! So was lenormand. So are dominos and dice and playing cards. The lots used for divination in the Bible were also used for gambling. Nearly everything used to tell fortunes can be *played with, toyed with, touched, tickled, and teased.* Sound oddly sexual? Good, it *should* be—in a totally consensual way. If you use a divination system which did not come from a game, make a game out of it. How could you use them to play solitaire or jacks? What if you made a casting kit only out of game pieces that you collect from yard sales and consignment shops and discount stores? What if you gave yourself a month to work only with a system you've never seen before—or a week, or a day? But, like, more than a day, okay? Seriously. If you deny yourself your most familiar tool, you'll be *forced* to find answers in an unfamiliar one.

Let's do it right now. Watch:

An Entirely Made-Up-On-The-Spot-But-Still-Very-Effective Method of Reading Playing Cards

I don't read playing cards for anything other than yes/no questions. I don't feel like learning some historical system because, while I'm sure it's effective, I don't learn well by memorizing things. I need to work from a place that makes sense to me. This is why, for example, I don't use the traditional elemental correspondences for the four

---

35 For context, the *grand tableau* (big picture) is a cartomancy technique popular in lenormand and kipper cards, where the entire deck is laid out in one giant spread and read in a host of different combos.

36 Here, houses are similar to the astrology houses in a birth chart. For example, in the lenormand grand tableau many readers view that spread similar to a tarot spread that has positional meanings (like *past, present, future).* In the case of lenormand, the implied spread positions are the names of the cards when the deck is in order. Card number one in lenormand is the rider, and so when a grand tableau is laid out whatever card falls in the first position is falling in the "house" of the rider. This adds shading and color to the card, not unlike the way that Venus in the seventh house of astrology highlights that Venus is most active in your relationships and partnerships. If the clover (which is often thought of as something lucky or small) falls in the rider's house, we might be looking at a "short ride."

cardinal directions. Because of where I sit on the planet, North is cold and cold is Air; East is wet because the ocean is east of me; South is hot, and heat is Fire; West is Earth because there's the entire rest of the continent to my west. That makes sense to me and is easy to remember. It also helps me remember which seasons correspond to the elements, also not traditional: North/Air/Winter, East/Water/Spring, the ice thaws and we move toward the South/Fire/Summer, and then West/Earth/Autumn, circling back to Air and Winter in the north. My friends always make fun of this because it's not how it's traditionally done. Doesn't matter. I've been doing this my entire adult life and I can never remember the traditional correspondences and I always remember mine—and it has the benefit of reflecting where I am on Earth. If I moved to California, I'd maybe have to switch Water and Earth. I don't know, because I'm very much an East Coast person.

Okay, with that context provided, let's start working through our new method:

Diamonds represent anything that glitters, anything that costs, the finer things, and because of that the suit also represents wealth (or lack of it).

Spades dig, so they represent anything in the ground or related to workers and working—death might live here, because graves are dug, but so could birth as a seed is buried and grows, too. Spades would relate to the working class and to tools.

Hearts are machines, they pump—fluids get pumped, so this is a suit of fluidity, but active fluidity; it's going to give us action and it's going to give us moods, it's also going to represent moody professions: arts, but also politicians and public-facing people who have to manage perceptions. This is very middle class, because only middle-class people have the luxury of caring about what people think of them. Rich people are too rich to give a damn, and the working class and working poor are too busy surviving.

Clubs hit; they're weapons, so they're going to represent force, energy, sometimes brutality. We're going to find "law enforcement" here, as well as anything related to justice—actual, or what the systems of power would have us believe is just. On the other hand, though, we're going to find enthusiasm and passion here; the force of this suit is going to energize the other, more lethargic suits.

What else have we got to work with? Numbers. I seem to have fixed on kind of a social structure for my system here, so I'm going to think about re-interpreting my numerological keywords (also, incidentally, not traditional—see my other books for why) through this lens. Here goes:

1. *Seedlings:* anything dependent and vulnerable
2. *Attractions:* anything that pulls and draws, or anything that polarizes
3. *Interferences:* interruptions, surprises, and blockades, but also breakthrough
4. *Structures:* power, influence, status quo, conservatism
5. *Revolutions:* upheavals and mergers; riots, protests, and unrest
6. *Reconciliations:* healings and forgiving; reunions and remembrances; anything "re-"
7. *Appraisals:* reviews and evaluations; self-reflections and considerations

8. *Labors:* works and efforts, anything that uses up energy (and because it is twice four, it can also indicate major conservative tendencies)
9. *Transformations:* changes and shape-shifts, revelations that change perceptions, and points-of-no-return
10. *Resolutions:* truces, ceasefires, handshakes; completions and finales; yielded results

Now, I just have these three people: knave, queen, and king. I don't feel like dealing with the monarchy, right now—so let's think. What's a knave or a knight? They're a hired gun, essentially; often a journeyman, they go where the work is. Independent, likely; potentially not a fan of authority, but their relationship to authority will probably depend on the suit. Queens are complicated. Do we relegate them to the role of royal uterus, or do we elevate her to head of state? If head of state, what makes her different from a king? Let's stray from the typical gendered stereotypes slathered on the queens in other systems and go further. In chess, a queen is the most powerful piece and can move basically anywhere (in a straight line, so there are constrictions) and any number of spaces. So there's massive power and freedom, here. What can we equate that to? Who's got massive power and freedom? People in charge, I guess; so this rank in our new system can represent anyone in a position of more-than-average power. Finally, the king. I could fall back on my tarot conceptions, but let's play the same kind of game: A king is an heir, someone with a literal birthright, someone theoretically called to the throne by a god. This, then, can represent anyone who is doing what they should be doing—if the client, then they're in the right role; if someone else, then they're well positioned to mentor and/or benefit the client. It could also signal anyone who plays a similar metaphorical role in someone's life.

Do we use the jokers? What are they? A joker card was introduced into playing cards as a trump in the game Euchre, and it's gone on to serve in the role of wildcard. I like the term wildcard. What does it mean? A radical, someone unexpected, unprecedented; out of step, but willfully so. Someone on the margins who doesn't play by the rules and doesn't give a damn about them. Let's let this wildcard be wild in that way by representing similar people or situations.

There, we now have a whole system for reading a standard playing card deck. Does it work? Let's find out. Say we have a client asking whether or not they would benefit from experimenting with micro-dosing. Why not, right? We're just playing. I'm going to shuffle a playing card deck and draw, and in doing that I come up with a line of five similar to my previous examples. (The number in parentheses next to the card name is the order in which that card was drawn and laid out.)

Jack of Hearts (4), Six of Spades (2), Queen of Diamonds (1), Jack of Clubs (3), Nine of Clubs (5)

Lots of people! Totally unexpected! Love when that happens. Without looking too closely at the cards, I do worry that the impacts of micro-dosing could have an impact on this client's personality. Would they triangulate in some way (because of the three face cards)? I'm not sure, but it's the first thing that came to mind. But of course, we don't simply jump to conclusions—we do the reading and explore our theses.

The queen of diamonds actually tells me a lot about my client: they've got a lot of expendable income and a lot of time on their hands. This comes from the meanings we assigned to the queen and to the diamonds. Now, if this were a real reading I would never say that out loud, mostly because I'm not yet certain that's a true perception. She may be free and easy with the money, but she's surrounded by two heartier cards: the six of spades and the jack of clubs. I said that spades represent working and digging and also things buried and unburied (or metaphorically dead and born). Sixes are reconcilers—and also anything "re." This is a fascinating combination. A reconciliation of the buried. That's not clicking yet, but it doesn't mean it won't. Would else could it suggest? I included healing in my concept of reconciliation because healing is the body reconciling with itself. This is a "wellness" question (to avoid the judgmental eyes of the AMA) and of *course* for entertainment purposes *only*, but six does speak to this very theme. If I think about things "working" (spades) and healing (six), then this could actually be the answer to the question—yes, this will work (the healing tool will heal). But I'm not done with the reading, so let's not celebrate too soon. The jack of clubs has something to say, and we already know that clubs bludgeon. Jacks are workers, journeyman, hired guns—there's something clumsy and oafish about the club as a weapon that is concerning to me, here, in the hands of this free-wheeling jack—but, of course, journeymen are skilled laborers. So, they're skilled with something clumsy. *Ah!* That's promising: *skilled with something clumsy....* This field of micro-dosing could be considered clumsy in that it's in its relative infancy (in pop culture, of course indigenous people around the world have used psychotropic plants for medicinal purposes in all sorts of ways before we experienced better living through chemicals). So, again, promising. So far, if my client works with a skilled practitioner, this could be quite healing.

Let's explore the two cards we've yet to consider: the jack of hearts and the nine of clubs. I seem to be drawn to mirroring in this reading, so that's why I'm considering these two cards together right now. The jack of hearts is also a skilled laborer in the area of flow and fluidity and feeling. Promising! Earlier, I wrote that hearts also represent moods and moody professions—so, hey! That fits, too. The nine of clubs is the last card, and here we're faced with transformations of the club variety. Revelations that change perceptions, points of no return. Clubs, again, being force, energy, enthusiasm, and passion. This also bodes well.

(Those of you who read playing cards traditionally are likely screaming into your void right now. Which tickles me. But, of course, you need never use this system and of course I've never said for a second that this is "real" or "authentic" or anything else. It is *literally* something that I *made up on the spot* while writing this chapter. The point is less that you like what I'm doing and more that you understand that you, too, can—*and should*—play this way.)

If I consider those mirrored pairs again, then we have a skilled practitioner who could really make this work and create some healing, and we have a skilled practitioner in a moody profession who could create a big transformation for the client. Now, the tone *suggests* that this is positive, but of course the reading itself doesn't say this is going to be a *good* transformation. And the dominant suits are the spades and clubs, which are more down to earth and less glittery than hearts and diamonds. Also, the only suit that repeats is clubs, and we know that's a weapon. But, again, it's also *force*—energy.

Let's return to the queen in the center, who I initially felt was someone with a lot of time and money on their hands. I held that in my mind, and now I'm going to see if I can re-contextualize this in terms of the question. My initial "feeling" about the client was a little vapid, a little spoiled. That's potentially my bias, although it could well be true. What I do know is that there's some *need* for healing, otherwise a healing or reconciling card (six) wouldn't have shown up. And the six chose to show up in the suit of laborers. Healing is necessary in the realm of labor. Now, I don't know what this client's life is like, but I know they're "doing" something (labors/spades) that needs healing (six). I also know that there are two jacks—two laborers—in this spread, so this person has work at the forefront. If they're showing up as the "most powerful" role in the deck (recalling the queen as the most powerful piece in chess), their queendom may be based on hustle culture, and we may be looking at someone who is burned out. The "glitter" I suggested in the diamonds could actually be *fire*. (Though I did not give these suits elemental correspondences; they were based purely on the suit icon. That said, if clubs are force and energy, they're more likely the Fire suit. Still fires glitter, and that makes sense contextually.)

This client likely has the money to do this. No one who can't afford it would likely consider it. So, the power here may be one of having pushed too hard too long and some healing is clearly needed, something to restore the efforts and labors of those jacks and the six of spades. Because the jacks suggested law enforcement in my earlier descriptions, and because the queen is the most powerful of the people in the deck, then I'm guessing this person is in charge of some major business. So it would make sense that they're burned out. I also know that they're capable of feeling better because of the jack of hearts.

If I pair the cards that sit next to each other (the jack of hearts and six of spades; the jack and nine of clubs), then I may learn more. I'd wager that this person started this business (or whatever it is they do) out of something they deeply love (jack/hearts) and they have worked hard at building good work relationships (six/spades). But they have been fighting so hard (jack/clubs) that they're going to *have to* change (nine/clubs). So, this is a moment that really requires them to engage in their wellness. The reading doesn't get into what happens if this client doesn't get some help, but we don't need it to. We all now know what it feels like to be burned out and unable to function. In fact, the lethargy I detected earlier in the reading with the queen of diamonds may have been their feeling of depression. When I read the entire arc from right to left, I get something a little like this: *A person who loves their work and is good at it needs to heal themselves from their work because they've reached a powerful pinnacle and are on the verge of burnout. They need a skilled and effective energy practitioner who can help them find the change they need.*

Bringing all this around to the original question, it looks like—*in the hands of a* qualified *and* skilled *practitioner*—micro-dosing may help my client deal with their burnout. Note that I didn't emphasize "qualified" and "skilled" just to protect myself from the gaze of the fortune telling police, but because the reading italicized it. We got two jacks. That doubles the importance of a skilled practitioner. It's literally saying, "Look at this twice! And from at least two angles!" It's not just me that wants to make sure the client understands that the practitioner's credentials need to be impeccable, it's the cards and whatever makes readings work.

There it is. I'd call that an effective system. It gave me lots to work with and lots to play with and I'd have no problem trying this with a client. And it has the benefit of being totally mine, which means I'm more likely to remember all the correspondences I came up with than I am for those I try to memorize from a book. Which reminds us: learning doesn't need to be something imposed upon us; it can be something we draw out of ourselves. And, most often, that's going to be way cooler and more effective.

To Everything, Learn, Learn, Learn...

We are perpetual students—both of the world and of our divinatory art. I do want to add that there's a lot of benefit to taking time to learn about things that have nothing to do with fortune telling or divination, too. Take breaks to read about literally anything else that interests you. You need to take breaks. You can burn yourself out from trying to learn too much when you need a rest. Listen to your body. If you don't feel like practicing that day, don't. It's okay. I know I've encouraged you to read as much as possible about everything possible, but you'll also notice this isn't the first time I'm telling you to take breaks. I promise, this advice comes from hard-won experience, too. *Don't be like me! It's exhausting!*

CHAPTER NINE

WHEN THE TEACHER IS READY

What's in It for Me?

I have a habit of assuming people don't want to hear what I have to say, so I begin a lot of these chapters playing defense attorney. But there's something to be said for giving people a WIIFM. That's corporate jargon for, "What's in it for me?" Learning tends to be more effective when the learner sees value in what they're about to experience. In this case, the single biggest WIIFM I can give you is this: *the best way to up your skills with just about anything is to teach it*. I learn more from my workshop participants than I do from any book. Not everyone wants to teach in the formal sense, but you can mentor, coach, or counsel (in the non-clinical way) someone, and you will learn new things. That said, enjoy!

Education vs. Intrusion

In one of my favorite movies, *The Prime of Miss Jean Brodie*, Maggie Smith plays a deliciously non-traditional schoolteacher at an *extremely* conservative girls' school in the years before the Second World War. She's bright and elegant and interested in art and music and beauty and she "adopts" those special girls whom she feels are ripe for her guidance. She becomes an icon to these girls as she takes them to the opera and on tours of historic Edinburgh (the film takes place there) and exposes them to maybe more than she realizes. At the same time, she's also a worshipper of Mussolini and though she's a breath of fresh air in the girls' lives, she's also as bad an influence on them as the conservative surroundings they're used to. She's just a more fun kind of toxic.

She's called on the carpet by the head mistress for her unorthodox teaching methods and straying from the school's curricula, and instead of cowering, she delivers one of the best summaries of what teaching *really* is. The word education, she explains, comes from the Latin root words meaning "I lead out" or "I bring forth." As a teacher, she feels it's her responsibility to bring out of the students what's already there. (Of course, this isn't remotely what she does: she's a cult leader manqué. She isn't truly interested in the girls as individuals, but more as proxies for parts of her life she is too conservative to give into.) The ornery head mistress suggests that there should be some "putting in" of information to the students, too, and Miss Jean Brodie explains that this simply wouldn't be education. It would be *intrusion,* from the Latin root meaning "I thrust." It's a dramatically delicious scene because Maggie Smith is a queen, but also the acting and writing are so good and so riddled with irony. Neither of these women truly care about the girls; both cares for what they think the girls need. And, in Brodie's case, she cares about having acolytes.

All that said, and for all her problematic relationships to her students, Jean Brodie gives us an excellent definition of what it means to teach, to educate: bringing out what's already there.

Wait, but if People Don't Know How to Do Something...

If there's a little voice in your head right now telling you that when people don't know how to do something they can't have that brought out of them, then I have news. That's ego. Everyone knows how to do everything; they just need to discover the link between what they already know and what they want to learn how to do.[37] The skills required to read tarot, already exist in most people who are alive and well and living in the world: recognizing patterns, making connections between contextually relevant items, disregarding irrelevant contexts, answering questions, asking clarifying questions, telling stories, summarizing, and caring for the feelings of other humans. Everyone knows how to tell the truth and everyone knows how to recognize when they're not comfortable doing something. Everyone knows what it feels like to be "in the zone" and really cooking with something, just as everyone knows how to recognize when we're not getting the results we want and we have to course correct. We know how to listen, how to engage with others, and even how to make educated guesses about the potential course of events based on known information. Everybody has said, "Oh, that's not gonna end well," because we know life patterns and what they mean. Everybody has said, "I've got a funny feeling about this," because we all have intuition. Barring any restrictions, physical or mental, these are things most people do just about all day, just about every day. That's all it takes to do a reading.

What a teacher does is help the student draw lines between skills they already have and goals they want to achieve. This is truly the job of the educator. Beyond that, the teacher gives feedback and support and asks questions and pushes students to slightly uncomfortable places while making it safe to fail. Now, looking at modern education, you're probably not seeing much of this. It's one of the greatest tragedies in life that most people don't experience *learning;* they experience *lecture.*

37 I hate using "everyone" this way, because it's obviously a major generalization. It's just that more accurate phrasing is clumsy. Apologies.

These are not the same things. Lectures have a place, but they are not teaching and are not educating. It is instruction. Intrusion. That's different. Some things are better off instructed. History, for example. The history of a divination system is better explained. No one needs to internalize that to the degree that they can then recite it. Lectures give information that will likely be forgotten.

Modern education centers the teacher as an authority. Authority is a funny word because of how close it is to "authoritarian." Much of modern education, at least in my experience, is authoritarian. And what we as learners are conditioned to expect over a lifetime is to be told what to do and then to repeat it. The teacher is central and the focal point of the experience. The teacher makes the rules, the teacher holds all the power, the teacher grants and denies permission to speak, act, think, or use the toilet. Everyone is there *because the teacher is there*. The teacher is the active one and the students are passive, unless following instructions and repeating set tasks that are performable and measurable—measurable, of course, by the teacher's standards. The teacher is the expert, the all-knowing, the deified. The students are supplicants who should be grateful for the wisdom of the sage standing before them.

Much of what we think of as school isn't education. And a major problem with that is most people who go on to teach anything learn what teaching is from this way of experiencing "learning." And so they go off and create the same kind of classes for students who are, again, expected to sit, listen, obey. And the cycle continues.

It may sound like I'm being hard on teachers, and that's not it at all. I love teachers. Teachers get too much shit from us, while they try to babysit our brats *and* get passing test scores *and* hopefully instill a little wisdom in the kids, all on a basically volunteer basis with zero budget to speak of. Teachers *lose* money teaching in American schools. They do it because they have to. It's not the teachers. It's the system. In fact, if more teachers could educate rather than intrude, the teachers would be less exhausted. I'll admit that I have some evidence that classes are less teacher-centric than they used to be, but the power dynamic remains—as does the exhaustion of everyone involved. Where we suffer in life and work, it's generally because of systems that are so familiar we don't notice them but are insidious and sapping us of our life force.

To bring this from the macro to the micro, we see similar behavior in readers. There are readers who do all the talking and the client sits passively. That's why exploring this topic is relevant, even if you don't want to teach. The goals of a reading are similar to that of a learning event: discover something new, discover what to do with it, and remember both of those things later when you need them. A reading that centers the reader is the same as a class that centers the teacher. It's not necessarily going to be totally ineffective, but everyone will feel better and more excited when it's a collaboration. And the people who need to will remember more, too.

How Adults Learn

If you're about my age or older (mid-forties, at the time this will be released)—and for sure a little younger, too—you likely recognize the passive learning environments I've described. Most learning events are about ninety percent lecture and ten percent participation. If it's school, then the practice—homework—comes later and alone. If you're familiar with more current educational trends, you'll note that this is backwards. At least two thirds of any learning time should be spent with the students, the participants, taking center stage—talking, doing, trying, failing. *No more than* one third of the time should be spent with the teacher lecturing. This can be an alarming ratio to folks who are teachers and are used to talking most of the time.

"Who the hell are you to tell me how much I should be talking in my own classes?" Glad you asked! Hi! I'm an adult learning specialist, with master trainer certification through Langevin Learning Services, and a stack of other certifications in the field—along with more than twenty years working in this field seven days a week since I was about twenty-one years old. I'm in fact uniquely qualified to talk about this because it is the way I've paid my rent and kept myself in jeans and gin as far back as I can recall. And, I started out as a lecturing monster. When I began training new hire classes, I talked for three weeks straight with only cigarette breaks stopping me. I was exhausted at the end of every class and my students were sort of left to figure things out on their own. My aim was to get them to pass the final so I could get them out of my training room just in time for another group of twenty to sit in front of me and listen to my three-week monologue. Not surprisingly, I burned out. Nearly got fired, in fact, because I was kind of a mess and floundering and no one reached out to help me.

Which is why I'm doing that for you, right now!

I learned to love learning and I learned a lot about myself by discovering what I'm going to share with you now. I know it's going to help you—even if only to advocate for yourself as a student. You, as a paying student, should settle for nothing less than what I'm about to describe. Because, and this is the most important thing, *the lesson is about the learner, not the leader.*

Memory, All Alone in the Moonlight...

In a classic text on adult learning, *Telling Ain't Training* by Harold Stolovitch and Erica J. Keeps, we learn some fascinating and potent points about the human memory. I'll give you some of their insight here, but I will say that if you do enjoy teaching, you should absolutely read that book. It's coming into icon status in the learning world.

Memory is key to learning and it's harder to memorize things than we'd imagine. We all know so much after being alive for so long, we forget that we had to re-encounter all of those things in order for them to stick. This is because there are two kinds of memory: short-term and long-term. The long-term memory is kind of our hard drive or our cloud storage; it's where everything we've "saved" lives pretty much forever. It may not always be at the forefront of our mind, and sometimes pieces of "files" there will chip away, but once something gets saved to the long-term memory cloud, we've got it as long as our circuitry functions as designed. Short-term memory, on the other hand, serves as a filter. It catches everything we encounter over the course of a day and decides what means something and should be pushed through to long-term memory—and, of course, what means nothing and should be discarded. Things can't get to our long-term memory without making it through the gatekeeper of the short-term memory.

The problem is that the short-term memory is somewhat haphazard in what it decides is important and not. Important information frequently gets filtered out and trashed, while absolutely unimportant information gets saved. Quotes from stupid movies make it through while the birthday of your new partner keeps getting rejected. It's bizarre. Life would be much easier if we could *decide* what needs remembering, rather than having our short-term memory decide—but it would also be much slower, because we'd have to stop after every single contact with new information and decide what needs to make it through. That would more or less be like having to stop after reading each word in this sentence to decide if each matters—and then having to do that after each sentence, each paragraph, and so on. We'd lose all context. No, we need this automated system, faulty though it may be.

Happily, there are some conscious and semi-conscious things we do that can help us remember what our short-term memory might otherwise forget. There are essentially three categories of things that we tend to hold on to: 1. Things we repeat; 2. Things we value; 3. Dangerous things.

Obviously, repeating something makes it memorable. This is the basis of rote education: practicing your scales, keyboarding, or language. Repeat things enough and they'll (usually) stick. This is probably why we remember phone numbers and addresses for things we no longer need. We also remember what we care about, what we value. We'll *eventually* remember a loved one's birthday or anniversary or other important information because we care about them. We'll remember to go to an event we want to go to, we'll be able to recite scenes from our favorite movies, we'll know our best friend's favorite songs. When things matter to us, we force them through short-term memory into long. And, of course, if we're scared of something, we'll remember it in order to avoid it. We may not want the alarm clock to go off, but we set it so we can go to work and not get fired. We remember to take our meds or whatever other thing we don't actively care about but that there would be consequences for forgetting.

As educators, as teachers, one of the ways we can best serve our students is helping them connect a topic to one of these three realities. Find a way to make them care about it, find a way to make them repeat it, and—if appropriate—make them unwilling to forget it. (In our world, it's hard to make something too "dangerous.") This is why the learning experience should only be about one third explanation. It is through doing that people start making these neural connections. Which is what happens when we're learning, *really* learning, not just listening, we're creating new neural pathways in the brain that make recall possible. It's actually magic! We're changing the brain! So fucking cool.

Unhide Your Valuables!

One of the best ways teachers can help people connect something to their own value is to help them find a personal connection to it. Many of us are *interested* in a lot of things, but we don't *pursue* most of them. Even when we do pick something up, we'll often put it back down again as quickly. I've currently got three crochet kits I ordered when I thought I'd learn to do that and I've never gotten past getting the "magic circle." When we stick with something, it's because we connect with it enough that we're willing to give it attention and time when so many other things are vying for both. One thing that helps us fall in love with something is getting results from it. The sooner people start seeing their potential and experiencing progress, the more excited they get about it. And then, at a certain point, they're hooked and there's no going back. Even when things get tough, they'll stick with it because they've already dedicated energy to it and forged a deeper bond.

When working with students, it's helpful to give them opportunities to realize and recognize that they're doing well. It's one thing to tell them, but it's much better if they discover for themselves. Creating activities designed for success and used at strategic moments throughout a course can go a long way to motivating students and helping them form the all-important bond with the topic at hand. When people feel successful, they're more likely to try new things and experiment because their ego has been placated and put down for a nap. With that out of the way, it's okay for the student to play. They're not trying to prove themselves anymore, they're now just in the sandbox having fun.

"Gamification" is a hot topic in adult learning theory, so much so that it's actually gotten rather tedious. Yes, people like games; no, they're not easy to build and really good ones tend not to fit in the limited time available for most classes in any adult environment. But it needn't be sort of a tedious, development-intensive thing. Simply *calling* an activity a game relaxes the ego of most learners and allows them to switch into a more fun, even more competitive mode. Competition isn't bad if the only actual opponent is the learner themself. Low-risk, low-stakes activities make it possible for people to think with parts of the brain less concerned with ego. Low-risk failure—or the opportunity to do weird things with zero negative consequences—*allows* for learning to happen because we're not self-conscious. Incidentally, this is valuable for the teacher, too, because you'll feel less nervous when the whole event has the quality of a meetup rather than a formal "learning environment." (Evil music.) In fact, every time a teacher does something that makes the course more learner-centric, their job gets easier and easier and much more fun.

Okay, but I'm Still Pretty Smart. They Need My Wisdom.

No, they need your *guidance.* It doesn't matter how smart you are. When that becomes a part of the equation, you're centering yourself and your ego. *They,* the learners, are smart and they need to be reminded of that. They need to discover how smart *they* are. They already know how smart you are; that's why they're taking your class. They want to get to be where you are, and they can only do that when they find their own path to success. When you're giving them the benefit of your wisdom, you're denying them the opportunity to access their own. That isn't learning, it's lecturing.

I have never met a tarot student who couldn't read. Ever. And I've worked in adult learning for more than twenty years and I have seen a lot of people who simply could not do things. Not once have I encountered a student who couldn't read. I have encountered folks who go off on discursive tangents during readings that distract the client and confuse themselves; I've met readers who don't believe in themselves or their abilities; I've met people who have such a unique point of view that their readings are totally unorthodox—but I've never once had a student who couldn't do it. Ever. I've also never had a tarot student who needed me to tell them what to do. Any time a tarot student has asked me a question and I've responded with, "I love that question. Before I answer, tell me what your thoughts are," they've wound up answering their own question and never remember to ask me what my answer would have been. Yeah, sometimes I add it, anyway. Hey, they asked. But I never negate what they think. *Because what they think is the answer!*

As teachers, we have to be careful with our wisdom. Of *course,* our experience matters, but there is a power dynamic we have to be aware of. Ignoring it can make it a less productive class. Students inevitably look at teachers as experts, and everyone looks at experts with a mix of awe and resentment. We wish we could be like them and we're annoyed that they're where they are and we're not. Most folks don't even know they feel that way, it's just so natural and common. Especially for those of us who had really less-than-ideal school experiences. Teachers may be wonderful, but we're also fully aware of those who had the power to protect us and let us get our asses kicked, anyway. Everything contains multitudes, and the *system* of education certainly doesn't benefit anyone, students or teachers—and it complicates our relationships with both learning and educators.

The ways that your experience will *most* benefit most students is by sharing your *failures.* The successes are for sure impressive but the more impressive you become, the further you get from their level. They start to view you as an icon and not a facilitator of learning. They'll fall in love with you, but they won't learn much.

Their egos will tell them they'll never get where you are and so there's no point in trying. You'll likely find that people start to drop out of classes before reaching the end—maybe more than you expected. It's because the power dynamic constantly creates a poisonous atmosphere, an unsafe atmosphere, and we can only learn when we feel safe. The more impressed you are with yourself, the more impressed they will be, and the more the class becomes a keynote series with you as the awe-inspiring host. They'll remember some of your best bon mots, and when they want to show off, they'll say they were your student, but they won't learn anything—or not much. They'll be impressed, you'll feel good, and no actual exchange of knowledge will have happened. Most of what you say will get forgotten over time and you've ceded your opportunity to have an influence on that person.

On the other hand, when we share our failures, our missed opportunities, and the mistakes we've made and what we've learned from them, we pitch ourselves where we actually are: here on Earth, standing on the same ground as our participants. This is one reason I always awkwardly avoid the terms "teacher" and "student" in my classes. I don't "teach" workshops, I don't "have" "students"; I facilitate workshops and work with participants. It is clumsy and unsexy and more of a pain in the ass to say, but it's also more precise and more accurate. I always try to aim for those. (But, again, that's a practice, not a destination. I aim for it; I don't always hit the mark.)

It is in spaces where we discover the humility of our teachers that we discover our own power. When teachers center learners, the learners are bound to grow. Even if they don't accept any of the teacher's concepts, they're being forced to deep dive into them, to experience them more fully, and so whatever conclusion they do draw comes from a deep understanding of these concepts. It's not simply an act of rejecting a bullet point shared during a two-hour lecture; it's the thing of getting into the weeds with a concept and discovering how it feels and what reactions it causes, so that when we reject it, we know why and we also know what we've chosen in its place.

And this is the reason why, even if you have no interest in teaching fortune telling, it's worth knowing these realities—because the same happens for clients. They, too, are given the opportunity to grow and discover for themselves during readings that center them and not the reader.

He's So Shy

There are students and clients who really dislike taking an active approach. This is less an issue with clients, particularly when you're in a position to read for a lot of people successively. There isn't time to focus as much on dialogue. But that doesn't mean there should be none. We need to ask questions, check in, and make space for the client to participate to their level of comfort.

Passive or shy students can be trickier, and I know because I am one. I'm going to tell you what: knowing everything I've just told you and having seen with my own eyes the power of activated, learner-centric educational sessions, I still prefer to be quiet and observant and obedient as a student. I'm always slightly relieved when I take a class and find out it's lecture-based and I don't have to talk. I get to sit back and...what? Get distracted, actually. It just gives me a chance to turn my camera off, crawl onto the bed, and scroll through my phone while I half-listen to whatever I'm supposed to be learning. I don't want to be asked what I think or to demonstrate a technique. I want to be left alone. And I am. Both by the teacher and by whatever the teacher is teaching. I do not remember.

This is one reason why what we want isn't always what's good for us. Yes, it may be more relaxing for us introverts to experience passive, one-way learning. But it's not going to get us where we want to be, and like all fortune tellers, we have to challenge ourselves. This might mean making ourselves participate when we don't want to, but it might also mean exploring alternative kinds of learning. An asynchronous class, one that is pre-written or pre-recorded and includes homework that can be turned into a guide or teacher, may be a good bet. These have become more common as instructors discover the joys of passive income.

The main problem with asynchronous courses is that they tend to be designed to be even more passive than live lectures. Often, it's nothing more than a recorded video—a lecture—and *maybe* a handout or a quiz before moving on to the next lesson. For these kinds of classes to be effective, and worth the sometimes ridiculous cost to the pupils, they have to be even more action-packed than live classes. Recorded or not, a lecture is a lecture. A good class demands work from the learner, whether that learner is sitting in the same place and time as the teacher or not. That said, shy students may get more out of an asynchronous class because they don't have to "perform" their activities in front of others. So it makes it safer for the learner; they're not going to be judged or forced to give their energy away to strangers. Both of these are important to an introvert.

Introverted or not, though, people won't participate regardless of the delivery method if the coursework isn't most of the following:

- Relevant to the learner
- Clear and accessible, regardless of prior experience
- Fun, safe, and unlikely to damage the ego or self-confidence
- Likely to improve the learner's abilities
- Credible—i.e., the learner believes that what is being presented has value and potential to improve their life

Without these, it doesn't matter what we do.

This is one reason it's worthwhile for teachers or educators to survey their classes and see what *they* want to learn. Too often, nobody asks students what they want or need; educators just decide on their behalf, usually without ever talking to them.

There's nothing particularly wrong with this, it's how most courses work, but if we really want to center the students, we'd ask them what the heck they need.

In *The Anti-Racist Writing Workshop: How to Decolonize the Creative Classroom,* author Felicia Rose Chavez explores, among many things, the ways in which modern education is focused on a sort of male-ego-driven sense of competition. This is particularly true in writing and artistic workshops, where students are asked to bring in their work and subject it to obliteration from their classmates and professor. In my MFA program, we had something called "abattoirs," where—following the reading of a student's play—everyone enrolled in a certain class would go down into the greenroom of the theatre and be encouraged to say whatever they wanted about a piece to the author's face without having to bother with niceties and the author's feelings. The idea being to both toughen up the author's skin, making it possible to endure the constant shit being thrown at writers everywhere we go, but also to kind of minimize the ego. Happily, the years I took this course, most of my classmates weren't interested in being nasty. Things did get uncomfortable, but they often didn't leave scars. But it comes from a weird and cruel desire in education to, in fact, leave *the first scars* on the creative professional.

What this *actually* does, particularly when it works as intended, is that the biggest blowhard in the group gets the floor and usually holds it. Then comes the second biggest blowhard, etc., each trying to impress everyone with the astute ability to dramaturg a play to the point that it no longer resembles the piece the author originally wrote.[38] This goes on until all the blowhards have had their say, and the occasional useful critique is offered in the space between blowhards by someone actually interested in what the writer is trying to make.

Bullies *love* this kind of learning and they claim to be able to take it. Arts in particular trains students to expect and appreciate this kind of abuse, and it's one reason why so many people in the arts are so mentally ill and why we have such fucked up boundaries. There are a few areas of life where that kind of immersive preparation might be appropriate: how to deal with cops, say, or joining the US Navy's Seal Team Six. Most things in life benefit from a little less cockblocking and preening. Most learning would benefit not from attacks but thoughtful questions. "What would happen if you explored the more misogynistic tendencies of Character A in different ways?" "How do you think audiences will react to this monologue about why rich people need love, too—and how close is that to what you're trying to achieve with this?" Inviting students into the conversation is helpful.

The other thing is that the student is totally de-centered. They are forced there to sit and listen, take notes, not respond, not defend, and not ask clarifying questions. Again, this is meant to give the student a little bit of a taste of the real world.

---

38 "Dramaturg" is to the theatre world what a developmental editor is to the literary world.

Writers who defend themselves tend not to get selected—unless they're the random cishet man whose misogynistic and racist work is considered edgy and a powerful exploration of toxic masculinity. It's amazing the grace we give toxic men in the arts because so many men drawn to the arts are femme to some degree or queer and we fetishize toxic masculinity. Which is of course why we like to toughen artists up, so that they, too, can join the *fuck your feelings* entourage and go around making other writers feel like shit.

Learning shouldn't be like this. That kind of experience is the opposite of safe and healthy. When you put people in the position of having to absorb everyone else's derision, they're not learning anything other than shame. *Some* people—almost always cishet men—*love* the "break me down and build me up" attitude that is so common in this kind of learning, but I don't really see them ever getting better. I just see them finding new ways to deflect. It's like a test of their masculinity to "take it" and still do what they were always going to do anyway. Their work may *change,* but it doesn't get *better.* Not in my experience anyway.

Feedback is a…Cliche?

We need feedback. Although the cliche "feedback is a gift" is a fraught one, because it implies that *all* feedback is valuable. It's not. Any learner needs to figure out how to separate feedback that is actually going to help them grow and feedback that is based purely on the ego of the giver. As teachers, we need to understand that because the way we give feedback can be the make-or-break between someone continuing on a journey and finding their confidence and throwing in the towel. As a teacher, I never want to be the reason people throw in the towel.

"Some people just aren't cut out for certain things and they need to know that." Maybe. I don't know. I'm not sure I get to decide what's good and what's bad and who has the right to do something or not based on my admittedly biased standards. None of us gets to be the arbiter of what's good or bad. If a student isn't meeting your standards, the assumption is frequently that they just aren't up to it. Maybe it's that you're a bad teacher. At least for them. Ya know? A teacher's job is to open up, not close down. If you sense a student isn't suited to your style, it's okay to let them know—privately—that you're concerned you're not having the best impact on them.

The way we give feedback matters because of the power structures we're talking about. By taking on the role of teacher, you are also taking on the care and feeding of your charges for the duration of the class—and, in a way, beyond that. If you're a good teacher, people will come back and you'll sometimes hear back from students with questions and reflections even years after you worked with them. Giving feedback is as much an art as anything else, and it requires a nuanced understanding of—*guess what!*—the human ego.

The authors of *Thanks for the Feedback: The Science and Art of Receiving Feedback Well* explore what they call three feedback triggers:

- *Truth triggers*—That feedback isn't true, so I don't need it.
- *Relationship triggers*—That feedback might be true, but who the hell are you to give it to me?
- *Identity triggers*—That feedback has just attacked something about myself that I hold to be true and essential and I can't handle it.

I would add a fourth: when people understand the feedback but fight it because they don't know how to act on it. We might call this an *uncertainty trigger*. It's helpful to understand these reactions because the way we give feedback can sometimes skirt them. You'll note, too, how much these triggers are based on ego. And it's real. The third one is particularly difficult, because we will experience this as readers, too. "What you just told me has destroyed a sense of myself that is keeping me going, and so you're absolutely wrong." Christine Jette in *Professional Tarot: The Business of Reading, Consulting, and Teaching* (which is in many ways a spiritual ancestor of this book) explores that this is a psychological reality people use to protect themselves.[39] As readers we may not know we're coming up against that, which is another reason why it's important not to use the client's feedback as the only barometer of our success.

If we want people to receive our feedback, it helps to build an honest-to-goodness relationship with them first. It sounds simple—and it is. If people trust us, they're more likely to take feedback from us. If our relationship with someone is founded on mutual respect and generally positive conversation, the times where corrective feedback is required—for either participant—is going to be easier to engage, because there's already a strong bond there to soften the blow. This takes care of the relationship trigger. If we can build a decent one first, then it's easier down the line to engage in coaching. When people's only experience of us is harsh critiques, we can never relax around them; the ego is always going to resist engaging with that person or what they're saying. It's inevitable. They make us feel like shit about ourselves more than anything else, and no matter how smart they are, who the hell wants to live like that?

Truth triggers are easily overcome by phrasing feedback as an open-ended question (any question that can't be answered with yes or no). Rather than saying, "You should have interpreted this card this way," try asking, "What would happen if you kept trying to dig for another possibility?" The first scolds; the second invites. It puts the learner in the position of considering a possibility, rather than defending

39 It's out of print today and somewhat dated from a technology standpoint, but still worth reading and not too hard to find.

their thesis. Frankly, though, however you do it, asking a learner to interpret a card differently isn't really helpful. You're just taking the place of the guidebook or cheat sheet. When situations arise where a student struggles to come up with a coherent or relevant answer. Try asking the following questions:

- What do you know about this card? (If it's tarot and a major arcana, I won't even reference the card. I'll ask, "What do you know about fools?" or "What do you know about emperors?")
- What do you know about the question?
- Where can you draw a line between what you know about the card and the question?

Often, these three questions will be enough to unlock the reading for the student. Somewhere along the way, they'll make a connection between the card and the question before you even have to ask the third one. But, either way, by inviting them to return to what they *know*, you're distracting them from what they *don't know*—which, in this case, is what the card means in this reading. By asking open-ended questions that thoughtfully direct the student to what they're already good at, we lower the stakes, turn down the heat, whatever metaphor you want to use for making things less stressful. Really, that's the main thing we can do when a student struggles: lower the temp, lower the pressure. It's generally not that a student can't do the thing, but rather they're putting too much pressure on themselves to get it "right." And of course they are. So much of education in the industrialized (read: colonized) world is based on passing tests. But that's not learning. Ask a student what they remember about a topic once they know they passed the test on it and they won't be able to tell you. Because it's not valuable or useful and no neural pathways were created. They held onto the information in short term memory until they could let it go.

When I was in undergrad, I had this experience with a class I was forced to take. In my "Math for the Humanities" course (a class supposedly designed for non-math people), I found myself frequently in tears trying to get through the homework because the teachers were stretched too thin to do anything and the tutoring agency hired by the school to make up for that gap served only to confuse me more. (Guess hiring a whole outsourced tutoring company is better than just paying college professors a living wage so they don't have to teach twelve classes a week to survive.) Anyway, I managed to pass each test, but I forgot everything by the time I reached the end—and so I failed the final. I still wound up with a passing grade in the class, but my GPA—which I had managed for the first time in my life to keep at a perfect 4.0—slid all the way down to 3.96. Not a major slump, objectively, but one test ruined a perfect score I'd spent three years working toward. Because I learned that I was a moron from my grade school days, I was really proud of that GPA. And the shitty design of that shitty math class ruined it for me. And, yes, I do blame the course. If it had been designed correctly, I would have remembered how to do what was on the test. The class would have trained me, not demonstrated once and asked me to repeat it.

In terms of identity triggers (those times we can't take feedback because it has attacked our sense of self), there's not much a teacher can do other than attempt to create a safe space to experiment. I hold teachers to a high standard, but we are *not* therapists. We cannot make a student love themselves or see the magic they hold; we can only provide opportunities for them to discover it themselves. When someone's identity is on the line, when they're holding themselves to such high standards, there is little the teacher can do about it.

I was talking to a friend of mine a few years ago, an excellent acting teacher, who was having issues with one of the students who'd been cast in a play she was directing. I said to her, "You know, she just wants to know you like her." My friend said, "I do know that, but I can't give her that. She needs to realize I like her on her own." My friend was right. She could have told her student that they'd be BFF's and that she *adored* this young person's acting—but the student wouldn't have believed her. They needed to find it in themselves. They needed to like their own work before they'd believe anyone else did. This is a lesson I've had to learn myself during my lifetime—over and over and over again. Learning isn't a straight line.

We cannot learn for our students, we can't love them on behalf of their parents who didn't, we can't make them see how wonderful they are—even if they are a truly unique gifted individual. In the same way we can't live our clients' lives for them, we cannot "fix" a student. They need to find it themselves. That may sound annoyingly like a ruby slippers response (you had the power inside you the whole time), but it's one of the few times when that's really the case. The only way for people to learn how to love themselves is for them to learn how to love themselves. We cannot do it for them. What we can do is make places that are conducive to learning. Safe places, as much as many people hate that term, are required. (For what it's worth, it seems like such an "American" thing to hate the concept of "safe spaces." Like, the implication is that somehow feeling safe or needing to is effeminate and un-American. The great irony, of course, is that the people who most demand safe spaces are largely the white men who get pissed at the idea that anyone would want to feel safe.)

The fourth trigger, uncertainty triggers, is when people understand the feedback but resist taking it because they secretly don't know what to do about it. I didn't know this to be a thing people did until I realized *I did it all the time*. When I started writing, I avoided showing my work to anyone because I didn't want them to tell me what was wrong with it. When I eventually started showing people, I would get pissed that they didn't "get" what I was doing! I remember one friend of mine would always look at a piece and go on to say they loved how I did whatever happened to be *the exact opposite* of whatever I was trying to do. I got really in my head about feedback because I didn't want to deal with it. I didn't want to have to do a re-write because I felt like my work was "fine." What I didn't realize until years later is that I just didn't know how to fix what wasn't working—whatever had made someone have a reaction I didn't want. I didn't want the feedback because then I'd know something was wrong and I wouldn't know what to do.

Honestly, my way out of that tendency was accidental. When I went back to school to finish my bachelor's degree, I wound up having to deal with *constant* feedback—mostly bad—because that's just how classes work. I had to take feedback from everyone and eventually I just stopped caring about it. There was too much to get offended by and a lot of the time it was clear the person giving feedback hadn't really given much thought to what I wrote. Accidentally planting myself in a situation where I had to get feedback on everything also accidentally helped me deal with my ego. I also learned that experimentation is the only way to fix something that isn't working and that failing—getting it wrong—is the only way to eliminate possibilities that *could* work. By doing it "wrong," I was able to realize that option wasn't the solution to the problem, and I had to go on to the next. I will say that I eventually got to a place where I could tell within about thirty pages of a longer draft that I needed to scrap the work and start again. That's been a useful skill, but I never would have achieved it without that immersion in feedback.

Teachers don't need to wait for students to realize this, though; we can make space for them to figure it out. For example, one piece of feedback I often have to give is something like this: *That's a great answer! But it's not the answer to* this *question.* This happens when a student comes up with a brilliant card interpretation and/or answer to *a* question—just not the one we're working with. It may be close, but it's not quite there. And this isn't uncommon for readers. We get so excited that we've actually gotten an answer—we celebrate that we didn't freeze—that we stop right there. We forget that we have to actually answer the question the client asked. The interpretation of the card(s) isn't the answer; it's a path on the way to the answer. We have to come back to the question and make sure it makes sense and that we phrase our answer in such a way that it correlates to the question. They have to make sense together. When I tell some folks that, they look stricken. They realize it's true, but they panic because they now can't see any other interpretation of the cards. And the *interpretation* may be just fine. It's the way the question is answered that needs work. What we need to do in that case is guide the student toward the answer—by asking them questions that will help them move in the direction they need to go. We make it safe for them to try and give them some guidelines to use so they're not going it alone. But they still remain the focus.

Okay, but like, I'm Really Smart...So...

Yeah, you are! Write a blog. Write a book. Make videos. There are plenty of ways to share the amazing things you know. There is even space inside the classroom. Remember, we have about one third of the time to yap if we want to. But if you're teaching to show off, then you're teaching from ego—so you're not teaching. This may be upsetting, it may be hurtful to hear, maybe you don't like me anymore. You may be thinking, "Well, *other* people who do fully lecture-based classes might be egotistical, but not me. I'm a generous lecturer and I really know things they don't!" That's your ego, though. It is, I'm sorry. I know it's annoying. I feel it, too. As someone who has felt so dumb so much of his life, I feel the need to show off my brilliance all the time. But I can't do it in the classroom because that's simply not the gig. Having an ego isn't bad, it doesn't make you a bad person. We all have them. If you do ego-driven things, you're not a failure or a monster—but you're also not teaching.

If we're teaching, we have to ask ourselves why. Are we interested in having a mini-cult? Or are we interested in helping people discover and grow? If it's the latter, you have to cede the spotlight to your students every single chance you get. You are not the star of the show. They are. On the bright side, your students will all think you're fabulous and charming when you allow them to take center stage because their egos are going to love that feeling: we all want attention, caring, and focus—and we definitely want encouragement from cool people we respect. It's human. But if you feel the need to impart your wisdom in a one-way flow of information, teaching may not be for you. Again, write a book. That's fine. I'm doing it right now! A class where learners do nothing isn't a class, though. It's a staged reading or an audiobook.

So much about the life of a fortune teller is about de-centering our egos. I almost wrote "de-centering ourselves," but that's not it. So many of us in the divinatory arts have had to de-center ourselves (or, worse, been de-centered by others) that we need to remain the heart of our own orbit to some degree. We don't, though, need to center our egos; that, everyone can do without. And if you're worried about your ego, I cannot tell you how rewarding it is, how joyful it is, when I get to sit back and listen to workshop participants share their insights on concepts, readings, and cards. My body just radiates happiness. It's one of the things I love most about doing what I do. Back in the old days when I started in corporate learning, I trained the way my high school teachers taught: I lectured my class for half the time and spent the other half giving them tests to prove they were listening. And I wound up burned out, exhausted, and in the emergency room thinking I was having a heart attack. Today when I teach, I feel energized after. I feel great, I feel happy. It may shock you, but I feel *hopeful.* That's probably the only time this cynic feels that way. Hope isn't part of my makeup—except for when I'm guiding a workshop. You might think you feel like your students don't need you and you might feel like you might be bored. You won't be. I promise. The joy of watching people discover their gifts will uplift you—and, again, this is coming from one of the bitchiest, snarkiest, crankiest guys I know.

I repeat to you now things I repeat to folks in my day job: The learners should be more exhausted by the end of the class than the teacher is. Also, the more work the teacher is doing, the less the class is learning.

You probably have loads of wisdom to share. Share it! If you insist on doing lecture-based learning, at least set the expectation that this is going to be a fireside experience where one person does all the talking. Better yet, *record* your lecture and give it to the learners to listen to on their own, and then use live class time to discuss and play. If you're absolutely a lecture-lover and you cannot live without monologuing, do that. There can be a place for lecture. That place just is not the classroom. We enjoy listening to smart people talk about things they're passionate about. But when we're trying to learn how to do something, we need practice and feedback, not lecture.

If, like me, your early school experience left you feeling less-than, self-loathing, and feeling like crap, it should become your mission never to let anyone feel that way in one of your workshops. Ideally, we'd do the same for our client when we're reading for them. Much of what it means to be a good teacher can be applied to being a good reader.

Thoughts on Workshop Topics

I usually don't offer introductory tarot workshops, primarily because everyone else does. I've found it useful to focus my classes on folks who have a foundation and want to grow in specific areas. I also tend to limit the number of participants in a class to no more than ten. For some classes I'll allow more, but rarely. This means that everyone in the class gets the attention they deserve and allows for a lot of discussion without anyone feeling like they're unable to contribute, or too shy to contribute. While this limits the income I can make from any one class, I've found that the experience is much better for all of us. Everyone gets to contribute to their level of comfort and even more introverted and shyer learners are more likely to participate when there's less of an "audience." It also means that folks are able to connect more and over time will feel safer with one another. That's harder when classes are much larger.

For our purposes, though, I've decided to create an outline of an introductory tarot class that you can adapt to suit your particular tastes and style—as well as the topics you choose to use. I offer this as a gift, use it as you like, the only condition I ask is that you always center the learners. That's the whole point of this. If you take nothing else from this chapter, take the fact that the learner should be more impressed with themselves than with you at the end of a course.

Some Pre-Course Considerations

It's important to realize that you cannot teach everything there is to know about most divinatory systems during a single, five-week class. Focusing on what is possible means working *with* time constraints rather than against them. This is why I find more niche classes helpful. For example, at the time I'm writing this chapter, I'm in the process of wrapping up a five-week course with the same name as this book. Each week we focused on one element of fortune telling:

- Week 1: what it is and how to understand your own reading philosophy.
- Week 2: agency, how to see who has it, who doesn't, and what can be done about it.
- Week 3: predictions, what it means and what's possible.
- Week 4: bed-side manner, how to work with clients—especially when their questions are surprising or unusual and maybe butting up against your ethics.
- Week 5: free for all. I always leave the final week for whatever the participants want to talk about. I let them know at the beginning that we'll do this, so they have the whole course time to think about it. Some folks will e-mail me ahead of time, giving me time to do some exploration or experimentation of my own, but often we just wing it. It's not as crazy as it sounds, and we've never once had a boring fifth week. And I always prepare a little something, just in case.

If you like doing larger groups, consider opportunities for breakout sessions. Most teleconferencing programs allow this—and, of course, in person it's much easier. Giving the group opportunities to talk in smaller huddles means that introverts will feel safer (although they will groan when you announce a breakout, because they know they can't hide anymore). Expect a few drop-outs—but don't let that stop you! As a facilitator, you can pop in from group to group and check on them, answer questions, etc. This will allow you to provide more tailored feedback and conversation than you would with a larger group. In small huddles, you can focus more. Then the groups can come back together and share key things they learned or experienced. It's a great way of making a larger group more intimate. It does require some effort in most teleconferencing apps, though, so I definitely recommend practicing beforehand.

When leading a class online, visual aids help—particularly for folks who have a hard time focusing. They needn't require a graphic designer, although as the elder brother of one I definitely encourage it. Most modern presentation apps (PowerPoint, Keynote, Canva) will guide you through the process. The main thing when creating visual aids is to make sure that color contrast between text and background is high and easy on the eyes. For some reason, people love green text on a blue background and that ain't it, kid. Limit yourself to *one single idea or concept per slide*. Slides should have no more than six-to-seven lines of text and no more than six-to-seven words per line. Use a combination of image and text to make the point more memorable. There are plenty of free stock photo sites out there now. At the time of this printing, I tend to use Unsplash and Pixabay most, although they are increasingly relying on unattractive AI art, so I do have to hunt more than I used to.

When using images and text, make sure they're making the same point. Visuals should never be purely decorative. It's okay to have decorative elements, but the main visual should "say" the same thing as the main text. Don't exhaust the eye by trying to do too much. Simple is always better. And if you can share the slides as a handout, so much the better. I'd also save them as a PDF as compatibility always seems to be an issue with slide decks.

Avoid using Google Images unless you select the options that allow you to see only royalty free, open source, and creative commons images. This will prevent you from stealing somebody else's work. Creative commons licensure is when the artist or creator makes their work available to anyone to use for non-commercial purposes, usually with proper credit. It's good vibes, frankly, to credit artists and if you see that an artist has an image that isn't royalty free or in the creative commons, the artist *may* allow you to use it in an educational setting without paying for it—but every artist is different, and artists are rightfully wary of giving away their work. If it's not something you're displaying to the general public, they may be fine with it. You have to ask. Another solution, of course, is to take your own photos and this is increasingly accessible, as most smart phones these days have better cameras than pros were using twenty years ago. They don't need to be perfect; they just need to make a point.

Know going in that almost every class session will speed by faster than you think it will, especially when people are into it and contributing and have a lot to offer. It's wise to over-prepare, but know that you should handle your most important learning points first. Anything optional or inessential should be saved for the latter part of the session. Know when you're planning your course syllabus that you likely won't be able to cover everything.

Consider how much access participants have to you while not in session. Are you okay with students calling or DM'ing you any time? I'm okay with DMs, but I never give out my phone number because I detest talking on the phone. I spent the first three years of my corporate life taking calls in a call center. I used to talk on the phone all the time. That killed it. When my phone rings, now, I turn it off. E-mail is chaotic for most of us, these days, and younger folks don't even know what to do with it. Instant messaging seems to be the easiest. I don't mind it. It has the informality of a conversation but the ability for me to put off responding until I'm in the mood or have a good answer. Like clients, though, it's important to have boundaries—so consider them before the class starts and communicate them early. You can for sure change them over time, but know what they are before your first class.

Difficult Learners

Only once in my career have I kicked a student out of a class, and it wasn't my favorite thing to do. It was the right thing to do, because this person was making both me and the other participants uncomfortable and wound up saying some things that felt outright racist. In this case, I contacted the student after class, explained that I don't think I'm the best teacher for them and that this class isn't the best format for them and refunded their fee. I then created a new conference link for the class and sent that to the remaining participants. It wasn't fun and I felt like a heel—in part because I wish I hadn't brushed over what they said in the class in an attempt to normalize and protect the other participants. But I did begin the following week by thanking those students who let me know they were uncomfortable. It is a teacher's job to prioritize the safety of the class—even when the danger is one of the other participants. So, knowing how you'll handle difficult students as well as when and how you'll kick someone out is wise, too. Will you refund? Most folks wouldn't. I'm conflict-avoidant, so I usually do. But the older I get, the less likely I am to take people's crap.

After this experience, I provide a PDF attached to each class registration that includes a description of the course and the following language:

Workshop Details

My workshops are always participant-centered but introvert friendly. I tell my groups, "Participate to your level of comfort." Some folks jump right in, others take a week or two, and others lurk. All of this is fine, but to those lurkers I encourage at least a little participation. And the reason is that these sessions are *interactive.*

Throughout our time together, we'll have our cards out and we'll be reading, sharing, and discussing. I prepare a lesson guide for myself, but I'm a facilitator, not a dictator—and the joy of learning is doing, and the greatest lessons come from each other.

This is why I don't sell recordings of past classes, because the content is as much the group's as it is my own, and the specifics and focuses change based on each group.

Agreements

Before committing to a class with me, read the following. These are the "rules of the road" for the learner-centered space I work to create.

- We recognize the realities of history and modernity that leave people oppressed, disenfranchised, and traumatized. While this may sound dramatic, my expectation is that, at a minimum, class participants accept that homophobia, transphobia, other queerphobias, white supremacy, racism, ableism, classism, ageism, misogyny, and other systematic dogmas are alive and well and hurting people as we speak. This is my first rule, because:
- Learning only happens when we feel safe, dammit! The workshop space should be an actively safe place where queer people, people of color, people of any age*, people of any body type and ability, people of any

nationality or faith**, any gender expression, etc., can be comfortable to relax and experience the class. (*Except for the fact that my classes cover topics considered 18+; **Unless that nationality or faith makes you actively harm others and you're actively doing that now or plan to.)

- Nobody's perfect. Any one of us might use the wrong pronoun, mispronounce a name, stumble on an accidentally awkward sentiment, use a word we don't realize is no longer acceptable parlance, or say something dumb or weird that we didn't quite mean as it sounded. We'll all actively attempt to make the generous assumption with each other. (Unless a trend of not-very-thoughtful, easily avoidable behavior appears.) If someone corrects us, we thank them; if we notice we've said something incorrect, we fix it. We're human. And, for many of us, the pandemic did a number on our brain's speed and flexibility.
- If you're consistently being a dick, I will kick you out and I will not refund you. Sorry.[40]
- No comparing ourselves! My workshops are designed assuming you have a foundational tarot practice but are created to compliment the development of your foundation if that's still in progress. Some of us will have been reading for 20+ years, some of us for 20+ minutes. That's okay. Some of us charge money for readings (which, supposedly, makes us "professional") and some of us don't (which, supposedly, makes us "amateurs"). In my workshops, the definition of a pro is someone who wants to learn, who is open, who gets excited by new ideas—even when they don't agree with them. And the mark of an amateur is someone who is closed, refuses to learn, and doesn't want to encounter anything that runs contrary to their assumptions.
- It's your time! If you can't make it, no worries. We'll miss you, but life happens.
- Introverts: I won't make you do anything that you don't want to do. I will occasionally ask you if you want to add anything, and this is to give you the opportunity to chime in if you've been too shy so far—but you can feel free to decline. I think you'll eventually warm up, though.
- Extroverts: You make my job so easy! Your enthusiasm lights us all up and gives the workshop a motor! Once in a while, though, you need to shut up and let others talk, okay? Just a reminder!

Having something like this that comes from you and sets the tone before the class or as part of the beginning makes it easier to deal with issues down the line. They rarely arise, but when they do it's good to have expectations set. Surprises cause drama, but it's hard to fight about not getting a refund when the reasons why are

40 I added this after my experience having to kick someone out. This is generally the only time I will not refund someone—when they're getting canned because they're an asshole.

laid out ahead of time. Prepare for the shitty things and you likely will never have to deal with them.

Over-Excited Learners

Some folks will take over a workshop just because they're excited to show what they know or share what they've learned. This can be annoying to everyone but that student, and yet we don't want to destroy their enthusiasm—only bring them back down to earth and make sure everyone gets a chance to speak or share. The best way to handle this is to begin the class by explaining that your goal as facilitator is to make sure everyone gets heard, and so you will ask folks who talk a lot if they can hold their thoughts from time to time in order to make space for others. Those excited, ambitious over-sharers will forget, but letting everyone know ahead of time makes it easier to point out when it's happening and less likely for it to hurt the enthusiastic know-it-all's feelings. (As a certified know-it-all, I try to be really sensitive about this.) Sometimes know-it-all behavior comes from insecurity, so if you make it clear that this isn't a competition and no one needs to impress you from the get-go, that helps.

Under-Excited Learners

We never know what lies beneath still waters, so it's okay if folks don't participate too much, especially if they're showing up. Some people don't like to talk or share and that's A-okay with me. You'll usually find that you think these folks don't like you or the class and then afterwards will tell you it was one of the best learning experiences of their lives. In my corporate life, when someone doesn't participate, I have the unfortunate duty to "encourage" them to—this usually means pushing them to do things they don't really want to. In the divinatory landscape, though, I don't need to prove that you've taken the learning and it's none of my business whether you get anything out of it if you don't say anything, so I don't force anyone to participate. I will occasionally say, "I'd love to hear from some of the quieter folks. We want the benefit of your wisdom, too," but I don't push it. If a quiet person is pushed to talk in a class, they'll likely drop out. It's not important enough to make them feel unsafe and they will almost always raise their hand to speak at least once during the course of the workshop.

All that said, let's proceed to:

A Basic Course Model for an Intro Class

Session One - Prework: Learners are invited to read a short history of tarot and some basic foundational keywords for the cards prior to class. They are also prepared with a course framework and have been told about any supplies they need for the class.

Session One Outline

Timing	Topics
15 minutes	Instructor intros Class intros My typical icebreaker is asking everyone to share who they are and what they hope to take away from the class.
15 minutes	Introduction to the suits/elements of the minor arcana What each suit represents and a little bit about lines that the learners can draw between the suit and elements and life today.
30 minutes	Suit/Elemental Breakout/Discussion If it's a large group, use breakout sessions; if it's under fifteen, this can be a whole-group discussion. Learners will take each of the suits and think of all the areas of life each applies to. For example, they might look at the suit of swords and discover that this suit could apply to: soldiers and law enforcement, wealthy people who show off their status, anyone who works in the kitchen or operating room, and divorce lawyers. The aim being to think of as many modern correspondences for each suit/element as possible. Doing practice readings with the minors during this time would be great, too.
5 minutes	Stretch break Breaks are helpful even in short, two-hour sessions because they help people focus and let them check their phones.
15 minutes	Introduction to numerology Learners experience different numerological systems that explore numbers one through ten.
30 minutes	Breakout into pairs Learners will come up with what they think are their most useful meanings for each of the numbers.
10 minutes	Debrief and questions and answers Set up the homework.

Intersession work between Sessions One and Two: Learners will be presented with practice questions and use the elemental and numerological practice they have to answer the questions as best they can. If there is a group chat or forum, they should be encouraged to share their work there and give each other feedback. If doing this, encourage the class not to compare their answers to each other, but rather to explore the ways they got those answers. Everyone sees something different in the cards and that should be celebrated. The feedback should be more about encouraging each other and asking each other to explain how they got what they got rather than saying, "No, that's wrong, I read it this way."

Session Two Outline

Timing	Topics
15 minutes	Homework sharing and discussion
15 minutes	Introduction to the pages and knights
30 minutes	Practice readings using the pages, knights, and minors
5 minutes	Break
10 minutes	Introduction to queens and kings
15 minutes	Practice readings using queens, kings, and minors
10 minutes	Contextualize the courts through a modern lens Who are they and what do they correspond to in modern life?
10 minutes	Debrief and questions and answers Set up the homework.

Intersession work between Sessions Two and Three: In the space between classes, learners should dedicate some time to practice. In this case, they should solidify their theories about the court cards and do some readings using the courts and minors.

Session Three Outline

Timing	Topics
15 minutes	Homework sharing and discussion
30 minutes	Introduction to the majors

15 minutes	Practice using the majors intuitively
5 minutes	Break
15 minutes	Contextualize the majors and their jobs in modern life Who are the majors when moving through daily living?
15 minutes	Practice readings with the majors
10 minutes	Practice readings using the whole deck
10 minutes	Debrief and questions and answers Set up the homework.

Intersession work between Sessions Three and Four: Learners should spend as much time as possible looking for examples of the majors in their day-to-day life and journaling what they see and what reminds them of it. They should also do practice readings using the whole deck.

Session Four Outline

Timing	Topics
15 minutes	Homework sharing and discussion
15 minutes	Introduction to spreads and how to use them
30 minutes	Practice reading with different spreads Special attention should be placed on how it feels when the spread doesn't work for the question
5 minutes	Break
15 minutes	Introduction to the finer points of crafting good questions and how to work with clients on their questions
25 minutes	Practice writing good questions and helping clients come up with good questions
10 minutes	Debrief and questions and answers Set up the homework.

Intersession work between Sessions Four and Five: Learners should experiment with questions of all kinds and journal how they worked, how they felt, what was successful and what wasn't. Since the final session is a free-for-all, they should also prepare questions or topics they want to discuss with the group.

Session Five Outline

Timing	Topics
15 minutes	Homework sharing and discussion
Remaining time	Anything the class wants to explore
10 minutes	Closing and asking learners to reflect What can they do now that they couldn't do before, along with what their next steps are and what their next learning goal should be

Other Considerations When Teaching
Because of the way I teach, I don't sell recordings of the classes to people who didn't register for it. This is because the class material depends so much on the participants and what they say and share and ask. It's as much their content as it is mine, so it's not for me to sell it to anyone. There are times when folks will register for the class and not come to the live sessions. To be honest, I'm not wild about this because they're not contributing to the class—which means they're benefitting from everyone else's wisdom without being there to share theirs or even say thanks for the good ideas. This is more of a personal bias on my part, but I really do prefer that people only sign up for the class if they're going to show up and be present and part of it. That said, I've also never pushed that and as an introvert with strong social anxiety, I never will. I, too, sometimes freak out even before things that I want to do and will chicken out. So, I get it.

I tend not to make much in the way of handouts for classes, but those are another useful thing—especially in something like the above, where there's a lot of information to cover in a small amount of time. Reference materials are helpful.

The workshop outlined above is a little more tightly structured than I typically prefer. I usually only focus on one topic per week, but doing an entire foundational course in five weeks is a little more difficult. My advice is to plan for being able to cover less and if you can cover more, great. I can't think of a time when I had extra time in a class, though. I think a six- or seven-week course might be more appropriate for an intro class, but that's also a big-time commitment for everyone. Keep that in mind. People can be hesitant to take classes that are going to demand every Saturday for six weeks or more. Also consider your own schedule. I only teach on Saturdays because I work Monday through Friday and so Saturday is generally the only day I have any energy to do it. But it also means I'm giving up one of my days off. I rarely teach or agree to read at events on Sundays because I need that day to wallow.

Finally, if you're going to teach introductory courses, just be prepared to really sell the class. *Everybody* teaches intro classes these days. It's a good way to make additional income, because most folks don't make much doing readings. Problem is, there are only so many students who need or want an intro class. Also, I've found that most people, even beginners, don't want to take beginner classes because they either feel they're already above that or they don't want anyone to know they're a beginner. So, it may be helpful to pitch your class to a particular kind of student. You might get more interest in a class designed for working parents who want to learn tarot, rather than a general interest course. Reason being people like affinity groups and it shows that you're creating something relevant to the needs of the working parent. Just make sure if you do that, you actually design the class accordingly. Don't promise what you can't deliver.

Most of all, though, have fun. Teaching divination workshops is one of my favorite things to do and frequently lifts me out of my doldrums or my mean reds. It's a rewarding experience.

By Your Pupils You'll Be Taught

To close this chapter, I want to express a bizarre truth: the best way to learn about something is to teach it. I have learned more from teaching tarot than from any book written about it. That's not to say the books aren't useful, but the classroom—virtual or in person—creates such a cauldron of learning, such a potent energy, that revelations can't help but happen. Your participants are going to say things that will blow your mind. To them, it's just something that seems logical; to you, it might be the most amazing thing you've ever heard. It was through teaching workshops that I discovered the trouble with questions phrased with the word "should," and how the best thing to do with "should" questions is to do a reading for each of the possibilities, rather than have one reading try to tell you the potential outcomes for everything. It had never occurred to me before, but it was brilliant.

Now, if you're a beginner, should you be teaching others? Maybe not for money. But if you want to do a workshop for your friends or community, why not? It's how I got my first training job, and I wasn't super far along into my journey at that point—probably not more than a year. If you create a workshop where you're the facilitator rather than the teacher, which allows you to participate, too, you don't have to know all the answers, but you can still benefit from a group's collective wisdom. You will learn a lot. And you'll likely get better participation at first because, to be honest, when people do search out a class for beginners, they're going to drift to names they know—the folks whose names line the shelves of the local bookstore. Starting out with an informal, free meetup might be the best way to go. And because of technology, you don't even need to leave the house.

In any case, teaching is one of the most amazing things a diviner can do and it's such a rewarding way to keep our craft up to date. It's just a matter of remembering why we're doing it, for who, and what the end result should be. If we keep that in mind, we're golden.

Okay, you've been good. We can talk about readings again.

CHAPTER TEN
ADVICE

I realized recently that I'd gotten kind of pedantic about giving (or rather *not* giving) advice during readings when a student apologetically mentioned they do them. So, I want to be clear as we dive into this chapter that there's nothing wrong with giving advice readings. I would wager that at least two thirds of readings have some advice-giving component. It's not that giving advice is bad or wrong; most of us do it all the time. It's more that people just don't take advice well and so advice readings may not be the most useful.

Before we get into the reasons why advice readings may not be as useful as we wish, let's talk a little bit about why readers may enjoy giving advice readings more than others. I'm going to give you three guesses as to why.... Ready, set...

It's a Trap!

Michael Bungay Stanier is the author of a book called *The Coaching Habit*, which is an excellent resource for anyone who even skirts the edge of doing coaching work. I highly recommend it, particularly if you're the kind of person who tends to take on other people's problems for them. If you're a fixer by nature, then this book can help you put the onus back where it belongs: on the person who actually needs to solve the problem. All that said, it's a more recent book that's relevant to us here. His latest, at the time that I'm writing this, is called *The Advice Trap*. And it's a must-read for, well, anyone who has ever given or gotten advice.

I clearly cannot distill the fullness of that book (though it's a quick read) into a few paragraphs and I'm not sure it would be right of me to try. But one of the first salient points Stanier makes is that when we give advice, we're frequently solving the wrong problem. In part, we do this because we jump to conclusions, and we don't really do any root cause analysis. This means that we're often putting bandaids on gaping wounds. It doesn't work for long and rarely does it work at all. It is the ego who loves to give advice because the ego wants to feel smart and useful. Giving advice makes us feel both of those things. And if it's good advice and the recipient takes it and runs with it and it solves their problem, bravo. The problem is that the recipient frequently does what they were always going to do, and it's probably not what the advice guided them toward.

I don't think this is because people are jerks and don't value the advice we get from friends. I think it's more an issue of the old hot stove situation: You can tell a child not to touch the stove over and over and you can present them with evidence that doing so will burn them. But it's often not until the child actually does burn themselves that they truly remember to stay away from it. People have to learn their lessons the hard way, sadly, because it's really only after winding up with an unwanted result—sometimes repeatedly—that we decide we don't want to feel that way anymore and change our tactics. Some folks never get to that point, no matter how many times they make the same mistake nor how often well-meaning loved ones try to get them to see the light. It's one of the truly annoying things about being a person. No doubt you know people like this—and no doubt there are at least some areas of your life where you *are* this person. Most of us are. The most effective lessons come from times we're stuck and we have to figure our way out.

The giver of advice isn't harming the recipient, but they're often wasting their time. I know this first-hand because I am the king of advice-giving. Damn if I couldn't solve everyone else's life issues. Alas, my own remain as irritating as ever, but I for sure know how to solve your problems. And that's the annoying thing: I'm actually pretty good at giving advice. For some reason, I became the kind of person who can intuit exactly what needs to be done to solve issues (other people's issues, anyway). And I'm known to launch into advice-giving the second you start complaining about something going on in your life. It wasn't until recently—maybe in the last five or seven years—that I've realized that nobody takes advice. I mean, I'm generalizing, but you get my drift.

Not only do people not take advice, they frequently don't *want* it. A lot of times, people just want to vent. They don't need a list of instructions; they want to be heard. Giving unwanted advice is a sure way to cause moderate-to-severe rage among our friends. Again, I know because I've done it. *A lot.* Even though I actually get really annoyed when people try to give me unwanted advice. I, too, frequently just need to vent and I have now begun prefacing rants with that. "I'm pre-thanking you for your advice, but please don't share it. I just need to get this off my chest." It saves me a lot of annoyance at people who mean well but haven't really thought things through. So I've largely stopped giving advice to friends and family—and if I have something I'm certain will be helpful, I will frequently say, "Hey, I have an idea that could help. If you ever want to know what it is, I'm happy to share." Much of the time people will say, "Oh, please tell me!" So, I do. If they don't, I keep it to myself. And you know what? Not only do I not annoy my friends with unsolicited feedback, I also save myself from the inevitable frustration that comes when they don't take my advice and I take it personally.

Incidentally, it's frequently true that people who ask for advice won't take it, either, so that's where the fortune teller's job get tricky. If there's a good chance people won't take the advice the reading gives, what are we even doing?

Finding Your Roots

To borrow a title from Henry Lewis Gates, Jr., one solution is to think in terms of finding the roots. Not so much our ancestral roots in this case, although they may wind up being one of the roots we're after, but rather something a little more banal: root cause analysis. Oh, I know it sounds terribly corporate and dreary, but *dahling,* it is simply the *absolute limit.* Really, dear, *everyone's* doing it.

Or should be.

Now, allow me to preface the following with an announcement about myself: I tend to do most things really quickly. (Shut up. *Most* things.) That includes most kinds of readings. In a fifteen-to-twenty-minute sesh, I can generally do an entire nine-card box spread and a follow-up reading on that or another topic. I'm not saying this is better than reading slowly; I'm not saying it's the right way, or even that I'm doing something right. I just read quickly. I read books quickly. I write quickly. I'm very lucky and very thankful for that. It's not a sign of any abilities; it's just that I have a brain for "reading," so to speak, and so I do work quickly. (This is why I typically charge by the spread and not by the hour. I truly do not know how I'd fill a whole hour. There are times when twenty minutes seems too long!) I can do a grand tableau in a similar amount of time, although I don't think I've done any face-to-face grand tableaus because they're a pain to lay out when time is limited.

This is all to say that what I'm about to propose may not work for everyone, particularly if your readings take a gentler pace. That's very okay. *That said,* if you would like to speed up your readings, I recommend doing a little something like this...: If you do readings out loud, record a few, give yourself a few days, and then come back and listen to those recordings. What you'll notice as you listen is that there may be places where you're repeating the same thing over and over, or where you're maybe teaching the cards rather than reading the cards. Teaching the cards happens when we start explaining correspondences and similar things that give the client information about the *system,* not the answer to their questions. For example, if you notice that you spent five minutes talking about Aries' connections to The Emperor, you're likely teaching rather than reading. How much of what you said is related to the client's question? As you listen, use a stopwatch (a default app in many smartphone operating systems) and activate it every time you're monologuing about something unrelated to the client's question.

This will give you a sense of what you may want to edit.

It's harder to edit as you're reading when you're doing readings aloud. Editing a written reading is a breeze. Editing ourselves as we speak takes practice and means that we may leave long silences in the reading. That's okay. If we can do most of the math in our heads and deliver only the most relevant information, the more the client will remember and the more impactful the reading will be. For many of us, *this isn't easy*. Of course it's not. We need to talk through what we're seeing in order to make sense of the reading. So it's not like we can do all the work in silence, and also some context will help the client understand what you're doing. This isn't something we're just suddenly good at. What this is about, really, is practicing. Like so much else, this is an experiment, and it isn't a straight line. I have days where I'm better at this than others, and the more I do it the better I get—usually. There are times when I can't stop myself and even times when there's so much to say about a reading and a situation that I simply can't not say a lot. But listening to ourselves and thinking about how much of what we say can be done internally, the faster our readings will get. Also, the more readings we do and the more practice we allow ourselves, the faster our readings will get, too.

Now, back to root causes.

When you or a client require an advice reading, consider beginning by offering a root cause analysis reading first. Divide the time accordingly and begin by doing a reading about *why* a situation is happening. This will often show you what to do about the situation, so you may not even need a second reading, but what this will do, in any case, is ground the advice reading that follows in such a way that it speaks directly to the cause. If you need to solve a problem, you need to know what the problem actually is. Many folks don't know why things are happening to them, or they think they know but they're misreading the situation or being clouded by bias and/or ego.

Let's try an example together. Let's say we have Niobe (they/he) and they've been facing a lot of issues with their father. He suddenly questions everything Niobe does, including Niobe's "choice" to live as a non-binary person. Niobe's father (Dan) has known this and been okay with it for a while, but suddenly seems to be suggesting that Niobe dress more like a "man" (i.e., more stereotypically "butch") and even wear a suit and tie at work. But it's not just clothing and gender expression; it's music choices, food decisions when they go out to dinner, and even the TV shows Niobe enjoys. They want to know what they should do about their father. We're going to talk about "should" questions in a bit, but for the time being, let's explore another question: *Why* is Niobe's father acting this way?

Let's turn to tarot again, as it's my true divinatory love, but you can do this with any system. For the "why" question I've drawn (as always, the number that follows the card title is the order in which it was drawn and laid out):

Death (4), Strength (2), Five of Cups (1), Ace of Swords (3), Knight of Cups (5)

First, a few things I notice out of the gate:

- The way Death and the Knight of Cups are riding in the same direction—to the right
- The way Death and the Five of Cups "contain" Strength, because both turn to that card
- The lack of wands and coins/pentacles
- Cups and majors are tied for "dominant" element
- The Air/swords energy is fairly limited, given the only swords card is an ace

All or none of these may matter, but these are useful impressions for me to discover. I also note that the focal point, the Five of Cups, is an emotional card and one of upheaval. Given the fact that Niobe is experiencing a lot of emotions based on their father's attitude lately, that tracks—but remember, this reading is *about Dan,* Niobe's father, not Niobe themselves. I have to stay focused on Dan. (That said, I would also like to point out that though I randomly named our client Niobe, the Five of Cups is giving "Niobe's Tears" vibes, which is so cool to me.)

The central trio (Strength, Five of Cups, Ace of Swords) suggests to me that Dan is sick and tired of being strong and actually feels he's got a deficit of strength left to offer. The Five of Cups disrupts the emotional stability and evenness of Strength (which, in this deck, has the number eight—which is a steady, even, stable, but also very effortful number; strength takes energy) and he wants to cut off his emotions (Ace of Swords). Something powerful may have happened to him to make him feel this way, and it looks as though he's been strong through a lot of loss (Death) and it's perhaps inevitable (Death) that he would feel this way.

The Ace of Swords presents a bit of a punctuation mark in the reading, separating the Knight of Cups from the rest of the cards. That's fascinating. At the same time, that same ace mirrors Strength, suggesting a cutting off of strength. Now, because I live with depression, I understand that I may be looking at someone experiencing depression. The listlessness, sadness, and lack of energy are all elements that come from depression. Again, I'm not a psychotherapist, so I'd be thoughtful about offering diagnoses; still, depression is pretty damn common, and I heard someone recently refer to it as the "common cold of mental health" issues. So, I don't feel super nervous about saying Dan seems depressed.

The Knight of Cups frequently has a sexy, romantic quality; often this is the romancer, the fuck boy, or the lothario. In this case, though, we must contextualize the card in terms of the information this reading is giving. I think that Dan is trying to drive people away (Death/Knight of Cups) and he thinks that once he can get people to divorce (Death) themselves from him, he can move on to something better (Knight of Cups). The desire to cut people off (Ace of Swords) is powerful

(Strength, mirroring the Ace). He's in such a deep funk that he may actively be trying to separate himself from people. But I can't neglect the connection between the two cups cards. The Five of Cups and the Knight of Cups, if we ignore for a moment the ace between them, suggests someone who actually wants out of a situation. If Dan is in a relationship, that may be the cause of it; if he's grieving the loss of a relationship, then that's the cause.

The combination of Death and Strength, both on the left, tell me that whatever triggered Dan's depression wasn't minor. This was a life-changer, and could be divorce or even the death of a spouse. This isn't something you just "get over." Knowing that the Four of Cups precedes the Five when the deck is in order, I know that it's possible he's been holding feelings at bay (the unseen Four of Cups) and can no longer do that (five shakes up four's stasis). So, it's possible he's been very good—very strong (Strength)—at ignoring the grief he's experiencing (whether actual or metaphorical), but that dam has finally broken (Five of Cups).

If we pair the Ace of Swords with the Knight of Cups, the knight's natural fluidity and tendency to roam is heightened by the immaturity bestowed on him (Dan, in this case), so the Knight of Cups is acting based on more juvenile thoughts, or more immature thoughts. I'd be careful about word choice, here, but knowing me it's possible that the word "immature" might slip my lips. I have a tendency to use it neutrally, even though I know it's got pejorative tones. I simply mean that it isn't mature, it isn't grown, it's not fully thought out. Dan doesn't have a plan but wants to go anyway. This could be bad news, but we can't forget that watery cards are intuitive, so this may suggest, too, that he's capable of navigating this based on his sense of direction. The combination of Air (wisdom) and Water (feeling) suggests that he may be able to find his way to where he wants to go. This is important because it means Dan could act impulsively and may surprise people (ace), which means that Niobe has to be aware of this. Also, the potential for Dan being suddenly triggered to run away is real (the Ace of Swords could be the "trigger") so that poor or thoughtless communication (again, Ace of Swords) could be a strong (Strength) motivator for him getting out of Dodge (Knight of Cups) and not caring who he leaves behind (both the knight [caring] and Death). So, Niobe might want to be thoughtful about the words they use when talking to Dan.

To sum up, Dan's been through some shit and he's feeling really low. There's some major depression or sadness going on and it's making him want to cut people off—and, in fact, he may just be looking for an excuse for him to end his connections and run off into the sunset. I do not see evidence that Dan is suicidal, because I don't believe that's part of the Knight of Cups; that said, the depression factor in this reading and the tendency for knights to act impulsively (they're action-oriented) and Dan's currently quick trigger finger (Ace of Swords) could suggest that a tendency toward self-harm is at play. Because the Knight of Cups *is* so fluid and so moody, I do not think that his dark (Death) moods are permanent. But just to see, in this case, I'll draw another card to follow the knight. Here, I get the Six of Swords.

Swords can often be associated with negativity, but they're objective and they're not emotional. Sixes rebalance and are the restorative follow-up to the emotional upheaval of fives, in this case the very emotional Five of Cups. There is progress frequently associated in this card, though often depicted as mournful. Sixes tend to exist in a beautiful, balanced place. This tells me that if Dan's thoughts aren't progressive now, they will be. The "mood" of the Knight of Cups will pass into a more objective, clearer, more balanced kind of progress—one that isn't quite as impulsive, and one that isn't super dangerous. I think Dan will come through to a healthier phase of his grieving, and I don't think it's that far away—but likely it's going to be a bit of a journey for him (and for Niobe), because sixes come in the second half of a suit. They're not as immediate as the ace, and we have to think that now the Knight of Cups is bookmarked by the ace and the six, so he's on his *way*—but only just beginning. I don't think Dan's in any physical danger, but I do think he's in a dark place.

There is an answer to Niobe's question already here: be careful what you say, because he's looking for a reason to cut you off. He's baiting you, and if you take the bait, it'll work—he'll shut you off. But that's not the full answer. Now, I could read this exact spread with a view toward Niobe's question—or I could draw another spread. Let's do both and see what happens. Why the hell not, right? This is an experiment and fortune tellers love experiments!

When re-contextualizing a spread of cards to answer a new question, we need to start from scratch—we, in a way, have to forget everything we've just done. This is one reason why people don't generally do this. One new set of cards for each new question makes sense. But we knew where we were going before we drew this array—we knew the ultimate goal was Niobe's question, but first we needed to know what was going on with their father. The intention was already part of the draw, so there's no reason not to see if it can't offer something. Again, there's no reason to do this, but there's also no reason not to. We've got the cards out already, why not give it a go? I can see most people wanting to draw a new spread, and why not? We like shuffling and drawing and it's certainly more entertaining for the client. That said, why not squeeze the orange and see if there's any juice left—to coin a clumsy metaphor.

Once again, I return to the center. The Five of Cups tells me that Niobe is really connecting to Dan's distress. They may sense that there's something deeper going on with Dan right now—and, of course, asking for a reading to begin with is a sign of that. But we're looking for advice. Often, I look to the first card in a reading to give me confirmation of what I already know. Niobe is upset, probably also feeling depressed thanks to their dad's constant judgment. This is an unpleasant experience for both.

Pairing Strength with the Ace of Swords, I see that Niobe needs to be careful with their words. Here, I'm reading Strength in a slightly strange way: because real strength takes focus and effort, I'm reading that as "careful." You need to use your strength wisely (Strength plus swords generally) and wield your weapon (Ace of Swords) with grace and courage (Strength). It's a bit of a journey, I know, but it's the first thing I thought of. Strength in this context is playing double duty as another virtue—prudence. Strength is frequently thought of in terms of blunt force, which would be a common use for a sword. But we already know that if Niobe goes in with a *what the fuck is wrong with you, you're pissing me off* attitude, it's going to give Dan the ammo he needs to run away. Thus, contextually, Strength can't reflect blunt force—which is an older image for the Strength card. Look at old Italian decks, and you'll see a man bludgeoning a lion. In this case, we benefit from the gentler version given to us by the Marseille-style decks and of course, Pamela Colman Smith's gentle scene.

Pairing Death and Strength, I feel that Niobe needs to understand that an ending (Death) is a strong possibility (Strength), which underscores the fact that using their strength wisely (Ace of Swords again) is important. The Ace of Swords and the Knight of Cups suggests Niobe put down their weapon (ace) and go into conversations (swords) with Dan in a more caring (Water/cups) way, maybe even giving Dan the emotional space he needs (note how the Knight of Cups walks out of the reading, leaving all the other cards behind). This gives me the sense that the best thing Niobe can do is take the pressure off the relationship by letting Dan have some emotional space, even some emotional distance. When I pair Death with the Knight of Cups, what I really see is someone letting go—in this case, letting go of the need to do Dan's emotional labor (knights aren't laborers, but with the absence of any more active card, the knight in this case becomes the main actor, the main doer, of the spread).

Death reminds us that our control is limited. There may not be much Niobe can do at the moment to fix their relationship with their father; Dan is going through some shit and needs to deal with it. The best thing Niobe can do is allow Dan's journey to take place without attempting to constrict it too much. Now, this isn't what most of us want to hear, particularly if a loved one has started negating our personhood and especially if this is sudden. But it does give me an "absence makes the heart grow fonder" vibe, which is sometimes a simple necessity. Sometimes we just need space. Niobe may not like this advice, but they did ask what they can do about their dad's behavior. In this case, Dad needs to figure it out and needs some time. Niobe attempting to interfere could backfire in a big way. If they can't deal with Dan's 'tude right now, they're probably better off avoiding it altogether. Once Dan is out of his funk, this behavior is likely to chill. (I return here to the reading ending with the clarifying Six of Swords card and recall that in my case swords correspond with North and Winter, giving me "chill.") In fact, the Six of Swords can suggest Niobe think about other stuff until Dan's over his journey.

For the sake of speed, I'll limit the next reading to three cards. These cards are drawn specifically to answer Niobe's question, "What should I do about my father?" Here, I've drawn:

The Magician (2), Temperance (1), Ten of Wands (3)

Right out of the gate, Temperance suggests a moderate approach. But because the card sits in the middle of two, and because it's often thought of blending two things together, it makes sense that we would consider, too, that The Magician and the Ten of Wands are the two things being blended. At first glance, I wondered how possible that was; both cards have a fair amount of energy at play. The Magician is directing energy, and the Ten of Wands is carrying it. It seems like blending the same thing, but we can't really "blend" identical things; they're just two parts coming together. To be honest, I find this trio of cards a frustrating combo and not really given to giving particularly good advice. But that could also just be my general mood, which is mercurial (to say the least). So, I pause, get over my irritation, and consider each card individually before I consider them as blended elements.

The Magician is frequently the card I look to for liars and frauds, con artists, and narcissists. But also entertainers of any kind, deft and agile tradespeople, and those given to both misdirection as well as intentional or spiritual workings. Whether for good or ill, the pre-Golden Dawn image of the street performer is generally more useful to me than the iconic mage designed by Smith and Waite. Like them or not, they're incredibly quick, they're incredibly agile, they're incredibly charming. They could not succeed in their task if they didn't seduce an audience into attending their act. So, there's a seductive, manipulative element to the card. There's also a great deal of persistence and skill—if their show isn't any good, nobody will stay and watch it, let alone hand over their hard-earned money. This means the card represents people who are good at reading the room and sensing when attention is drifting. Lots here, really, when I pause to get over myself. For our purposes, the deftness, ability to read the room, the seductive/manipulative/charm quality, and the agility are all relevant.

In terms of the Ten of Wands, we can link it to The Magician with tenacity, for sure, but let's not worry about the pairing for a while. What do I know about this Ten of Wands: Tens complete a cycle, they're endings; they're also, in their own way, beginnings of things (we take the marriage of one and zero to make the numeral 10, so that not only brings us to the beginning but brings us to an *elevated* beginning. In a base ten number system, every new ten is a new beginning but at a higher level). The wands, the suit of Fire, are, of course, fiery—passionate, energetic, enthusiastic, definitely tenacious. In the well-known Waite-Smith image, we've got someone *literally* putting their back into it. In fact, they're doing something quite impossible. If you look at Smith's art, that's not an actual posture anyone could hold for long—but there they are, doing the impossible. Wands are creative (not unlike The Magician) and potent; they're driven, hungry (fire needs fuel and air to burn or it will die). The shadow of that, though, is being destructive, using up resources too quickly, and being needy (fire needs fuel, etc.); there's a tendency to hurt with fire. Fire needs to be managed, but our instinct is to fight it. Compare Indigenous fire management techniques to modern governmental ones. The people who belong to this land know how to work *with* it; the rest of us know how to play "hero."

If this were a descriptive reading, the Ten of Wands would tell me that this uncomfortable situation is very nearly over. But this isn't a descriptive reading, it's an advice reading. The card needs to speak to that. So, again, I think about what's relevant to our purposes. Actually, as soon as I do, the Ten and The Magician suddenly leap into action together: *Put your back into a charm offensive.* This is the way that the two cards get blended in Temperance—the one card we haven't actually talked too much about.

It's true that some cards are fairly quiet in readings, but I don't know if Temperance's main purpose here is simply "to blend," or if it has more to say/do quite yet. Let's consider: Temperance literally means moderation, but when I think back on US history, I recall that it was an extremist movement. The Temperance Movement in the US was a largely racist act, because the white middle class believed that crime was caused by drunken immigrants, the poor, and other unwanted riffraff. It was, as the cliche goes, "the curse of the working class." (Now why would the working class need such an escape...hmm...probably not the exploitative ruling class forcing them to work in dark, humid mills or in the blood-soaked meat packing plants. It must be their moral character. *Of course!*) Conservatism always finds a public-facing cause that seems appropriate. So the mission "became" a pro-woman, anti-violence campaign: get rid of alcohol, and men (of course, that meant poor men and foreigners, not the refined ruling class who never intended on giving up alcohol—and didn't) wouldn't assault their wives. Upon achieving this lofty goal, violence didn't decrease, but crime in general *increased. Everyone* was engaged in bootlegging, whether as a runner or consumer. This, of course, includes the ruling class who would never suffer the consequences of violating temperance laws, but which became a *wonderful* way of jailing the impoverished and other huddled masses.

Bit of a history lesson, but why this matters is duplicity, deception—themes in sync with The Magician. There's also something binary about Temperance, given that it's frequently depicted blending two items, sometimes at an impossible angle. The impossibility, visible in the Waite-Smith, connects it to the posture of the Ten. Here, too, the word "posture" inspires me. There's mucho deception at play, here. So, the advice goes further: *Pretend you're fine with him.* This underscores the previous message: *Put your back into a charm offensive.* Be delightful, agreeable, amenable; accept his cancellations and his moods; avoid him as much as you can, but when you can't, be a joy—understanding, validating, open. Then, get home and strip it all off and take a shower. This answer makes sense for a few reasons, given how close Dan is to cutting everyone off. Though we don't want to hide our pain from our loved ones, there are gives and takes and sometimes (annoying as it is) we have to center other people's shit over our own, at least when we're with that person. It's a problem if the balance is always on you making that space, but if it's even, there's not really anything wrong with it. This isn't telling Niobe to deny their personhood, gender, or anything else; just to let Dad be in his mood and to be totally charming about it and eventually he'll get over the funk. Annoying, but temporary—at least if we actually follow the advice. And that's the whole point.

The Whole Point

By beginning with why Dan was being a tool, I set up an important motivator for Niobe: I was able to show the consequences of ignoring the forthcoming advice. Right? Niobe knows that if they don't give Dan space and if they're not solicitous of his moods, then Dan may use it as an excuse to blow off Niobe completely. There's a cost now. In this case, Niobe's relationship with Dan. They know that giving Dan some time to go through what he's going through and allowing themselves to center Dan's grief for a while, the relationship will eventually self-correct. On the other hand, if they're cranky right back and push too hard, Dan will bolt. Now, we see not only the advice but also the actual problem we're dealing with. We've also allowed the first reading to completely dictate how we read the second, which makes us feel *so much more confident* about what we're saying. We know that the advice is likely to be good because we have so much more context about the conflict.

Obviously, every preliminary reading will tell a completely different story with different outcomes—but it's *always* going to tell us the thing that *really* needs to be addressed, so that we know what advice really matters. There are probably a lot of wise things we can say given the guidance of our divination system, but the less context we have the more we have only instinct and generalities to go on. We're more likely to draw on our own experiences and judgment of a situation because that's all we have to work with. We can only call on what comes to mind, and what comes to mind as examples are going to be things we're super familiar with. This is fine, this works. And this is how most of us read most of the time. It creates a bit more of a metaphor for the client: "You're experiencing something similar to this, right? So, we should probably do something like this." It's not unlike communicating in a different language using a guidebook. It's not perfect, but it gets the job done.

On the other hand, if we learn the language and experience it in situ, we're going to be able to have much more specific conversations. You'll not only be able to ask where the library is, but you'll be able to understand who built it, out of what, why, how many books are inside, and what it used to be. You'll have a much fuller experience of the library. If you can understand the language, you can experience the fullness of a menu description. By doing a preliminary reading, we can learn the language of the situation—allowing us to be exponentially more specific and accurate. The more we know, the more the cards start to speak *to that specific situation and moment,* rather than in generalities. I mean, look: generalities can work. Nothing that came out of Delphi makes a lick of sense to us today, but clearly those inscrutable messages meant something to the many, many, many who went to seek the oracle's advice. But why not have it be a little easier, why not learn the code rather than using a Cracker Jack's decoder ring, you know?

There Are Shouldn'ts and Shoulds

The time has come, the walrus said, to talk about one of the most fascinating words in the fortune teller's lexicon: *should.* It's fascinating because it's probably the most common word we hear in questions. Everyone wants to know what they "should" do. Everyone wants to know how something "should" go. "Should" pops off the tongues of clients with the frequency of "I", "a", and "the." The liberal use of curly quotes here isn't purely due to my long-standing yet over-abundant relationship with punctuation; it's because "should" is such an imaginary concept. And that's why it's so hard to read about, and actually, I think that's why it's such a common word in questions. Not just divination questions, no, questions of all kinds in life's funny little journey.

Here's why I think the concept is imaginary and why we (people who grew up speaking English) tend to use it: "Should" implies certainty and a binary path. When we ask "should," we're saying, in essence: *There is a thing that isn't real, but I want it to be. I would like to know how to make that happen. There is only one right answer and only one path to reach this thing. Right now, I need to know if what I think is the right thing to do will get me there.* Also implied, from my teensy little vantage point, is a certain amount of *I would also like someone to blame when this inevitably fails to manifest, because it cannot be my fault—for I have done the Correct Thing™, and as such I'm entitled to getting what I want.* There is so much human psychology connected to such a tiny word, a word tossed off with little consequence or forethought. Merely a modal verb (yes, I had to look that up) that we probably use hundreds of times a day.

And yet, within it is a lot of desire and deflection! How cool is language, y'all?

I'll pause and assure you there's nothing wrong with any of this. It is how we who speak English speak. "Should" is *filled* with, *riddled* with, *fecund* with possibility! In fact, that's what modal verbs do: they indicate intent and possibility. No wonder we love this one so. We love possibility. We *need* possibility. We would perish without it, because the bleakness of life—too bleak already—would be impossible to bear. We must have *something* to look forward to. And we must have control over it happening, at least to some degree, and we must do everything correctly to ensure it does.

The only problem is, many "should" questions innocently confuse possibility with inevitability. When we do that, and the inevitability turns out to be false, we often look back and wonder where it went wrong. Where *we* went wrong. What did *we* do to make this happen *to us*. We get angry, we get depressed, and we beat ourselves up for having fucked up so royally and ruined any possibility of happiness in our lives.

But what we didn't know, what we never bothered to ask about, was whether the damn thing was possible to begin with. If the goal was to turn a straight guy into a gay guy, that was never going to work. Nothing you "should" try will achieve that end, because that's not how sexuality works. If you managed to "turn" him, then he wasn't straight to begin with. See what I mean? Now, most of us aren't attempting to do that; most of us are simply trying to get promotions or dates or movie deals or stars on the Walk of Fame. We live in a time of possibility, and if it can happen for the winner of *The Voice,* why can't it happen for us? There's nothing saying it can't.

I'm not here to say it can't happen for you, not at all. I'm not even going to dwell on the law of averages and the potential for "making it" in any big, long-lasting way. What I'm going to say is that when we operate from a "should" perspective, we're operating based on assumptions and setting ourselves up for frustration because we don't have a full view of what we're working with.

"Should I do X?"

It's a yes or no question, a closed question. Yes, you should; no, you should not. It's a binary. Most things aren't binary, though. Let's take this apart a bit. Say Ravi (he/him, gay, cis, mid-thirties, "young professional" at a consulting firm known for high pay, long hours, and lots of turnover) has been renting in DC while working at his corporate HQ in Bethesda, Maryland. A house he drives past every day on the way to work, much closer to Bethesda—and much further from the reason he moved there, DC—has just gone on the market. He's always thought it was cute, and that if he had to live somewhere it would be like that. He's wondering if he should buy the house. He knows he'll never be able to afford to buy in the DC metro area, he knows he doesn't want to leave the area, though. Should he buy the house?

I picked this partly because I know nothing about real estate, so I can't go on any tangents about it. But let's consider a few things. First, the question implies Ravi's offer will be accepted—in a market known for competitive buying. It's an in-demand house in an in-demand area and if Ravi has driven by it and thought about buying it, so has every other commuter on their way to *his office alone,* to say nothing of all the other commuters in what is a major hub for corporate headquarters. Now, it might be somewhat pedantic to take the question apart, but it does make me wonder how invested the client is in what they think they want. That's, of course, none of my damn business, *but* it does give me an indication of how much effort they're going to put into getting it—which is going to have an outcome on whether or not they do. It's not what I'll base the reading on, but it's a clue as to how things will go.

When people are *serious* about something, they've generally thought about it every which way, some will make flowcharts and Venn diagrams, some will journal and make notes, others will toss and turn thinking about it. By the time they sit with a fortune teller to ask about it, there's not really anything casual about their question. That's not to say they won't ask *a should* question, but what they're likely to add to that is a tonnage of context. They're going to give you all the potentials they've considered, all the possible roadblocks, and anything else they've considered. Most will, anyway, and I'm speaking in generalities. Point is, someone who has *really* considered it is likely going to give you more intel and will certainly *not* be casual about it. Chances are, this person has considered all the options and what they're *really* asking is which one is right for them. Let's come back to this good doobie presently.

In the meantime, we return to Ravi. When a question comes in casual wording, I've found many folks are really asking, "Do I even *want* this?" The question isn't so much "Should I buy this house?" as it is "Should I care?" It's a question based sort of on the *possibility* of possibility. "This is a thing I didn't know I wanted? Should I try to get it before somebody else does?" The idea of doing it may never have occurred to Ravi (or any client) before, but the fact that it's available suddenly creates an opening he wonders whether he should step through. It's a curiosity about action. "Will acting on this be in my best interests?" There's a bit of ambivalence, in that—if they *really* wanted it—wouldn't they be going for it?

In Ravi's case, we know he's likely going to leave his consulting gig soon, because he's at the age where most people decide they want to be treated more like a human being. Whether he moves on to another local company or not, whether he decides to take a pay cut, etc., these are all unknowns, because Ravi hasn't given much thought to any of this yet. Now, again, I'm making assumptions, but what I'm trying to pare down to is the *why*. Because with a question like "Should I do X?", if he *really* wanted it, he'd be making an offer. He wouldn't have asked for a reading—*or,* he would have asked a different question: "Is this a good financial decision?" "Will this tie me down to this region, when I may have to move?" "How likely is it my offer would be accepted?" There would have been some considerations of the specifics, of the realities of buying a house; there would be evidence that he's at least thought about some of the pros and cons—and would likely share at least some of them with you.

So, what does all this amateur psychology mean for us readers?

Well, it's just interesting, isn't it?

No, there's more to it than that. While I don't rephrase a client's question, with a casually worded phrase concerning a major life decision, I would likely ask the client for more deets. "Could you tell me anything that would give me more context about the situation?" Something like that. Some folks will say no. It's annoying, but it doesn't happen that often. Most will give you at least a little bit to work with, and when they do it will help guide your reading. You'll likely be working with a different question mentally than the one Ravi asked, but you'll give him the answer he asked for. There's always a little mental gymnastics in these kinds of situations, and what I'm *not* advocating for is a superior attitude toward the client or an assumption we know better. That's not it. As a reader, what I'm really doing is getting two messages from the divination at the same time. It's easier to demo than explain, so…

Let's say I draw the Five of Wands (2), the Five of Cups (1), and The Tower (3).

Whoa, right? Out of the gate, big NO! Well, not necessarily. But maybe. Allow:

Fives destabilize, which is *exactly* what Ravi is asking about. He's asking if he should shake up his status quo, in this case in a very specific way. So though the imagery in many decks may offer stress and mournfulness, I'm not ready to accept those alone quite yet. The Tower, of course, also destabilizes. And it's a building—a house. So that's also contextually relevant. Whether the lightning bolt and people falling from the highest floors will be relevant comes later; right now, I'm gathering information. It's always worth mentioning, I suppose, that I've developed a weird reading style over the years. I take nothing for granted. I try to quickly consider everything I know—as well as anything that jumps out at me—and not to decide on anything right away. This happened over time and was only partly conscious. So, again, if you come to different conclusions based on the same cards, that makes total sense.

The Five of Cups suggests emotional upheaval, or a sensational shift—sensation, in this case, meaning the five senses. I often think of cups/Water in terms of sensations rather than only feelings. The Five of Cups is restless. We always assume the cloaked figure is mourning, but what if they're just throwing a big tantrum? Restless. Water is restless, or it should be; still water can be dangerous. The spilled cups on the ground feel like missed opportunities. Ravi has missed out on things he's wanted before, probably due to inaction (note the story of the blasé Four of Cups missing out and then throwing a fit in the Five). I can, of course, ask Ravi if that's true. I mean it sounds good, but does it *mean* anything? Only one way to find out: *ask*.

The Five of Wands is giving energetic upheaval. I wonder if Ravi's been through a breakup recently (again, only one way to know for sure)—but either way, there's more restlessness. There's a lot of pent-up restlessness desperate to burst forth—which it does, in The Tower. If this were a relationship reading, it would be quite sexy. But it's not. Wands are fiery, so they can be temperamental. Fire and Water (cups) make steam, and that can be explosive, too. All this pent-up energy is building up steam and it's *going* to be released. This is very potent, possibly dangerous energy! It doesn't seem to be talking much about the banality of buying a house, no matter how much money it costs or what a big move it might be. This is a different kind of energy. There's a bursting forth from fetters. It's very aggressive.

Before I go further with all that drama, I'm going to consider a few other realities: First, no Air or Earth. Never a good sign when dealing with matters of finances and home. Where Fire and Water are unthinking and active, Earth and Air are more stable and grounded. You'll note that I'm not pairing the elements as they traditionally are when working with elemental dignities. Typically, Fire and Water don't have anything in common, like oil and vinegar. But it is that refusal to blend that unites them. They're forces of nature. Earth and Air simply *are*. When air moves, it's because it's getting hotter or colder (Fire), or when humidity builds up so much it starts to rain (Water). Earth also is most noticeable when its tectonic plates are shifting (thanks to volcanic action, Fire) or when it's being flooded with storms (Water). Yes, Air can be stormy, too, but not because of its own initiative; it's because of temperature changes. This isn't to say the traditional elemental dignities can't be helpful, but the actual behavior of the actual elements can give you so much information in a reading.

In this reading, nothing is grounding us and we're not thinking; we're all passion and energy and feeling and sensation and gratification. This is the impulsive side of us, this childlike side of us who doesn't have to worry about bills or planning for the future. There's nothing to stand on, no foundation. This could indicate problems with the house, especially given The Tower's crumbling state. Maybe the house is falling down, maybe its a beast to take care of. There's also nothing to breathe in, so there's nothing to sustain the fire or to keep the water moving. Eventually, the water will evaporate from all the fire, and then the fire will eat up all the air and will suffocate. Not ideal, to say the least.

Now, I return to the initial impressions I got about Ravi's whole situation being about shaking up the status quo and how this trio of cards could indicate that's exactly what he needs. Having worked my way through the reading, though, what I see is that Ravi feels deeply trapped and needs to break out. My guess is that it's his job causing this. Ravi is highly burned out and looking for any kind of *something* to make him feel excited and like his energy is going to something productive. But if he were to buy this house, he'd likely regret it. The Tower, in this case, isn't promising sexiness. Sometimes a cigar is just a cigar, and in this case when we're doing a reading about a house and the crumbling Tower shows up, it's not likely to work well. The place may need major renovations.

Actually, if we accept The Tower as the choice to buy the house, and then work backwards, we see someone living in regret and under the great energetic burden of keeping the damn place up and running. That's not something I usually do, but I just thought of it and found it interesting.

Now, I return to Ravi's question: "Should I buy this house?"

"Ravi, it doesn't look like it's the right thing for you. It doesn't look like the solution to whatever you're going through right now, and it may end up being a major headache."

But what happened to all that psychological analysis we just did?

Shrug. It got us the answer we needed, didn't it? Anyway, Ravi didn't ask that. He asked if he should do it and the answer was no because it's not going to solve his problems.

Do we owe him the whole story? It depends. In this case, this reading took a twisty path. That happens more in written readings, because the mind is forced to work differently, more slowly than when reading live, and it can allow more thoughts to form. But, either way, this was a uniquely deep dance, even with only three cards. Some of that would likely have come out during the interpretation. Remember, if this was live, then I'd be asking him questions the whole time: "It seems like you've got a lot of pent-up energy and emotions right now, is that fair to say?" "Have you been through anything like a breakup recently?" "How much do you know about the current state of the property?" Those kinds of questions would contextualize for us. Some of this information would also come out during the conversation. That means if I got an impulse that wasn't accurate, I would be able to validate it. If Ravi says, "No, no breakups, and I'm not feeling particularly pent up," then I have to rethink what I've gotten, and I will. No big deal.

If this were a recorded reading and Ravi and I weren't live in living color, a lot of what I gathered would remain internal. Not that it's not important, but that it just doesn't make the final cut. Here's what: When writing a research paper in school, we didn't include every quote we pulled or every datum we found because there just wouldn't be room. Sure, in school we'd probably use a lot of it to pad the page count—who doesn't? In a reading, though, I return to a few points I've made elsewhere in these pages:

Sometimes readings speak literally and sometimes in metaphor. I don't know which until I ask the client, but I can't do that if it's a recorded reading.

Sometimes what I see in a reading is *getting me where I'm going,* but is not the final destination—especially the impulses I discover as I'm first scanning the cards and letting them wash over me. Like, I need to go through certain interpretations in order to get to the ultimate one that answers the question. What got me there may not be relevant or even make any sense to the client.

I try to use as few words and make as few points as possible. The less I say, the less options I offer, the more likely the client will remember what I do say. Again, this isn't easy or simple, and quite often a reading will be a bit of a monologue. But I'm still trying to monologue as economically and crisply as I can. If it's not going to be relevant to the client and I know that, I try not to say it.

The experience of writing out a reading as I have to do in this book is *dramatically* different from speaking one. It uses whole other parts of the brain. There are of course overlaps, but the way the brain functions while communicating in written language is very different from speaking.

This demo was really about showing off the "gymnastics" of getting to an answer while looking for different things first. I knew I was going to get to Ravi's "should," but I needed to see a lot of other things first, including *why* the answer is no. Another thing I've said before and will say again: this is one reason I enjoy tarot so much. I can get so many layers, even when I'm reaching for simple answer. Those layers help me feel more confident that my ultimate answer is sound and as correct as possible.

Now, to return, as promised, to those people who have thought about all the possibilities and potentialities and still ask a "should" question. In these cases, I think the best thing to do is a few smaller readings exploring the vibe of each outcome.

So, if there are two possible choices (don't buy the house and buy the house), then do a reading on each. What is the likely outcome of each scenario? This is because humans love the safety of binaries, even though most things aren't binary. Both of the options may get the client closer to their goal(s). Knowing what could happen for each possible choice is a more nuanced, more realistic view of the situation. Things are rarely entirely good or entirely bad, entirely right or wrong. Everything contains multitudes. And so buying the house may offer one set of outcomes—probably a mix of good and bad, *maybe* tilted in one direction; likewise, with not buying the house, it's also probably a mix of good and bad and *maybe* tilted in one direction. What you may find is that both options take you to the same place. Or that neither takes you anywhere.

This sounds like more work, but it's not; it's just a series of smaller readings rather than one big one. Instead of a nine-card box, which is my go-to, I might do three or five cards per option, depending on how many options there are. You might lay all the cards out at once, or you might shuffle and draw between each. There are benefits to both. Laying them all out allows you to see themes and weights of numbers and suits. Shuffling and redrawing for each one allows the potential for cards to repeat. It's all a matter of taste, and you'll often decide in the moment which to do. Neither is wrong or right, and they each have interesting potential. But what's most important is that the client gets a bird's eye view of their situation and can choose which option has the most pleasing outcomes, assuming any of them do.

I guess that's the other thing. "Should" implies that good things are possible, and sometimes that's not the case. Yes, we all know what a cynical fatalist I am, but I didn't get that way by accident. I know a lot of lovely people who are single and don't want to be; I know a lot of people wasting potential in a job they hate because they lack self-confidence, in part because their self-esteem was stolen by that job; I know people who have had just awful health scare after awful health scare. The reality is, and we need to know this as readers, that not everyone gets the brass ring. It's shitty, it sucks, and that's not fate; that has more to do with the hoarding of resources, including access to what we consider success. But it's real, nonetheless. No reader wants to tell a client, "Hey, no matter which you choose, it's going to suck." But sometimes that's the answer. Because sometimes that's life.

More often than not, though, any option is fine. Those times can be frustrating for clients, because we frequently want a clear sign that we should do X or Y. Life doesn't work that way, though; in fact, most of the time it's a crap shoot, even when you have a reading. But what's comforting about that is that there are a lot of times where the seemingly irrevocable decision turns out to be not-so-irrevocable after all. Sometimes clients may feel disappointed when a reading isn't dramatic, but they're better off. Anyone who has lived through drama knows that's the truth.

If I Were You...

I *love* the topic of advice, and I love that there aren't clear, succinct answers to be had for whether or not advice readings are truly worth doing. It doesn't matter, because people want them and we're going to give them. It's just like predictions, which is what the next chapter is about. What I've shared with you is more to get your brain pondering the topic, not so much to provide you with firm answers. There aren't any, and anyway if there were, that would be dogma. What I do hope is that you'll start thinking about advice readings and paying attention to the ones you do. How they go, how the client reacts, how you feel about them—and, if you can find out, what the client ends up doing and how it went. Don't get too caught up in whether or not the advice was right. Remember, it's likely that even if the client told you they followed it, they probably didn't—or, at least, they did it in their own unique way. Which is as it should be, since we're not the boss of them. Not to say you shouldn't care about whether it was or not, but you should (there's that word again!) consider it with curiosity. "*Why* did this go as it did?" The thing is, life is full of choices, and even the best advice can't make people do what's best for them or force things into being. That's the annoying thing about fate.

CHAPTER ELEVEN

CALLED IT

When I asked folks what they thought a fortune teller was, I realized that most people think of the role exclusively in terms of prediction. It's funny. *Only* prediction seems to be considered fortune telling. This interested me. In this case because it's not "*future* telling," and not everyone has a fortune in the future to tell about. I guess *fortune* has always been viewed as another name for *fate*, and so it makes sense. But what's so funny to me is that it didn't really occur to me that the equation was so specific in people's minds. As you've seen in the prior chapters, I lasso a lot under the fortune telling umbrella. This is partly because we're talking about fortune telling for modern life, but also because the act of predicting is no more or less common than any other kind of question. Many people will ask for advice or to know what their partner is thinking or what to do about their ex. It's also because I think I've always viewed predictive readings as part of the process—even when I said I didn't do them.

Over to Gary with the Weather

I have a thing for TV meteorologists. I love it when there's a mild snowstorm and they've all got their suit jackets off and their sleeves rolled up like they're really in the thick of it. I know some overpaid consultant did a focus group that told producers to make them do this, that this makes them look more trustworthy and less nerdy, and I think it's fully the stupidest thing on the planet. And yet, it tickles me. I enjoy it. Look at you cosplaying labor, TV guys! So cute! (I'm curious, now, whether this happens outside the US. It's never occurred to me, but do TV weather people usually roll up their literal sleeves during storms like they were out there shoveling people out? I wouldn't be surprised if it's only in the US, but I hope it's not.)

In the US, meteorologists get a bad rap. Consumers of TV weather always talk about how constantly inaccurate weather people are. It's a joke and probably one of the easiest jobs to make fun of as a result. The problem is, that's such a weird stereotype. They're right way more often than they're not. If they weren't, they'd get canned. On any given day, they're right about what's going to happen. The thing is, the times when they're wrong are the ones we notice most. It's the big snowstorm that suddenly goes off course. It's the hurricane that turns west rather than east. The main reason for this is that these are the most unpredictable weather patterns. They can't be fully predicted, because the conditions under which they form and move are so changeable, so mercurial. (Add to this the fact that news agencies want to scare the shit out of us as much as possible so we keep our eyeballs glued to their advertisers, and you've got another reason people don't trust meteorologists.)

Life is this way, too. Not only in the sense that the biggest, most dramatic things are weirdly the hardest to predict, but also because we're constantly forecasting without even thinking about it. We literally do it every day. "I *knew* this was going to happen." "Told you so!" "Called it." We're constantly predicting outcomes and then bragging when our predictions come true—usually much to the annoyance of the people we gave advice to, who then proceeded not to take it. (Get the connection? Wink.) This isn't any metaphysical, magical thing; it's our ability to recognize patterns and associate them with outcomes we've seen before. This is how we learn, if you recall. It's touching the stove and realizing it's hot, and then realizing that if other people touch it, they too will get burned. It's knowing that if we date that same kind of guy again, we're going to end up in the same boat we did last time. It's knowing that if our best friend dates the same kind of guy again, *they're* going to end up in the same boat. It's knowing that not planning well enough will mean the big pilot at work fails and that not looking at the data we paid for will mean we miss our goals again.

Prediction is shockingly prosaic. It's weirdly the least subversive thing we do. At least, these days it is. Corporations have entire teams dedicated to forecasting. This is based entirely on reading past and present trends and predicting what future trends will be. I've been around call center forecasting enough to know that, unlike meteorologists, call forecasting is wrong as often as not. The thing is, most people who ask for predictive readings have some sense of what the outcome will be already. They're really looking for confirmation of their gut instinct and usually they find it. When they don't, they've got some new information. But many, many people can tell where things are headed without the benefit of divination.

As always, I'm not saying we shouldn't do it; only that it's not actually that shocking or dramatic. Most of the time. And the times when it is dramatic are probably the times when the predictions are most tenuous, least certain.

Back to the Future

If we think of life like the atmosphere (as above, so below?), then it's easy to see how prediction works. Some weather events recur under certain conditions. This makes them easy to predict. The now-familiar *El Niño* and *La Niña* are examples. They occur around the same time, in the same places, and under the same conditions. Meteorologists can see those conditions and make an educated guess (these days with the benefit of radar and algorithms) about these events occurring. Some weather events are less predictable. Hurricanes, for example, tend to form only during certain parts of the year—the late summer, early autumn in the northern hemisphere, when the oceans are warmest—but whether or not there are many or few in a year, where they make landfall, and how dangerous they are.... These are all variables that are difficult to predict because they are so sensitive to all the conditions they encounter. Sometimes they're reacting to conditions, sometimes they're absorbing those conditions, and other times they're being absorbed by or depleted by other conditions. For such powerful, forceful, and dangerous weather events, they're shockingly fragile and amazingly agile. One of the reasons why hurricanes are so dangerous is that they are so difficult to predict. Even when they make landfall, no one knows where they're going until they get there.[41]

Like the weather, there are some things in life that are surer bets than others. Like the weather, the time between a reading and an outcome can impact how sure a prediction is. The further away the hurricane, the harder to predict a path; the further away the event, the more things that can impact whether or not it happens and how. Of course, this all depends on our individual cosmology. If we believe that things are fated, or that we're pawns in a massive simulation, then we have no free will, and everything is predictable to the degree that the Fates or algorithms know what the next move is. One of the main reasons that fortune telling fell out of favor is a bigger focus on individual free will, self-empowerment, and the concept of rising above our station. We don't believe in Fate anymore. In fact, we've flung so far to the free will zone that we've actually reached that icky and problematic place of assuming that good things just happen when Becky manifests them.

When looking at fortune telling systems of older times, they are fatalistic. Individuals were confined to certain paths in life. Sue Tompkins, in *The Contemporary Astrologer's Handbook* (also a spiritual ancestor to this one; though I only discovered it while working through the second draft), has this to say about the journey of astrology from ancient times to the present day:

Astrologers such as William Lilly in the 1600s could make precise predictions because there were fewer possibilities and many more moral certainties—there were

41 It occurs to me as I'm writing this that there will be a time not far away when these analogies aren't effective anymore. We are heading into an unpredictable weather future, which means much more difficulty predicting what will happen by meteorological experts—and by fortune tellers. As the weather goes, so do we. The best laid plans are frequently changed by weather and that's going to become increasingly a factor in whether or not things happen. "Should I buy this house?" Sure. Oh wait, an unexpected hurricane just blew it into the ocean. Sorry. Climate change is going to make everyone's job harder, including fortune tellers. One of the many reasons it would be nice if the supposed leaders on this planet would get their heads and egos out of their asses and do something about it, rather than guilting us into buying expensive electric cars which still run on fossil fuels. Anyway. Point is, it's going to be more difficult.

only so many things that were likely to happen and people's views of the world wouldn't differ so much. In Lilly's day, clients were not encouraged to think in terms of personal autonomy and free will. The astrologer's job was to tell the client their fate. Nowadays, an astrologer looking at the chart of a child cannot even imagine the occupational possibilities (for instance) that might exist...even a mere twenty years down the line.

This is true of any divinatory system, and we see it reflected in the card-based systems that were designed for telling fortunes in the eighteenth and nineteenth centuries. The concepts depicted in *vera sibilla* cards, for example, include death, disease, pregnancy or motherhood, gifts, money, and villains (in sibilla, they're literally called "enemies"). The earliest meanings of lenormand cards, designed as a game but with the possibility of fortune telling, which seem to be based at least in part on tea leaf reading, also consider the limited potentials of life.

The New Thought movement, among other changes in society, including the scientific discoveries of "new" planets that have changed the shape of astrology, brought us a very different world. There arose revolutions, a middle class, technologies that made learning and information available to more than only the wealthy; kingdoms have risen and fallen; the entire experience of being human has changed. We feel less beholden to the Fates today because we understand that nature's cycles cause winter, not the death of a deity. We are more likely to survive diseases than ever and we're more likely to shift between classes than ever before. Even in places where caste systems have clung terribly, that is changing. And divination changed to reflect this much more empowered reality.

Prediction fell out of favor because it was fatalistic and because we could defy the odds now. Many people realized that they needn't be beholden to anyone or anything. It wasn't cool to get yer fortune told. It was gauche, tacky, outdated. Kind of. Because people are *always* curious, people *always* want to know what's possible.... But it largely became focused on potential rather than inevitability. And of course, the books of the modern tarot era reflected that. You can see a marked difference between Eden Gray's work, which is still relatively recent in tarot history, and what we started seeing in the modern tarot renaissance of the late seventies and the eighties, into today. Much of the work is dedicated to the psycho-spiritual puzzling out of problems, roadblocks, and internal issues. Also, science began to separate itself from what it viewed as pseudo-science, even though those pseudo-sciences laid the groundwork for what we understand today as science. Astrology and astronomy weren't separate fields for much of human history, and neither were inseparable from faith and medicine. Science began to dictate what "educated" people did and believed, and being (at least perceived as) an educated person became quite fashionable—because nobody wants to look "poor" (unless that's the style this season). "Smart" people don't believe in that "nonsense." Religion became the opiate of the masses, not a way of understanding the numinous—a word that has also fallen out of favor.

I bet a smart astrologer could tell me why, and they might also be able to tell me why the tide is turning again. Because the self-empowering movements that emerged from New Thought coincided with a generalized individualism that seems particularly American. Maybe our greatest export, aside from war and right-wing Christianity. We lost the sense of the communal over time, focusing only on the nuclear family (itself a problematic myth), and above all else the personal and private. Navel-gazing became a common pastime, and now we have social media to capitalize on that, too. I'm not anti-navel-gazing. I'm a navel-gazer to the max. I'm just pointing out that the collective gave way to the supremacy of the individual, which culminated in the psycho-spiritual focus of divination for the last forty or fifty years.

Today, I sense another sea change. I think the individual is slowly—*too* slowly—receding back and the collective is reclaiming center stage. Many of us are realizing that centering the individual has made us selfish, greedy, and cruel; many of us are realizing that this shift has accelerated climate change, inequities, abuse of labor, and lots of other ills. Further, *because* of climate change, social inequities, capitalism, and lots of other ills, what happens next is less certain than ever. So, here we are, once again, wondering what the actual fuck. And, here we are, once again, curious about using divination to predict things. Since life is by nature cyclical, it makes sense that we'd swing in that direction again. And I can't say for sure, but I have the feeling we're only at the very beginning of the swing back to this kind of thing. I know the sixties were supposed to be the dawning of the Age of Aquarius, but I don't think it was; I think we're about to face an Aquarian Age, and I think it's not about "harmony and understanding." I think it's about the abusive power structures falling apart. In any case, only time will tell what happens next.

Oh, and fortune tellers. We'll do that, too.

In *The Contemporary Astrologer's Handbook,* Tompkins compares a natal chart to a map. Each person's map is different. If I'm born in Boston to a wealthy family with a compound on Cape Cod and I'm given every leg up, that's my map and I navigate the world accordingly; if I'm born in Haiti to a poor family and my country is constantly being interfered with by colonial governments and my resources are limited, my map reflects this, as does my course in life. Point being, we do have a measure of free will. On the other hand, we're also at the mercy of conditions we can't change or have limited ability to change. The context of who we are when we're born, who we're born to, and the various challenges and privileges that life provides impact not only the options available to us, but the *number* of options available to us. In a way, those of us who were born into (what we call where I live) "low-income families" are closer to those clients of the 1600s that astrologer William Lilly could make such specific predictions for. Our options are limited. Meanwhile, a Kennedy can do more or less whatever he wants, and usually does.

Like all in life, free will isn't a binary proposition. Some of us have more than others thanks to our psychological makeup, health, physical abilities, class, race, gender and gender expression, sexuality, level of energy, location of birth, etc. These are all things we don't get to choose and things we don't have control over. We have *some* measure of control over how those things *impact* us, but it's not as simple as the modern narrative suggests. We don't live in a meritocracy and people don't just succeed by working hard and keeping their heads down. All the conditions described above and more impact those things, and it's only the people who had it easy who think that everyone else can do it, too. (It's why I roll my damn eyes every time I see a well-paid athlete making the sign of the cross after scoring. Easy to believe in "God" when you're getting paid more than most people will make in a lifetime to play a game. Same for the Elon Musks of the world. Sure athletes work hard—Musk doesn't—and we've seen how athletes have suffered health ramifications thanks to unscrupulous team management. But when you're making money playing a game and going on bro-y podcasts and endorsing whatever someone wants you to endorse, it's easy to feel like Jesus got your back and all it takes is believing in yourself.)

Not everyone has a "fair" start in life. And many people never find fair footing. So, sure, free will. But free will is partly a side effect of privilege. The free will of someone wed to an oxygen tank is limited dramatically in comparison to a "young professional" running enthusiast with an LA Fitness membership and a bank account full of expendable income. This is why I'm so bitchy about influencers manifesting their shit. You didn't manifest that endorsement, Charity; you benefitted from pretty privilege and the fact that your skin looks great because you've never had to work over a hot stove or steam table, fold laundry in a dry-ass laundromat, or mine coal underground. You got lucky that way. Sure, there are things we can do to improve our lives—*some*times. And, sure, "anybody" can get "lucky." It happens "all" the time. But the odds simply aren't in most of our favors. And when folks get out on the mic and make it look easy, they're doing psychological damage to those who see the videos and whose obstacles are substantially more difficult to overcome than Mx. Fresh-Faced From Home 2024.

Anyway, point is: free will isn't a zero-sum game, nor is fatalism. Life exists on the vibrations caused by tension, and so do we and our futures. This is the difficult and exciting thing about divination and fortune telling. Anything could happen! But if anything could happen, *how the hell do we figure out what will?*

The Art of Prediction

Doesn't that sound *fancy?* It seems like I'm about to reveal some big secret to you! Well, I'm not. But it's a cool concept. Prediction depends mostly on two things:

- How far away in time the thing is or should be
- What patterns are at play and will be at play during the lifespan of the reading[42]

42 By lifespan, I mean the time between the reading and the thing happening or the client realizing it's never going to happen.

We've already explored the way meteorological forecasts become more accurate the closer we get to the date. Similarly, the closer we get to an event, the easier it will be to predict. Different folks have different considerations of timing. I typically limit readings to six months because this feels like a relatively strong period of time to explore (but later I will show you a new version of an old spread that might let you take this a little further). The things we have been doing and are doing are still going to be in play, (the current conditions as weather forecasters say); they're going to be impacting what happens down the line. But we're also not looking so far into the future that certain as-yet unforeseen energies could be forming, too. These are the things outside of our control, the things we haven't considered because they either haven't happened yet or we haven't encountered context for them yet.

Let's say you're working toward a promotion at work. You've spent the last couple of years working with your boss on an action plan, taking classes, doing the things. You would like to know whether or not you're going to get the promotion before the end of the year. We'll say it's now early May. By limiting the reading to May through November, we're able to see the ripple effects of what you're doing right now and have been doing. Now, let's say your boss up and quits, throwing a wrench into all your plans. It might mean you advance sooner, or it might mean another boss comes in and doesn't care about your action plan. You have never heard any rumblings of your boss leaving. Everyone's happy with her and she performs well. What you don't know is that a memoir she's been working on has suddenly been picked up by a major studio and will have a Netflix limited series starring, oh, Pedro Pascal. This kind of shocking development would be easier to predict in the first three months of that six-month time period, but it wouldn't be impossible to see it in the second half. The further away we get, the less likely it is that we could predict this hiccup.

Again, we come to cosmology. How much of life is fated? I can't answer that question for you. If I could do that, I'd be really wealthy. (To quote my spiritual ancestor, *the* Ms. Dorothy Parker: "I hate almost all rich people, but I think I'd be darling at it.") Could this promotion be your destiny? If so, it would be easily predictable and your boss's movie deal wouldn't get in the way. If, on the other hand, life is a series of accidents caused by our energy bumping into one another, then your boss's sudden good fortune could indeed kill the chances of you getting yours. It's a slippery slope, to misuse the phrase, because getting into the theoretical physics of existence is a rabbit hole one might easily fall down while, say, drifting to sleep at night—preventing the drift or the sleep. But, by limiting the scope of time a reading can cover, whatever is going to happen is likely forming or formed, and whatever will be is going to emerge from at least some of that "weather."

When people ask predictive questions, they're usually not specifically worded. "Will I find the love of my life?" "Will I get this promotion?" "Will he propose?" These are complicated questions thanks to the implied "ever." Meaning, the question seems to be asking, "Will I *ever* find the love of my life?" Or, an even more common wording, "*When* will I meet the love of my life?" Here we venture further into the waters of chaos. What is a "love of my life"? *Is* there such a thing? For *everyone?* And will *everyone* meet the love of their life? And will it *always* be a person? What if the client is a straight lady and the person who is supposed to be the love of her life is her gay best friend? What if it's a puppy? This makes it all so complicated. We already know that not everyone finds a "love of their life"; we know that really wonderful people never manage to make that equation pan out. Some people never get the promotion or whatever the longed-for thing might be. And who the hell wants to give the client the news that they'll *never* find that thing? I sure as hell do not, thank you. And because I have no sense of how long this person will live, I don't know how long "ever" is—which also means there could be things thirty years down the line that haven't even begun forming yet (again, assuming there's no such thing as fate).

By limiting the timeframe of the reading, we not only improve the potential accuracy of the prediction, which is nice, but we also give the client a reasonable window—and, potentially, all-important hope. *And,* assuming some things happen without being pre-ordained, the time for life to shift a little and new paths to form. In *fact,* telling a client that they're not likely to meet their soulmate in the next six months could motivate them to prove you wrong, and that could lead to a wonderful outcome! I tell this story a lot, so stop me if you've heard it before. One of the earliest readings I remember doing for a friend involved this very question. He wanted to know if he'd be meeting anyone soon. All the cards were totally closed off. It was like The Emperor, the Queen of Swords, and like, the Two of Swords; I can't remember exactly, but very much that sort of vibe. And I said, "No, you're totally closed off, you won't let anyone near you." A few weeks later, he met someone and reminded me I'd been wrong. What I knew, that he didn't, was that his reaction to that reading opened him up. Sure, the *prediction* was wrong, but only because he changed his behavior.

One could say that, in the fate-based version of the story, that reading was the plot point designed to get him into that relationship. But that would be a boring story. I prefer the more hopeful version, where he heard what the reading was *really* saying ("If you want to meet someone, open up!") and then actually did it. Either way, from my vantage, that's a successful reading. The answer was logical given the question and the cards and, though the answer wasn't what he wanted, it gave him the chance to adjust his tactics, and he got the result he wanted.

The point of all this, though, is that limiting the span for a reading gets us out of potentially icky waters and into a more realistic timeframe for prediction. If your readings seem to be accurate within a year, great! Further than that? If you're confident, go for it. I'm not. I just don't see everything as that fixed and I do think that certain events can get waylaid by the unexpected, the unseen, the sudden. Anyone who drives a car with any regularity knows that the difference between a head-on crash and a near-miss can be a fraction of a second and a knee-jerk reaction. Life is a mix of the fixed and the mutable. (We'll explore these terms more later.) We don't so much stop something as life mutates and becomes something else. That's how I think about mutability. A slow-mo shapeshifting of focus in life. This is what I mean when I say that the second factor in prediction are the elements at play or coming into play in the space between the reading and the time the event happens (or doesn't).

All that said, this is just my theory and what the hell do I know about how time works? I only—and you only—know what our senses perceive, and we know that's not a good barometer of reality, because we know everyone perceives things differently. There's an expression in the corporate world everyone knows and hates: "Perception is reality." We hate it because it's not true. The way people perceive things is not the actual reality of it. Except, for that person it is and there's no other way to perceive it until, somehow, a perception shift happens. Perceptions are no way to objectively judge anything. They're chaos. Things may be far more fixed than I'd like to know, and the older I get it does seem some things simply aren't "fated" to happen. On the other hand, I keep being surprised by life—in good and bad ways—and who the hell actually knows? So, if you don't want to limit your readings to six months or a year, don't. Right? Screw it. Do what works.

Re-Inventing an Old Spread

The first tarot book I read was *The Tarot Workbook: Understanding and Using Tarot Symbolism* by Emily Peach. It's long out of print from what I can see, and may have been when I got my hands on it. I was in my very late teens at the time and I'd had a few encounters with tarot readers and I was just *curious;* I just wanted to know a little about *what this thing really was.* You know, because of course I'd always heard it was satanic. But I was a former Catholic queer kid ready to rebel. So, I found Peach's book, grabbed it off the shelf, shoved it in the stack of other books I was buying, and checked out—never once looking inside, and thinking I'd probably never look at it, anyway.

Of course, the first thing I did when I got home was throw myself on my bed and crack the spine (the books', not mine). But, to my annoyance and shock, *there were no pictures of the cards!* I mean, that's what I wanted to see! And in this book, there's a rectangle on each card's page where you would take *your* deck and put *your* card in that spot while you read her descriptions. *Dammit!* Well, there was only one thing to be done...I was simply going to have to buy a damn deck. Whatever. I was just curious, and it wasn't like I'd ever start doing card readings, anyway, because that's weird and dumb and *it doesn't even work* and *I don't want to know if I'm dying* so whatever. I bought a deck. It was the purple and gold U.S. Games *Original Rider Waite Tarot Pack,* the one with the light blue roses and lilies backing. The one everyone hates the coloration of. And I think as soon as I saw the *box,* I was in love. By the time I'd gotten the wrapper off and laid my eyes on The

Fool, I was a reader. Maybe I always was one and didn't know it. But I was hooked.

I'd never seen anything that caused such an emotional, physical reaction. I remember the experience of seeing The Magician, The Empress, Death, The Tower—all in that dramatic and captivating line work of Pamela Colman Smith. Even in that somewhat dingy, dirty "facsimile" coloration, I couldn't stop looking at them and thinking about them. It was obsession from go.

The point of all of this is that I probably wouldn't have gotten a deck if the book had had pictures of the cards. I wouldn't have needed to and would likely have been too scared to do it. But once I was so close and yet so far, I had to. So, this is really a digression about how that book may be responsible for what you're reading here—even though I actually didn't understand most of what the book was talking about. It's *very* Golden Dawn, all about Kabbalah and astrology, and it was way over my head. I didn't really give any more thought to it, and anyway it had done what it was put in my life to do: force me to buy a pack of tarot cards. After I did that, the floodgates were open, and soon my tiny bedroom in my parents' apartment was secreting piles of books and decks. Actually, I must have tossed the Peach book, because I have no idea where that copy went—and I have all my other books from that time. I managed to find a used copy a few years ago and picked it up. And then I picked it up again this summer as I began working on the design of a new class based on reimagining old tarot spreads.

This book has some deliciously esoteric spreads, like the Tree of Life, the Astrological Horoscope, and some dubiously named ones—including the Twenty-One Card Romany Spread. I will give this book credit that in 1984 (when it was originally published in the UK) the author used the term Romany, rather than the more common pejorative it's high time the tarot world retired. As I was thumbing through the book looking for some fusty old, musty old spreads, I had to stop and look at this one, because timing is in its title. Tarot readers are always looking for ways to figure out "when," and it's probably the hardest thing to do. It ultimately wound up being an over-complicated past-present-future spread. There are three rows of seven cards, each corresponding to past, present, and future. I was a little disappointed, but then I decided to mess with things—as I do—and since that was the point of the class I was creating, anyway, it was sort of the perfect place for me to start.

So, I hereby present to you the new version.

A Modern Timing Spread

Shuffle the deck and deal out three piles of seven cards each. Then, put aside the remaining pack and shuffle the first group of seven cards while thinking about the six-month period starting today. Stop shuffling and lay the cards out in a line of seven.

Next, take up the second pack of seven cards and shuffle while thinking about the six-month period that will begin the day the previous one ends. (In this case, that period will end a year from today.) Again, when ready lay out the cards in a line of seven.

Repeat with the third stack of seven thinking about the six-month period that will begin a year and one day from now. Again, lay the cards out in a line of seven.

Read each row of seven with the intention of discovering *how likely* it is the desired thing will happen during that period. The set with the most likely outcome is your timing. You could, of course, adjust the lengths of time. Make each stack reflect a month of the coming year, say, or make it weeks or days. However, you want to do it. I started with six-month time periods because it's what occurred to me when I got the idea, and also because this might be useful for bigger events or outcomes, the kinds of things that may take a while to form.

Let's try an example.

Say we have Malia who wants to know whether her girlfriend Ava will propose marriage any time soon. For context, Malia shares that Ava is much more interested in what she calls "traditional" relationships—monogamous and contracted. Malia is ambivalent, but she wants to know what to prepare for. For our intents, here, we'll stick with the three six-month chunks. But I'd read this more or less the same way whatever the timing. The main point is that we know what each chunk of time will be *before* we shuffle and draw. Frankly, everything else about a reading is somewhat arbitrary, including the number of cards and the time periods chosen. But as long as you know what you're going to do before shuffling, you're good.

For Malia's first row of seven, I've drawn (for this case, the cards for all three rows were drawn in the order they're listed):

The World, Two of Swords, Justice, Two of Wands, Nine of Swords, Ten of Pentacles, The Empress

It could be tempting to stop reading here. That's a lot of cards (seven is really a lot, but I'm sticking with what the book used for fun—use however many you want) and there are a few that indicate big things (The World), legal contracts (Justice), and family (Ten of Pentacles and The Empress). But we made an agreement with the cards, so we must forge ahead!

The second row of seven, representing the second six-month time period is:

Two of Wands, Four of Cups, Strength, Wheel of Fortune, Four of Wands, The Lovers, The Sun

Ah! There's some marriage stuff here, too, eh? Two of Wands (sexual attraction), Four of Wands (the Waite-Smith has a celebration happening that looks a lot like a wedding), The Lovers (obvi), and The Sun (generally a fun, sexy card).

The third row of seven is:

Three of Swords, Five of Wands, Four of Swords, Three of Pentacles, Eight of Swords, Judgment, King of Pentacles

I'm already tempted to rule out the third set because this seems more like the daily drudgeries of marriage: fighting (Three of Swords and Five of Wands), making up (Four of Swords and Three of Pentacles), fighting again and learning from it (Eight of Swords and Judgment), and growing mature (King of Pentacles). Here, they've *gotten* married; this is the daily stuff. The only card that really gives wedding vibes is the Three of Pentacles. Maybe Judgment, but only to a meh degree.

Working backwards, the second set of seven tells the story of a lusty, forward-looking dreamer (Three of Wands and Four of Cups) who is holding on to their impulses (Strength) until the time is right (Wheel) for a celebration of love and happiness (Four of Wands, The Lovers, The Sun). The first row of seven tells the story of someone who feels they have to really fight for what they love. The combination of The World, the Two of Swords, and Justice—in this case, The World is the thing loved, and the similarly guarded attitudes of the Two and Justice give me a fighting stance. This is also thanks to the swords. Further, both are biding their time, waiting—so while they're guarded, they're also stuck in a pose—almost frozen in fear. So, there's anxiety here, and a feeling of needing to be defended. The Two of Wands calms things and gets the sexual energy up and running again and sets the dreamer back to thinking about the future. But the Nine of Wands causes a hiccup. Panic! *What if they don't love me?? What if they leave me???* Eventually they realize they are loved and start to feel safer and more at home (Ten of Pentacles plus The Empress).

Given these three tales, Ava is most likely to propose—and get married to Malia—in the middle six-month time period. So in about a year or so, we should see these two wedded (assuming this is what Malia wants; remember this reading is about *Ava*). The first row of three sounds a lot like what many people experience in the early year or two of a long-term relationship: a mix of excitement, terror, happiness, anxiety, and expectation. It's in the second chunk of time where we see comfort and strength fully give way to the confidence to propose and marry. In the third, we see the life that kicks in once the honeymoon is over. The King of Pentacles at the end of the reading, though, does indicate longevity for the relationship. He's often the last card in the deck when in order.

A few points: I worked through this reading super fast. I didn't pause to think too much. The main thing was to avoid jumping to any conclusions until I had all twenty-one cards out, so that I didn't risk predetermining the outcome and forming a bias in my mind. I didn't dwell on symbolism or elemental relationships much; I just went for it. I said to myself, "tell the story of this row as quickly and succinctly as you can—just keep it on topic." And I did. And I got the answer. So, seven cards may *seem* like a lot, but it's really not. And what it did was give me a pretty detailed picture of each third of the time covered by the reading. That helped me feel my way through which time period would be most fertile for the event to happen. It's possible that the specifics of what I said in each story aren't fully accurate for Ava. Maybe she doesn't have all the anxiety I saw. I bet she does, though, because people who favor "traditional" relationships frequently fear being left or cheated on. Either way, it doesn't matter because that wasn't the answer to the question; the answer to the question was which time period would Ava be more likely to propose within. However I got there and however much it reflected Ava's mental state, I know that the time that would be most fertile, based on how I understand the cards, is the middle third. And *that's* the answer I needed.

Voila!

Cardinal, Fixed, Mutable

One final thing that can help when thinking in terms of prediction. In astrology, there are three types of signs: cardinal, which begin; fixed, which sustain; and mutable, which transform. We can borrow that concept and think of events or conditions this way. In life, there are some conditions that are "cardinal," or the impulse or beginning of something. We could think about this like the aces in tarot or playing cards; the way they suggest potential for something, more than they suggest the actual thing. A seed about to sprout. Good or bad, these need care and feeding to grow into power, so they could just as easily happen as not. Fixed conditions are those that are either permanent or semi-permanent, and also those things out of our control. These are usually obstacles to getting what we want, although if we're lucky they can also represent privileges that ensure our success. Finally, mutable events are those things that go on for a while and can peter out or slowly morph into something else. Like a friendship that eventually grows into a romance, or conversely a romance that slowly grows into a friendship; a vocation that evolves into a chore; a hobby that slowly stops interesting us.

As readers, we could use this in explaining why some things may or may not happen, or why certain obstacles feel insurmountable. We can have a conversation about which of the client's contextual conditions fit into each category before we read—or we could do a reading designed to help us understand that. And so I present to you, the CFM Spread! (Cardinal, Fixed, Mutable.)

A CFM Spread

It's simply drawing three cards (or however many you prefer) to represent the conditions in a client's life that are mutable; another three representing which are fixed; and a third set of three representing those that are mutable. Alternatively, you might ask which aspects of a particular situation fall into those categories.

Say we have a client named Hilda who is trying to get herself married! She wants a wedding! She's less concerned about who she marries, because she's single; she's basically ready to take whatever offers come her way. She's single, she's ready to mingle, and shortly after mingling she would like to rent a U-Haul. (That is a lesbian stereotype, but it is contextually relevant to know that Hilda is not a lesbian.) She has had zero luck finding potential mates and wants to know what the actual fuck. So, our question becomes: Why can't Hilda find someone to marry? (All cards were drawn and laid out in the order shown.)

Cardinal conditions: The Tower, Ace of Swords, Knight of Swords

Fixed conditions: Page of Swords, Nine of Swords, Queen of Wands

Mutable conditions: The Hierophant, Five of Cups, Eight of Cups

Because they will fade soon, the cardinal conditions are interesting in this case really only if there's some "hope" there—might the seed of something good be showing? And in Hilda's case, no. It actually seems like she just broke up with (The Tower and Ace of Swords) a prospect (Knight of Swords) who got out of Dodge pretty quick. This is what's on her mind (swords) right now but she's likely to be over it soon (swords are speedy, knights are speedy), even though it was a big blow (swords bludgeon, and The Tower does, too). If it wasn't a breakup, then she had kind of a blowup (Tower) with a guy (knight) that will cut (ace) off any potential. Or, she's thinking (ace) about a guy (knight) after the shock of finding him (Tower). Obviously, if she were here (and real) I could ask. This doesn't give me much—this cardinal energy is *very* cardinal. Nothing much to hold it down. Which may indicate that *she* does this. It's not the men she sees that move on from her; *she* moves on from them. She's always blowing things up (Tower) because she's on the hunt (knight) for something shiny and new (ace). That's good to know, but this is a *cardinal* influence—which means if she has that impulse, it's temporary.

The fixed conditions may be most important, because these are going to be the insurmountable obstacles. The Page of Swords suggests a really immature perspective (which is somewhat born out by my biased perception of Hilda's obsession with weddings, a thing I loathe). This page is really defensive, ready to strike anything that gets in the way. Next, we have the Nine of Swords, which suggests a certain amount of self-centeredness—that isn't a traditional interpretation, but nines work hard and swords think. What is she thinking about? The Page of Swords—meaning, herself. The Queen of Wands confirms this, at least based on one system that associates her with Leo (I typically don't use astrological correspondences, but it seems appropriate here). You'll note that I've jumped to really negative meanings for the cards, but that's because I'm looking for a problem. We're looking for why Hilda can't have what she wants, so I have to think in terms of obstacles. In this case, Hilda's immaturity may be a big issue; her self-centeredness is likely a reason she can't find a mate. The Queen of Wands is also likely temperamental.

Mutable conditions are highlighted by The Hierophant, Five of Cups, and Eight of Cups. In this case, I'm reading this as conditions coming into play, in the way mutable energy bridges. I think she's on the verge of losing (fives) faith (Hierophant) in traditional (Hierophant) romance/relationships (cups); she's maybe on the verge of a bit of an emotional breakdown or tantrum (Five of Cups) that may send her on a totally new journey (Eight of Cups), but it will be a lot of work to re-stabilize (eight as four + four) herself. This may actually be for the best, because her attitude is generally pretty childish. But I'm pretty sure I wouldn't say it that way. That said, this "breakdown" (for lack of a better word) may be what will finally shakes up (fives) her single life (again, eight is two fours—which could suggest doubly stable emotions). She could come out of this better off than she was. Good news—but likely not the news she wants.

In any case, now we know why she's not getting what she wants: her own attitude toward marriage is the thing that's keeping her from getting it. Because it's fixed, it's going to be difficult to overcome, but because the mutable vibes indicate a breakdown is on the way, she may actually be able to do something about the perceptions that have her stuck.

I Have Some Conditions

Whether or not you want to do a reading specifically around the cardinality, fixity, or mutability of the client's situation, it's worth recalling that—whether we read about it or not—all three conditions are likely at play in a client's life at any given time. Fixed conditions are those we simply cannot change, at least right now. This may include our income or what we do to earn it, our class and race, our family, our gender identity and expression, where on the spectrum of queerness we exist (though some would argue, and for them it would be true, that this too is mutable), where we were born and when, our mental and physical abilities and disabilities. This returns us to the chapter on agency, so I won't belabor the point. But as a reader, considering what conditions in a client's life are fixed can help you read better. You're less likely to give crappy advice if you understand that there are some things out of the client's control.

As readers, we may *think* a reading says to tell that asshole boss to fuck off and then quit, or to go to HR and complain about his harassment. If the client has no financial backup plan and if they're unlikely to be protected from their boss once they report the harassment, this isn't good advice. It may seem simple to us—go tell HR about it!—and *sometimes,* yes, that's what needs to happen. Ideally, no one would be put in the position of having to report harassment to begin with. But HR works for the company, not the employee, and just because we may have worked for more ethical companies doesn't mean our client does. Understanding the conditions under which a client is operating is helpful for offering advice. Telling a client they have the power inside them when, even if they do, they don't know how to access it, is not a good reading—for (I hope by now) obvious reasons.

Do You Believe It?

I was winding up this chapter the same weekend as wrapping up a workshop I'd been leading with the same title of this book. And one of the folks in the class asked a wonderful question with no easy answer. In fact, it wasn't easy to ask, either, because we all took a stab at putting it into language. But in essence the question was sort of: do you actually believe in any of this? And also, why would anyone put much stock in a prediction or a reading about advice or even about someone who isn't there? You can probably see why this was so hard to ask and answer. In the question itself is a sense of, *I know this works because I've seen it work, but also how could it and why would it and why would anyone make any life choices based on what a deck of* cards *said about the situation?*

Those are all really good questions. And I don't know. I do know that it works because I, too, have seen it work. I know that it's objectively nuts to base much of anything on the message delivered through a deck of cards. I also know that's not really how it works. And I know that as we all tried to ask and answer the question, we all had a sense of having been in the same boat as the person who first tried to give it voice.

Ultimately, and this is such a bad answer but it's true, it comes down to trust. We have to trust it will work, trust in our ability, and trust the reading is for the best. Predictive or not, that's the gamble. Even if we're doing self-exploration or psycho-spiritual work, we're still putting our trust in the thing and that it will lead us in the right direction.

We have to trust in whatever makes it work and then do it. And that's just the weird part of being human. Since nothing in life is certain except the ultimate inevitabilities, then why not do it? Why not predict? What the heck? What if it helps, ya know? And that's kind of the whole thing, at the end of the day.

What if it helps?

CHAPTER TWELVE

MR. BIG STUFF

Much of my work in divination education has involved de-mystifying reading, by which I mean stripping away esoteric dreck that gets between the reader and clear answers. My derision has largely focused on the notable men of the Golden Dawn and the pretentious and appropriative ways they decreed certain things to be true and other things to be both false and cretinous. It's no secret that many esoteric thinkers who borrowed liberally from the Kabbalist tradition were rabid antisemites. The myth came to be that the Jewish people had *stolen* this mystical tradition *from Christians*—which is quite on brand for Christianity to cry victim while harming others. This, of course, applies mostly to tarot; the esotericists either didn't know about or didn't care about other systems, like lenormand or casting. That pedantry irritates me because I grew up in Christian tradition that I grew to see as limiting and, eventually, poisonous. So, I spent many of the years I was learning tarot divesting from spirituality and the ways it has harmed me.

One could make the argument that "divination" of any form can't be completely divorced from divinity, because the word *divination* literally comes from "divine." And I won't push back against that. What I *will* push back on, though, is the assumption that somehow the daily things we encounter and struggle with are also somehow not spiritual. Either everything is spiritual/divine or nothing is; it's one of the few fundamentalist stances I take. Partly, this stance comes in reaction to a tendency on the part of many organized faiths to diminish the flesh-and-blood existences of life and focus on some fantastical never-future where one achieves perfect union with the divine—and, in so doing, separates oneself from the banal. It is the alchemical transformation of the base into the elevated, and it means viewing the world we live in with derision. And that's not great, because it cuts us off from the world and the world is suffering as a result, as are we. We need to live in harmony with the planet, with the actual world we're part of; if we don't, we damage the planet and its resources and put ourselves in danger in the process.

I've already said that it's hard not to speak in generalities. When I use the collective pronouns "we" and "us," what I'm doing is erasing the reality that there are *many* cultures in the world for whom this is not true. There are many global communities connected both to the *globe* and the *community,* two things the colonial world are not connected to—despite also being part of that global community. I'm generalizing "we" to mean those of us who are aligned with and entrenched in the neo-colonial viewpoints of self-supremacy, individual over the collective, profit about all else, and the fuck-your-feelings landscape created by those points of view. I don't mean those folks who have learned to work in collaboration with the Earth and with community. They don't need me to tell them any of this. The folks who need to hear it are the ones who, like me, are dancing with the devil, so to speak, or at least who have been most of our lives.

My anti-spiritual stance came as a reaction to the toxic waste dump of modern-day Christianity, in particular white Catholicism—which is very different from the Catholicism practiced in places where the old gods have been syncretized with the saints, where magic and divination are and always have been common, and where Hoodoo, Voodoo, Vodou, Santería, and other traditions have emerged from local indigenous spiritualities that survived by traditional beliefs with the safer veneer of Christianity. In fact, in recent years I've been majorly inspired by the spiritualities that emerged out of colonialism, particularly those in the southern US: Hoodoo and New Orleans Voodoo.

Recently, I took my first vacation since the COVID-19 lockdown and visited New Orleans. And while I'm not a practitioner of New Orleans Voodoo, I'm devoted in many ways to aspects of the tradition that have helped me navigate my own relationship to the religion of my youth. For example, I was wandering around one of the two museums that flank St. Louis Cathedral in Jackson Square and after making my way through the deeply intense Hurricane Katrina exhibit, I found myself wandering through the Mardi Gras exhibit, and then into a long anteroom that overlooked the square. Below me, on the steps of the church, sat table after table of fortune teller. There must have been at least fifteen of them, all plying their trade to tourists at the facade of one of the most famous Catholic churches in the United States. I had such a moment of spiritual joy, because I could *feel* the unique brand of spirit exclusive to people who learn to blend the hurtful with the healing; the mundane with the magical; and the colonial with the liberating.

Not long before this, I'd read Sherry Shone's brilliant *Hoodoo For Everyone: Modern Approaches to Magic, Conjure, Rootwork, and Liberation.* Shone's book is a re-imagined Hoodoo, designed for anyone who may want to explore it—including queer people, and we tend to be excluded from many things with Christian roots—in particular to develop magical and spiritual practices that are *liberation-based.* It is, in fact, a primer in liberation-based magic, inspired by the Black Christian experience, but embracing all bodies, faiths, and spirits—*as long as* the person being embraced understands how Hoodoo developed, why, and that it is and always has been about freedom and deliverance from the evils of enslavement, white supremacy, colonialism, and—these days—misogyny, anti-queerness, and the rest.

Shone's work is wonderful and I found myself relentlessly moved by the book, so much so that I picked up a copy of her earlier book, *The Hoodoo Guide to the Bible: Advice from a Real Hoodoo Worker.* In this shorter but equally compelling work, Shone, a queer Black woman, explores how she works with the Bible to create magic—and how she simply changes parts of the book she doesn't like in order to make them relevant for her work. For example, she might change the words around women being subordinate to their husbands to make it more equal or even eliminate the passage entirely. What's so amazing to me about this concept is that, as someone who grew up with the Bible (although most Catholics don't read the Bible; they read the bulletin) it never occurred to me that I could just change the shit I don't like. Shone's work completely blew my mind, because I realized suddenly that the power lies not in the text, not in the history, not in the rites or rituals, but in one's own ability to excise what has hurt us and replace it with what can heal us. And standing in that room above Jackson Square, looking down at all these fortune tellers working on the steps of a Catholic church, I realize that I, too, could take what I needed from a practice that hurt and amend it to my needs.

Beyond that, it taught me that spirituality needn't be something I have to avoid lest I risk having to give up any part of myself. It taught me that I can "steal" liberally from my childhood faith but leave behind all the crap that made me feel less-than along with all the garbage that justified colonialism, enslavement, anti-queerness, and misogyny. It was also a moving experience for me, as uneventful as it may sound, because it helped me find footing on a journey that had already started—one in which I began to re-examine spiritual and magical practices not as a self-centered, ego-boosting, manifesting-destiny kind of social media fodder, but rather a rebellious liberating act. I realized that spirituality can be used to push toward freedom from oppression and that that was, in fact, a central purpose *of* spirituality. This isn't to say that magical and/or spiritual work is a *replacement* for direct action, but that it's an exceptional complement; particularly when we're starting to feel weary from the lack of progress or even the backsliding that can demotivate us. When we feel we don't have anything left to offer a cause, we can always offer it magic. But a combination of action and magic are key; magic alone isn't enough.

This is all to say that I don't deride spiritual perspectives as much as I used to. That may be my advancing age, but I don't know. I suppose I always sort of wanted something to believe in after realizing that my childhood faith was a myth, and a dangerous one. I tried the books on Wicca when I was in my late teens, early twenties. I found great warmth and comfort in Scott Cunningham's work (I know there are a lot of negative feelings about his appropriative tendencies today, and two things can be true: yes, he—and *all* the witchy writers of the time—took stuff that didn't belong to them; and yes, he wrote with a kindness and an openness that may have led many of us to understanding the world in a way where we can see what the danger of appropriation really is), but I also found a lot of performative garbage that reminded me of the annoying crap I was trying to get through in learning the

Golden Dawn version of tarot. After a while, in attempting to connect with other like-minded folks in the proto-forums of the early AOL days, I found the same dogma, pedantry, and preening that I found in Catholicism; I found similar lacks of tolerance, similar ego trips, and similar fights, and I wanted nothing to do with any of that. It wasn't until recently that I began seeing that the "witch world" had started getting political, and that I encountered works by Sherry Shone and Denise Alvarado, that I was able to see there was a magical tradition that was based on progress, not the status quo. And that has unlocked a lot of my hangups around spirituality. Now, I'm unlikely to say I walk any particular spiritual path, but I would define my spirituality as liberation-centered. And this is why I'm able to talk about this topic here, unlike in my previous books which were really about kicking spirituality to the curb in order to make way for clearer readings. I still believe one has to do that, but then I think we can add the "big stuff" back in.

This is all my way of saying I'm not necessarily opposed to incorporating spirituality into divination, and it may well be "spirits" of some kind that make it work. If it is, I've been lucky that those spirits have been okay with me not believing in them or even sensing them. Although I'm also willing to bet most spirits are exponentially less egotistical than we are. They have no need for ego; they're not endangered by perceptions in the way we are. I think. Anyway, I don't know what I don't know, but I do know that it makes total sense that we'd divine spiritual issues as much as the banal, because for most of human history the two concepts were inseparable. There simply was no difference between the spiritual, medical, astrological, scientific, or anything else. It was all one, part of the human experience, and the spiritual stuff gave everything else meaning and context. And it recognized that not all physical symptoms have physical causes. And frankly, I don't *want* people's spirituality in my medicine, because the spirituality that's "allowed" to make it into the hospital is almost all Abrahamic doctrinal crap that is the reason humanity is so disconnected from our bodies and our earth. Both are diminished in many of these faith ways. We are encouraged to transcend our humanity, not relish it. And yet if we're denigrating our embodiment, and if—as at least Christianity suggests—we were made by "God," then isn't it fucked up to denigrate the body in that way? Incidentally, this is also why it makes no sense to me that environmentalism isn't a religious issue. If God made the heavens and the Earth, then God is gonna be pissed when we face them and say, "Oh, I didn't care about that thing you made because I know I'm supposed to transcend it."

This is, incidentally, how we know the right wingers are liars. If they cared about God and God's will, they'd care about the things God made—not just the Earth, but all the iterations of humanity that walk it. Including queer people. Including poor people. Including immigrants and migrants. If you believe in a god who created everything and you still believe it's okay to treat both the home and the neighbors that God gave you as pieces of shit, then you, in fact, are an absolute piece of shit yourself. And that's tough crap if you don't like it. Don't argue with me, go out into the world and prove me wrong with acts of inclusion and radical liberation.

What the Abrahamic faiths continue to demonstrate in the world is not a godly demeanor, but an egocentrism that puts the preferred faith and those who believe in it at the center of the universe, and everyone else in the trash. And no matter how well-intentioned the believer may be, it is still the reality that ego is at the heart of much of organized religion. And Christianity in particular has trained the world in how to do this in the most hurtful, damaging ways. Which is why many of us, including those inclined toward a spiritual worldview, are so hesitant about engaging with *any* kind of spirituality. Because the "spirituality" that takes center stage in the world's dramas is entirely centered on human bias and bigotry and not on connection to the divine. It is not possible to connect to the divine when marginalizing others. I guess I'm a fundamentalist about that, too.

On the other hand, this is all very general. The individual may not hold the ego-centric views of the larger faith and its dogma. There are plenty of Christians, Jews, Muslims, and others in the tangential faiths who aren't abusive predators or gaslighting dickbags. Without being too generous, I'd wager that *most* of the people who hold to these faiths aren't jerks. But that doesn't matter much to those who suffer the consequences of these dogmas and their deep intertwining into the laws and rules of our societies. Which means that many of us experience great fear and anxiety when faced with supposedly spiritual people, because we don't know if we're safe with them. Until we are presented with evidence that the believer isn't the stereotype, we're going to be reluctant to trust them and feel safe around them. And this is worth considering for us as readers because we never know who is going to be sitting across the table from us and what they truly believe. If they indicate a spiritual path, we can't jump to conclusions about what it is and whether or not they hate us. On the other hand, we can't just trust everyone because they're sitting down at our table.

This also makes reading somewhat complicated because everyone who sits down with us is likely to have differing cosmology and so we don't necessarily know how to talk to them about what it is they and we believe. And that's kind of a weird space to live.

I Believe!

In a recent class, the topic of angels came up because I shared a question I'd once been given as a test by a mentor: "I lost a child shortly after birth and I know he's an angel now. Can you tell me what he's trying to teach me?" That wasn't the exact wording, but you get the point. My own hackles went up when I read the question and of course they were supposed to. The question was a trick, at least in the context of working with a mentor, because I was supposed to point out that I don't have the ability to read about this. That's what the mentor wanted to make sure I said, because that was sort of the rules of the game at the time. We didn't do readings like that because it wasn't ethical. I knew what I was supposed to do and so I passed the test. I said something like, "I'm not really gifted with that ability, so I've chosen to do a reading asking how you can work through your grief." I've talked elsewhere about why this is a crappy thing to do, so I won't belabor the point, but suffice to say I would never do that now.

When I shared this with my workshop participants, many shared my experience of hackles going up. And, really, that's not because of the question or its ethical implications. Frankly, I don't see anything wrong with answering the question at this point. If it's approached with sensitivity, why not offer that comfort? For many of us today, it's the idea of "angels" that makes us cringe. Mostly because the term is so mired in a lot of emotional baggage from, in particular, the last forty years and the association with Christianity.

Angels, of course, predate Christianity and even Abrahamic faiths, but they became sort of iconic in the nineties because of a spate of books about angel encounters. I can't remember who the popular author was at the time, but I do remember the *Touched by an Angel* sort of craze that led to tons of non-fiction books, novels, and movies (the dreadfully depressing *City of Angels* with its iconic Goo Goo Dolls song may have been the culmination of this fad). And because the entertainment industry can't let a craze go uncapitalized, life in the US became consumed by this topic. Of course these weren't the fearsome angels of the Bible, who appeared to mere mortals as feathery clusters of eyeballs and rings of flame. These angels were, of course, humanoid, with wings, and inevitably white as cream. The former face of divinatory angel work, Doreen Virtue, emerged from this tradition—before finding "Jesus" behind the sofa and screwing all the people who paid her lots of money to learn the things she now claims are Satanic. In fact, Ms. Virtue's turn may be one of the major reasons that even people who were at one time attracted to the idea of angels now find the concept somewhat repellant or at least uncomfortable. For many of us, and I'm not immune from this at all, the whole idea just makes our skin crawl with discomfort. There's something sort of icky about these lily-white, muscular, heavenly hosts that scream CBS Sunday Movie. But that's not really a problem until we are asked to read about angels by a client who feels strongly that they're real.

I can't validate whether angels exist or not. I can't validate whether anything exists or not, frankly. But I do know that it's not my job to make my client feel stupid about their beliefs, particularly if those beliefs aren't hurting anyone and are helping them get through the day. It doesn't matter whether I believe in angels, like the band ABBA did, or if I think it's all nonsense. It matters how I treat that client and their question in the moment. And that's really what this preamble has been heading toward. Handling the big stuff when our cosmology differs from the client's or even the world's.

It doesn't really matter what I believe when I'm reading for a client; it matters what *they* believe, even if I don't like it or find it kinda cringe. I'm not the arbiter of faith. I'm a fortune teller.

Drawing Lines

One of the friends I met in grad school calls me occasionally to ask a question or for advice on something related to the work we did, and then she proceeds to say the most lovely things to me. She always tells me she's praying for me and I never doubt for a second that she means it and that she's praying for all good things. And I always feel so moved and so lucky when she does, despite the fact that I tend to get really angry when other people have said that to me. Usually because there's always an implication of superiority. But not with my friend; my friend means it and so I do, in fact, feel blessed when she tells me this.

It's also true that, while I tend to speak with general derision for Christianity and its colonial impact on the world as well as its distance from the messages of the man they claim to follow, Christianity has also been a major part of the civil rights movement in the US. It is through churches that the abolition movement spread through white culture in the years prior to the American Civil War. And liberation was *always* apart of Black churches, and many of the most iconic leaders of the Civil Rights movement were leaders in the Black Church. So, like all things, Christianity isn't one thing. The problem is the dominant forms of it that have made their mission one of repression, oppression, and forced obedience; it's the ways in which our laws have been informed by Christian theology—more often the bigoted versions of it—that are what make so many of us suffer. There isn't really anything Christ said that is particularly cruel, unless you're a wealthy resource-hoarder or trying to sell things in houses of worship. (Sorry, mega churches.) And so, though I hate the sin, I must love the sinner. (I can't believe I just said that.)

When a client comes to me with a question about angels or some other concept that's out of my cosmology, I remind myself that whatever we're talking about, these are "just" words for a larger idea. When we say *angel*, for example, it's simply a name for an otherworldly entity; someone beyond this plane, who probably understands this and the next world better than we do. They can serve as a liaison between the living and the dead. In many stories, angels are messengers for the divine. It's helpful to remember this, because it's not the *concept* itself that I have a problem with; it's a bias against bigots who co-opt those ideas and use them for hate. But just because someone believes in angels doesn't mean they hate queer people any more than it means someone who is queer couldn't be trying to hold up oppressive structures.

It's my job as the fortune teller to strip away my triggered reaction to the term and return to its essence: *angels are messengers*. Thus, the question becomes about getting a message from whoever may be delivering it. When looked at this way, I'm not going to get stuck in my head about how cringe the term angels is or how it reminds me of lugubrious TV mom drama. So many of the core beliefs people have are similar, it's only the words and character names that change—not unlike the way the Greek and Roman gods have the same personalities, but different names. Zeus and Jupiter have the same job, they just got different nicknames depending on who in the world was dealing with them and where in the world they lived. When we strip away the language—which is always mushy and imprecise, no matter what language it is—we come to similar concepts. And so I don't have to believe in angels or anything else; I just need to match the language I'm using to the words my client understands. When a client uses the term "angel," I should be happy rather than cringing; it means I now know something about how to communicate with this person in a way that will help them get what the reading is saying. I now come closer to a shared language with them.

If divination is a translation tool we use to speak with the divine, or at least get their notes, then all we're really doing when reading is drawing a line between the language of the tarot and the language the client knows and understands. The client may not "get" the term "ascended master," but might fully understand "beloved dead," say. No, they're not interchangeable, but that's not important. A reading isn't a theology lesson. My job isn't to teach them the words I use to talk about divinity; it's to use language that makes sense to them so *they* get the message. My cosmology doesn't matter. I don't have to throw it out the window. I just need to be able to equate my concept of the divine messenger and whatever I call it and what the client relates to. If they keep saying "angel" and I keep saying "ascended master," I'm not communicating well. I'm imposing my view on them. And that's not good.

It's easy to take what I'm saying as gospel and to feel like crap if you've done what I'm describing. You're not a jerk if you've had a client use a term you don't like and changed it on them. But you can be a better listener and communicator if you try to match their language rather than imposing your own. What the hell is an ascended master if you've never heard that term? If the client wants to know about a child who passed shortly after birth, "ascended master" isn't going to make any sense, even if that's what you feel they are now. The client still thinks of them as a child, not a master, and as an angel, not some esoteric entity with a C-suite title.

There are readers who create distance between themselves and the client by asserting that the client's use of a word or concept is incorrect. These folks are more concerned with being impressive and even making others feel small so that they feel big and smart and important. It's ego, it's gross, and it's a violation of the contract between reader and client. We are not there to judge them; we are there to provide an answer. That is all. If they've misused or mispronounced the word "Sephiroth," that's okay; it is not our job to give them the correct pronunciation or a gloss of its history and meaning. It is our job to answer the question. In fact, there have been times when a client has mispronounced a divinatory term, and I adjusted my pronunciation to theirs so they didn't feel bad. It's a small thing, but if that's the difference between them remaining open and getting the answer they need or not, then who the hell cares how the word is pronounced? If this were my day job and I was introducing a new hire and people kept saying his name wrong, it would be my responsibility to correct them. People have a right to have their names pronounced correctly. But if someone says "arcana" differently than I do, or doesn't know how to say "hierophant," then who cares? Only the ego. So make like Elsa and let it go.

I'm a Large Medium?

In my two prior books I've gone to great pains to explain I don't view myself as psychic. I don't. For me, that term suggests a certain amount of cosmic knowing, hearing, or seeing—what might be called clairsentience, say, or clairvoyance. (The different "clairs" indicate different ways of knowing. For example, clairaudience is literally *hearing* the message.) I don't experience that. I don't have spirit voices, I don't have messages come in dreams, and I don't have moments of knowing. In fact, what I do have are intrusive thoughts and anxiety. My mind is never at rest long enough for anything clearly divine to enter it. All I do all day is think about what might be about to kill me—cancer, traffic, American politics, whatever. If I were getting a message this way, I'd never know whether it was just my hypochondria or a real thing I need to know. The way I "hear" messages is from using divination. I need an interpreter or translator; I can't do it on my own the way people whom I think of as psychic can. Actually, the word "psychic" makes me as uncomfortable as "angels" does; it takes me back to the late eighties/early nineties and the Time-Life *Mysteries of the Unknown* series (an ad campaign that kept me sleepless for years—that's not hyperbole).

It is here that I must once again pause to consider the cultural influence on me and my behavior in life. I recall a work trip I had to take once and one of the attendees was someone who took the role of office pariah. Somehow, they managed to always do or say the thing that would embarrass or irk people. Clearly insecurity was at play, as it is for many of us, but because offices are as much a hot bed of ranking as high schools, these are the people who tend to get bullied or ignored altogether. During this trip, tarot came up and this silly goose said, "Oh, we'll be up in our rooms doing psychic readings!" It wasn't really anything more than an attempt to bond with me, but it made my guts curdle and I gave the kind of "you-don't-even-go-here" reaction I was so used to receiving from others. I'm sad to say, there's no bigger bully sometimes than the formerly bullied. I threw them under the bus so that I wouldn't look silly.

And that's because there is a part of me that thinks the word "psychic" is silly. Not that the act is stupid, but that the word, the *label,* just sounds pretentious. But I also feel that way about the clairs, too—sentience, audience, voyance, etc. Actually, there's a deeply hipster part of me that looks down on this part of my life. Isn't that odd? In fact, there have been very clear and very powerful signs to me over the last eight or so years that I'd benefit from focusing more on *this* work—this divinatory work—than the things I stupidly spent my future earnings getting degrees in. But...I haven't been able to do it. In part, because there's something "respectable" and "glamorous" about my MFA and something kind of embarrassing about my divinatory work. Like, I don't often talk about it with civilians because I worry they'll think I'm weird. (Which is bizarre, because I fully *am* weird and I know it and I'm proud of it. Aquarius is my ascendant. I relish weird and make it my brand!) Why do I care?

It's the same reason people think fortune tellers are frauds. Bias. And a lot of hardcore messaging designed specifically to make us look down on "those people." The bias isn't accidental, friends; it's deliberate. Recall, churches are corporations and have rent or mortgages to pay. In the US, many of them also have political causes to back. They don't want the competition. And of course the best way to demoralize people and make them obedient is to cut them off from their power—their gods, their ancestors, their rituals, for sure, but *anything* that gives them freedom and autonomy. That's why you can't get God to forgive you directly in Catholicism; you need a priest (being paid and housed by your donations) to forgive you. When I was a kid, the pastor of my church had a nicer car than any of the parishioners, *and he had a boat.* But my broke parents still gave their envelope every Sunday while they paid through the nose for Catholic school. They worked bingo games and did lunch duty for discounts on tuition, and we lived in apartments although my mom dreamed of a house and a yard. *And he had a fucking boat.* (My parents have their own condo, now; no yard, but a deck, some sunshine, and the occasional tomato plant.)

I've been a reader for about twenty-five years at the time I'm writing this. That's more than half my life, now. I've been reading longer than I haven't been. And I still sometimes feel shame about it. That's actually one reason I'm writing this book. If the community challenges the stigma, then the shame will disappear. But I still have to fight my own biases *about myself*.

Y'all, I don't know if this will be true forever (clearly I hope it is), but I'm *very* good at what I do. That's not ego, that's me saying something I struggle to. I'm an excellent reader and I'm an excellent teacher. And this particular part of my life, though it has had its ups and some *major* downs, has frequently been the most rewarding thing I do. The validation I've always longed for presents itself to me here; the self-confidence I've always wished I had exists here, too. The friendships I've developed are among the strongest (though there have been some real fuck-ups there, too) and the joy is almost relentless. I used to think I couldn't survive working as a reader at a fair or festival. I thought, being as introverted as I am, that I'd get too tired too quickly. Reader, the *opposite* turned out to be true! I feel *energized* when I've done a session of constant reading. Sure, on the drive home I start to feel a little worn out, but it's a *good* worn; the kind that comes from doing something you're really good at, rather than the kind that comes from living in a relentlessly cruel world. Same with teaching. I *adore* teaching. When I host workshops, I feel energized. And in both cases, all my hangups and insecurities take a backseat and give way to the ability to facilitate perception shifts.

I chose the word *facilitate* carefully, because that's what I do. I'm not the main actor, I'm just the thing that makes communication happen. It's not that I'm not actively engaged in it, but it's not *about me.* I'm the translator. The, I hate to say it, *medium.* All I want to point out is that I could be dedicating more of myself to this particular art, but there are degrees of shame that prevent me from doing it. And that has a lot to do with the messages I've internalized about myself, about the world, and about what the world thinks of people like me. Many in the divinatory and magical spaces talk of "coming out of the broom closet" in the same way queer people talk about revealing our orientation or expression. There's a need to reveal, and the very act of revelation implies that something dirty, diseased, disgusting is being admitted. "I can't keep this *shameful* secret anymore." I don't think queer people or diviners or witches or Hoodoos think of themselves that way; I think, though, that having to "reveal" something implicates us and makes us feel like we're somehow less-than or bad. Cis, straight people never have to "come out." And the fact that the dominant culture creates an environment where these things have to be revealed demonstrates why we're often hiding parts of ourselves that are perfectly wonderful and require zero shame.

Anyway, the thing is: when I described my experience of reading, I had a hard time avoiding certain words I don't like—conduit, medium, vessel. All of these imply a sort of stereotype of psychic that comes from everything I just described, but also my love affair with pulpy haunted house novels. I imagine the brutal experience of the medium in *Hell House* or the problematic camp of Ed and Lorraine Warren. And yet, like angels, those are perceptions of a word and my bias against them makes it harder to do my job. Because I don't want to be perceived a certain way, I avoid easy language; and because I'm biased against my own skill, I feel uncomfortable allowing myself to be classed with others of my ilk. People I respect and admire! People whose work has been formative! And yet—it's there.

Recently, I had the great pleasure of reading *The Book of Séances: A Guide to Divination and Speaking to Spirits* by Claire Goodchild. This beautifully designed and written book by the creator of *The Antique Anatomy Tarot* allowed me to think differently both about mediumship/séances and what I do just about every day. In fact, the whole point of the book is using divination systems such as tarot and bones to contact and "speak with" the spirits we want to engage, or who want to engage with us. Odd to say, perhaps (it is to me, anyway), but it had never occurred to me that tarot or bones *could* be used for mediumship. I think I had an accepted notion that a spiritualist used internal channeling or perhaps a spirit board, but that tarot or another fortune telling device had nothing to do with any of that. I simply viewed divination as a way of reading patterns and that was it. I had zero sense of it being spiritual, for reasons I monologued about above. But Goodchild's book made me think, "*Oh!*" It was surprising!

And so, it was a few months later that, sitting in the backroom of a local shop, a client asked whether I might do a reading aimed at getting a message from her ancestors, particularly an uncle she was close to. In most situations prior to this I would have said, "Oh, you know, I'm not a medium and so I don't want to try mislead you." Instead I said, "You know, I've never done that before, but if you're okay thinking of it as an experiment, I'm okay trying the experiment." The client readily agreed and we got the message—in fact, it was the same message we'd gotten in the more general reading moments before. It felt like a strong possibility her ancestors, maybe even her uncle, were confirming it. "Yes," they seemed to say, "you are in fact on the right track." It didn't provide any shocking revelation, but it did make the client feel more confident in the reading we'd done.

Can I ever know that it was one of her ancestors? No. Maybe it was one of *mine*. Maybe it was an ancestor we have in common, or the spirits of the people who stewarded that land before my ancestors got here (though that would be far more generous than my ancestors have any right to expect). It doesn't really matter, though, because it made the reading all that much more memorable and uplifting for the client. This client was about to embark on something new and needed to know things would be okay. The initial reading said it would be and then the ancestral reading said the same. I don't know about you, but that feels like a ringing endorsement of my client's choices. And the whole initial reading achieved the goal, what's the harm in getting an even more powerful validation?

A Digression on Repeating Readings

I pause now to comment on something else I learned not to do: read about the same topic more than once in too short a span of time. This applies regardless of who it's for and whether there's payment. The idea was that a client or reader could become too dependent on the cards and possibly develop an addiction to getting readings if they got them too often. It was also thought to be true that reading over and over again on a topic would lessen the power of the initial reading, because there was the possibility that we'd start getting vastly different answers every time. The metaphysical reasoning for some was that it would be like a kid nagging a parent. The spirits or guides would start getting pissed if you kept tugging at their skirts asking what was for dinner. Which is fair, I guess; I hate being nagged. Although I'm also not an immortal or otherworldly entity—and I've found that getting different answers about the same topic doesn't really happen that much, and when it does it's significant.

The number of clients who sit for a reading with me and then tell me they got the same answer when they read for themselves yesterday delights me. It doesn't make me feel like I've wasted my time and I don't think they're going to get addicted to readings. I think I just validated what they already knew, so they get two gifts: surety that the answer was right, and a bump in self-confidence since a "pro" just gave them the same answer. It's a win-win, really. And you hear readers all the time talk about clients who say, "Oh, the other reader I saw just said the same thing." Like, if readings work—and they do most of the time—then if something is going to happen, then the reading is going to keep saying it will. Right? And so often it does. That's the thing. We have all this circumstantial evidence telling us how often reading on the same topic yields the same answer. So what's it matter if we keep doing it? It doesn't. And if someone wants to pay me money to keep saying the same thing, well, I used to be an actor; I can handle that. (That was a joke, if I felt like a client needed a break I'd tell them.)

On the other hand, if you keep getting different answers, one of two possibilities is at play:

One of the readings was misread.

It's not a sure thing and could be dancing on the edge.

In the first case, look, we all have wonky readings. I know I'm not right every time and sometimes the times when I've apparently been the most wrong were the times when I felt the most confident I was correct. (This takes us back to whether or not we can trust the client's feedback. I still hold in *some* of those cases that I *was* right and the client couldn't see it.) Especially when we're learning, we can misread. It happens. *Especially* when reading for ourselves, *which is really difficult.* It really is. It's not impossible, but it is a lot of work for many of us. So, sure, we might get the wrong answer in one of several readings; in which case, make sure you do an odd number of readings and then take the answer that tips the scale as the surest bet right now. It really doesn't have to be any more complicated than that. Think of it as flipping a coin. Whoever gets the best on two of three flips wins. Odd numbers are helpful that way. The rare benefit of the binary, eh?

But the thing is, not all of life's moments are sure bets. I recall applying for a promotion in a former job and doing a reading to see if I'd get it. The reading said I would. I interviewed, did pretty well, and then weeks went by without any news. And then a month. And then three months. And because I already worked for the company, I knew the decision hadn't been announced, because we always contacted internal candidates when they weren't getting the job. So I read again and it said that I would *not* get the job. Again, weeks went by. I read a third time and got an affirmative: I *would* get the job. Not longer after, my boss told me that a client had pushed into the process, didn't like my experience, and wanted to meet with me. So I had to interview with this person (who, incidentally, I never wound up working with)—and finally I got the job.

One reading of this could say that at least one of my divinations were wrong. On the other hand, the more likely reading is that things took an unexpected turn. We talked about this when we did our number on free will and fatalism. This person who decided she needed to be consulted became an obstacle because she didn't like me. Only after she met me and discovered how fantastic I am was she swayed, and so the readings reflected these shifts. But I never would have known that journey was happening had I not done those three readings. The first one turned out to be correct, I got the job. But I don't think that it was looking at the ultimate outcome; I think it was looking at what the outcome was *at the time I did the reading*. Once the new person entered the chat, so to speak, the outcome potentially changed. The context is that I had already been doing that job in another part of the company. When we were bought by the new company, I accepted a move to another department because my role would eventually go away—a step down in seniority, but more money (oddly). So I would basically have been moving back into the role I had before. There was no reason not to give it to me—except for this person who intervened.

I tell this story a lot because I think it shows the value of reading about the same thing a few times. If you are getting different answers, it's an indication your agency is somewhat limited. There may be back-and-forth going on, tensions, or other things you can't see that are impacting the situation. Now, this brings us to another cosmologically complex question: If readings are communications with the divine, then wouldn't the divinity be able to see all of this and just give us the correct answer to begin with? And that, again, comes down to the degree of fatalism you view the world through and the question of whether a reading is a *dialogue* or a *map*.

Allow: A dialogue is a conversation. When using a pendulum, I tend to use it conversationally. I'll ask a series of questions to see what's going on, in part to get a sense of how accurate the pendulum is that day, but also because I have multiple questions that can be answered yes (up and down), no (side-to-side), or maybe/I don't know (clockwise or counterclockwise circle). A ouija board is equally conversational, although I've never used one, believe it or not, so I can't say for sure how conversational it *really* is. (I know, I know; it's just that *The Exorcist* is one of my favorite movies. Bias.) There's an on-going exchange happening. And a series of things being addressed.

A spread of cards or a casting is static. It's like a map. Once a map is drawn, it's not changing. If the landscape changes in some way, the map has to be redrawn. The map doesn't necessarily know what happens once it's drawn. A card spread is similar: once it's laid out, it's laid out. Sure, you could move things around and do additional readings, but a spread is a spread and as such it's a snapshot of the energy around a subject at the time of the reading. Not unlike our natal charts with astrology; a snapshot of the sky at the moment and place of our birth. And because we (or many of us) were trained not to do repeated readings on the same thing, we'd never see the evolution of a situation. Which isn't good or bad, it just is. But if we are doing multiple readings on a topic, we likely will see the shift in energies. As always, so much of this depends on the mix of free will and fatalism that makes up our existence.

The argument might be that, if a reading is a communication with a spirit or guide, then that spirit or guide must know more than we do—spirit guides frequently can see what's best for us in many cosmologies. So they will know the *ultimate* outcome of *everything*. Which, again, I cannot verify or deny. But I do know that if they're anything like guides in real daily life, there are times when they're going to withhold certain information for our own good. I also don't know whether their guidance is ever impacted by affection. When I love people, I tend not to want to tell them they look ugly in that top, even if they do. Ancestors or spirits may be similar. So we don't know whether they're always showing us the full picture, or if they're holding things back for various reasons. There's no way to know. And what you decide is ultimately a guess based on the facts of your own life and experience as well as how you tend to view the future.

My own life experience has told me many uncommon things about divination: that The Tower isn't always bad and isn't always big; that the image isn't the sum-total of the card's meaning; that it's okay to read for things that were once considered taboo and that it's better not to change a client's question; that things aren't entirely fixed, and doing readings about a situation multiple times may show you the shifting sands of a situation. Unpopular, sure, but they've been effective guideposts for me and have for sure improved the quality and accuracy of my readings—two things we all value. So even if you don't agree with me, why not try out thinking that way for a little while and see whether it shows you anything?

Ultimately, I think repeated readings on the same topic can be quite helpful. In fact, checking our progress on a particular goal is an excellent use of reading—and would require us to read multiple times on something. Try it. Set a goal for yourself a few weeks in the future. Work on it. Every other day, do a spread about it. What's changed? What hasn't? If you're getting the same reading every day, is it because you're making consistent progress? Or because you're already stuck in a rut? If the reading stays the same, you might be, too; on the other hand, a change in meaning each day should show progress—because *you're* changing. Even if the goal is a trivial one, you're *still* changing and the reading will reflect that. Give it a try and see what happens. If nothing else, it's an excuse to play with divination which is always a treat.

A Few Spiritual Considerations Worth…Considering

It's widely accepted in magical spaces that spirits, divinities, ancestors—they're not at our beck and call. Asking them for *anything*, including information or answers, without developing a relationship with them is tantamount to barging into someone's house without knocking and demanding they feed you or give you their electronics and jewelry. I'm not an expert in this area, but if you're not getting the kind of spiritual guidance you're looking for, you may want to work on developing a relationship with the spirits first. Without revealing too much of my private practice, I do have an ancestor lamp that I care for and keep lit most of the time when I'm home. It gets lamp oil as needed, but the basin of the lamp is also filled with offerings, herbs, sigils, and other items meant to make my ancestors welcome. I also have another lamp for another guide I admire and for a third, which is St. Expedite, I offer candles on certain associated days. X, as I call him, gets candles because they burn more quickly than lamps do, and Expedite is associated (partly) with speed; the candle just seems more on brand. I only give you X's name, because he likes public recognition and he's been good to me, so I have no problem shining a light on him here. It may seem an odd thing for a former Catholic to work with a saint, but X was kicked out of the saint canon—and as I result, I feel like he's got a kinship with those of us who have felt marginalized by our faith. I also respect that he's got a bigger following now that he's "no longer" a saint. He's my boy, as the bros say, and I'm awfully fond of him and he has come through for me as much as my living friends have.

Even small steps toward building a connection with the spirits you're attempting to communicate with can go a long way, because it seems to indicate a certain seriousness and also a certain respect. The analogy offered in many books is akin to this: I'd never walk up to a stranger and demand they solve my problems or give me money, and the same should go for spirits and honored dead, especially if they are truly honored. There are so many books dedicated to this that I tend to avoid recommending any. It's such a personal decision and one has to approach this from a personal perspective.

All of that said, I've been reading for decades now without incorporating any spiritual practice into my readings. I rarely if ever consecrate my cards. When I get a new deck, I rip the plastic off with my teeth, toss the extra cards to the side, and start working. When I'm reading, I don't cast a circle, invite anyone or anything in, or do much in the way of centering or grounding. In fact, I tend to resist anything that smacks of the performative over the substantive; I find it uncomfortable watching readers put on a big show of "getting in the zone." That's my own bias, my own judgmental tendency, but it's also true that what I do has always worked for me. And when I've tried to add ritual or spectacle into my readings, I just wind up feeling silly. I don't put this down to shame you; if you do this kind of work prior to readings, excellent. I could probably benefit from a more centered approach, sometimes. Earth is not heavily featured in my natal chart and keeping my feet planted has always been an issue.

The reason I bring this up, though, is that my readings *do* work, even without the ritual. What gives? If reading is a translation device between a spirit or divinity and the reader, then it would stand to reason I'm being awfully disrespectful by just assuming my guides will always be there when I need them. So why am I such an abysmal host? I guess because I get away with it?

But as always, we butt up against individual cosmology.

If pressed, I would say many readings aren't necessarily guided by an individual entity or guide, but rather by a sort of collective cosmic database available to anyone who knows how to tap into it. Like Wikipedia—a crowd-sourced repository of information. Teachers have been decrying the use of Wikipedia since it first came out because, being a wiki, it is constantly changing, because there's no editorial board curating what happens there, and it's not generally primary source material. That said, it is heavily policed by the crankiest people on the planet: pedants who want to show everyone what they know. And this isn't a bad thing, because it's an in-built quality control mechanism. I've often held that Wikipedia isn't where you want to go when you're ending your research, but if you're starting it, you can find a lot of referenced source material that that can get you on your way. And so, most readings are kind of like dipping into the cosmic Wikipedia of human experience. It is the reader's job to make sure the info we're pulling off "the cloud" is sound, and there's a possibility it may lead us in the wrong direction sometimes, but generally it's a good jumping off point.

Thus, most readings are searches into the collective unconscious. That's why they work and why sometimes we may go off course. We didn't check our sources close enough. It's not the most elegant of metaphors, but it does nicely for our purposes.

On the other hand, there may be times when we need the kind of reading or information that can only come from first-hand experience. In these times, perhaps, we call upon specific guides or beings or entities that know of what we need them to speak. This is more like going to the primary source. If you want to know about Anne Boleyn's thoughts, the only person you can truly ask is Anne Boleyn. Likewise, certain entities may govern certain parts of life, and one may want to call on a being associated with that part of life. Say you need guidance in your love life and you want to do a reading about that. Making a connection with Venus, however you do it, might be a good thing to do, then ask for her advice when you do your divination. As someone who is fairly mercurial (actually, Mercury, Venus, and the Sun are all right next to each other in my chart), I find myself reaching for Mercury (who technically wasn't a god, but rather a messenger) often. Because I'm so mercurial, I tend to feel certain Mercury retrograde periods deeply. Like the time I got to New York and found I'd lost my ID and couldn't check into my hotel. If we need *specific* advice or intel, it may be then that we're working with specific entities during a reading.

Again, this is all conjecture. I have read perfectly well for years without giving much thought to the spiritual. Maybe that's because it's something I'm "meant" to do. I don't know. I don't know how much I believe in "life purpose," but they may put up with my laziness because I'm doing work they need me to do. That feels arrogant to say, but what the heck? I don't know. But I do know readings work, and that's the main thing. There's certainly nothing to be lost by developing a relationship with a source that you would like to get to know and who you think may have guidance for you. Why not? The worst thing that can happen is nothing.

It's All One

I say there's no difference reading about the big stuff or the small stuff. Partly because we don't get to decide what is big or small to the client, and partly because it's all part of being on this planet and in these bodies. It would be too much like the esotericists I dislike so much to prioritize the spiritual over the daily, but I also think that prioritizing the daily over the spiritual can be problematic too—and I know from experience, since my relationship to the spiritual is so complicated. I think the main thing is to take whatever you're reading about as seriously as your client does.

You may recall from Chapter Two that I read for someone who had been having a lot of plumbing issues in their home—but water-related problems kept creeping up elsewhere, too. So, we looked at the same spread from two points of view: the banal and the spiritual. I didn't draw separate spreads; we just read the same cards two ways. I discovered that looking at the same situation from two points of view can enlighten both sets of interpretations. The causes and implications from one impacted and shed light on the other. And, to harken back to, well, *most of human existence,* we recall that there was rarely a difference between the spiritual and the banal. Both were inextricably linked.

For the sake of demonstration, let's do a quick five-card reading to explore how to read the same cards from two points of view.

Imagine we have Hector, who wonders why he can't seem to hold on to a girlfriend. He's been dating since he was sixteen (he's twenty-seven now) and has fallen head over heels for all the women he's been with, but he doesn't seem to get the same kind of emotional investment in return. Let's look at why this is happening from the spiritual and daily points of view.

I've drawn:

Temperance (5), King of Wands (2), Nine of Swords (1), The Devil (3), The Sun (4)

It's interesting to note right out of the gate there are no cups and no pentacles cards. These are the suits that we'd associate with "traditional" relationships, monogamous marriages, for example. We have three majors and two minors and the center of the reading—the apex of the arc—is the Nine of Swords. Various pairings that might matter include King of Wands + The Devil, Temperance + The Sun, Temperance + King of Wands, and The Devil + The Sun. Any or none of those combos may be useful.

Let's start with the banal answer. The Nine of Wands suggests massive insecurity to me. Neediness. That's not a traditional meaning for this card, so I'll explain: nines are exhausted, heavy, they feel like they'll never get there. They're uncomfortable and not sure they can get where they're going. Swords, of course, are thoughts. So, Hector thinks that he can't get where he wants to go—he's insecure. His mind is telling him he can't have what he wants. It's likely he's giving off mixed messages (this comes from the fact that the nine is flanked by two pairs of cards and swords deal with messages). On the one hand, he's saying to potential partners: "I'm a grown-ass man who knows how to handle my vibes (wands, energy) and I can give and take with the best of them (Temperance)." On the other hand, he's saying (and probably doing), "If you don't yoke yourself to me fully (The Devil), I will burn you (The Sun, heating up The Devil's hell). I must be the center of the universe (the Sun is the center of our universe)." The King of Wands turns his back on the Nine and The Devil. He isn't aware of the way in which his insecurity makes him so needy (the Nine and The Devil and his chains); in fact, he really does feel like he's an even-tempered dude (the King looking at Temperance).

His intensity (Devil and Sun) could be making women anxious (Nine of Swords), even while he's reaching out to them—and the ones he's reaching out to are likely to be much more temperate in nature (of course, Temperance) and less prone to drama. So he's likely attracted to the kind of woman *least likely* to put up with his neediness and intensity. These potential mates are going to be turned off pretty quickly, because all the intensity (wands, kings, nines, Devil, Sun) comes off right away. They (temperate women) immediately see what he is (he presents as the King of Wands, but not in the mature way he thinks he does; this is the King of Wands in shadow, if you like). Temperance rarely signifies a person in readings, but here it makes sense—and the fact that it's paired with The Sun makes me think of them holding a big spotlight up to him. They see what he is right away. They may enjoy a little *in*temperance (the Sun is hot, after all, and probably so is Hector, being so heavily represented with "hot" [wands, hell, Sun] cards), but ultimately, they feel trapped (Devil) and anxious (Nine of Swords) and turn on him (the King turns away from the rest of the reading).

Hector's question was *why,* so I'd tell him, "You're attracted to people who can see how intensely needy you are and they get either scared or turned off. You may be saying you're chill, but you're a zero-to-sixty kind of guy and you want to be the center of their universe." Most people aren't ready for that intensity so quickly. He didn't ask for advice, so unless he asked, I wouldn't tell him his best bet is to go after potential mates who match his intensity. Why? I doubt he can change. The neediness and intensity are so deep even in just these five cards (three majors, after all) that I think he'd *think* he was changing, but really would be reliving the same patterns and getting the same result.

Now, a more spiritual way of looking at it:

Hector defaults to grief and despair (Nine of Swords), it's his nature. He feels grief expansively (nine = three times three) and it's his worldview (swords can be perceptions). He is fundamentally a Hades, always working (nines) in the underworld of grief. He likely is rather a defeatist, too, because he knows, in the words of Sufjan Stephens, "all things go." In fact, that could be his motto. He connects to Hades, too, because of The Devil, who stands between him and The Sun. He is both Orpheus *and* Hades, and he believes that his salvation lies in the one who can bring him light. (Lucifer was the light-bringer.) He moves through the world as the romantic figure, both the predator and the hero (predator, Hades; hero, Orpheus—but also the fact that the King of Wands [hero] and The Devil [predator] mirror each other). He (Hades) must claim his beloved and possess her. She will become his everything (Sun). He may view relationships as his mission.

He may well be the romantic hero, and he may well have fetishized that to a strong degree (the hero in this card has to be the King of Wands, who beckons to Temperance, and of course wands are deeply sexual—particularly in this cis-masculine way). The way he calls to this gentle angel with one foot on land and one in sea, he views himself as the keeper of her salvation. "Come to me, beautiful one," he seems to say, "and I can save you." But what does she experience when she joins him? Literal, actual *hell*. That's what. He becomes aroused by this predation. He truly is a predator, like Hades or like the more romantic iterations of Dracula. He believes he has "crossed oceans of time" to find these women.

He's drawn to the innocent and pure—common associations with this Temperance, but honestly, it's got more to do with other things, including alcohol, so it's not *that* innocent. On the other hand, he gets off on the *idea* of innocence. He *perceives* women as innocent because he is there to protect them (but really to consume them, which in his mind is the same thing), even though it's clear that they're not that. (This comes from my feeling that Temperance looks innocent but isn't. He can't see the truth. So if his girlfriend turns out to be a drinker, say, or a smoker, he finds that deeply unsexy.) He wants virgins and likely will lose interest in women once he's fucked them because they're soiled (the romantic hero [King of Wands] mirrored by The Devil). Only then does he see (The Sun shining light) them as they are (my temperance-isn't-innocent stance) and loses interest. Because what he wants isn't a real woman, it's an ideal woman. In this case, women may be turned off by his intensity, but he also gets turned off by them being animals who pee and shit and eat. He doesn't want a woman; he wants an *angel* (obviously Temperance). Of course, Temperance is supposed to show the archangel Michael, not a woman—but I also don't think angels actually have gender, so take that.

The two readings are similar, of course the answer is going to be more or less the same—the cards are the same. But the first focused more on the *women* and what they see when they get to know him; the second more on him and how he sees women. The second one wasn't necessarily "spiritual" *per se,* but not far from it: it explored his sexual cosmology. He likely does see himself as Dracula or Hades or the Phantom of the Opera—one of those poetic souls whose talent and depth is supposed to save them from their abusive and predatory natures. (Look, I'm a Dracula fan, so I get it. But there's some baggage there, too, c'mon.). He thinks his intensity is romantic and what women *should* want. Here we for sure get incel vibes, although he doesn't seem to have any issue getting women; it's how he loses interest once he has them. The second was far more philosophical and more about his identity; the first, far more practical.

I'd rather give the first reading, to be honest, because I think it's going to be easier for him to hear and act on. There's some decent advice: you need to find potential dates who match your intensity and need to be consumed by each other. The second would be I think much harder for him to hear, because it really calls him out on some big shit. He *does* have predatory tendencies; he fetishizes the meaningless attribute of "virginity"; he has some major issues about women's value being tied entirely to "purity." And while he may be attractive, there's for sure evidence that he could be borderline abusive when feeling disrespected (all that king and Fire is egotistical, and The Devil isn't gentle—to say the least). This is going to the core of who he is as a man and what he believes he's entitled to. Oddly, though, because he does see himself as the tortured poet, he might actually respond to this—tragically, of course, *a la* his boy Hamlet, with lots of monologues and camp. Really, this is the main reason I've focused more on the practical than the spiritual as a reader. It's just easier for most people to connect to; there's more possibility to act on it; and it just hurts *less*.

But, as I've said before, there's no reason not to do both—and if this were a private session with a client who really needed to figure some shit out, I would have no problem going deep in this way. But what I love even more than the kind of reading we do, is the way that if we keep digging, we can find entirely new meanings in a set of cards we thought we'd already read! Like if we make just a small perception shift, we can dig deeper into the *same exact cards* and keep finding new information that will enlighten and enliven a session. And I think that's super cool.

CHAPTER THIRTEEN

DANCING WITH YOURSELF

Many of us struggle reading for ourselves. It's a notoriously difficult thing to do. On the other hand, many readers *only* read for themselves, so we know it's not impossible. It's interesting to recall the time when reading one's own cards was a major taboo is not that long past. I'm sure most people still did it, but it was commonly held that we can't read for ourselves, or if we can, we shouldn't. Mary K. Greer's *Tarot for Your Self* was really the first book that recognized people want to and actually can read for themselves and that was only published in 1984! Even with that wonderful book, many readers still bemoan the difficulty of getting decent information from a reading for themselves.

I'm guilty of the divinatory sin of *laziness*. When I read for myself, I tend to fall down even after all these years. I've confessed this before, but when I read for myself, I lose all my tenacity. I pose a half-hearted, not-very-well-written question, shuffle, draw, get annoyed that I don't immediately see the revelation life's been withholding from me, shove the cards back in the deck, and move on. Shockingly, that doesn't really yield the results I'd like.

Others cite our inability to be objective about ourselves and what's going on in our lives, and subjectivity doesn't make it easier—but, honestly, I hold that there's no such thing as human objectivity. We are incapable of it. We are creatures of perception and bias, alas, but that is also why most of us don't go around avoiding even our loved ones. If we were truly objective, we'd have a hard time finding anyone attractive or worth getting dressed for. I mean, if we're being truly objective, humans are really bizarrely designed. Looking too long at the human ear demonstrates it. Utterly bizarre. And don't get me started on our junk. This is all to say, I think subjectivity is inevitable in all readings. The key isn't so much to reach for objectivity but to take advantage of our subjectivity—by which I mean, our unique perceptions of the world are part of the interpretive process. Rather than pretending we're objective, we instead recognize that our understanding of the world will contribute to the way we interpret a reading. For me, it's not about objectivity but humility: the ability to understand that the conditions through which we move in life are not the same for everyone—and that some of us move through more obstacle-laden terrain than others.

What I think is a bigger issue than our subjectivity is the fact that when we're reading for ourselves, we're playing two parts at once: reader and client. Doing either of those is a lot of work as it is. Attempting to do both is double the work—and you're trying to use two parts of your brain simultaneously. If we can separate the two actions, it gets a little easier. Actually, it can get substantially easier if you're willing to really dig in, but—again—I'm adorably lazy when reading for myself, so I don't always.

There are a few ways to separate the two sides of reading for ourselves. The easiest is to record the reading and talk it through as though you're giving it to someone else. Don't worry about what you're saying and whether or not it makes sense. Just do the reading. (Incidentally, this is also beneficial for folks who, like me, have gotten really used to writing or thinking readings, but worry that when doing them aloud, they'll fall down. Practice reading for yourself this way and then you can listen to your readings and get a decent message—and then listen to it again and consider how it *sounds.* What words work, what don't, where you may want to say more, where you may want to say less?) It's best to take a break between recording the reading and listening to it. This gives you time to switch between the two modes. Go for a walk, have a glass of wine, do the dishes, whatever makes sense. Finally, listen to the recording as though you're not the one speaking. This can take some getting used to; people are shockingly cruel to the sound of their own voice. You sound fine. Don't let your ego get in the way of hearing what your brilliant reader has prepared for you. Attempt openness, curiosity, and grace. It's going to be okay. You could also do the same with a written reading, too.

Jeffrey Raff, author of *The Practice of Ally Work: Meeting and Partnering with Your Spirit Guide in the Imaginal World,* explores the power of automatic writing and connecting to something both inside and apart from ourselves. This book isn't divination-related per se; it's more Jungian (a word that, honestly, gives me hives). But the idea of allowing a flow of information to come by putting pen to paper (or fingers to keys, as I tend to) and giving space to the critical mind to step away is quite powerful. And because the experience of writing a reading is so unusual for many, it can be fascinating to start going and see what comes up—both as interpretations of the cards, but also freewriting inspired by the cards. It's easier to go on tangents in writing than it is when delivering a reading verbally. Many of us have gotten good at giving concise readings and we're trained to deliver only what is essential. This is good for our clients, but when reading for ourselves it's helpful not to edit. You don't know what's going to resonate later. A thing you scribble off-handedly that seems meaningless in the moment might be the key to unlocking the reading later.

You have to be able to read it later, though, so however you do this, make sure it's legible. I have to type when. While I've worked on my handwriting over the years thanks to my love affair with inks and fountain pens, I've learned that I can only write by hand for short periods of time before my script gets too sloppy, too lazy to read. My hand gets tired and I get bored and then I start to have a panic attack or a tantrum and it's not good. So, I type. I type pretty fast, even if my typo ratio dramatically reduces my words per minute. But I'm not concerned about typos when freewriting; I'm just concerned with getting as many thoughts down as possible without allowing them to float away. And so it doesn't matter if the words are spelled wrong; I'm more likely to be able to interpret what I meant with them than I am when writing by hand. Alas, I cannot be the luddite I long to be.

Try not to self-sensor. It's tempting, but when you're reading for someone else you have a lot of on-going contexts to work with that will help you shape the interpretation. You've got anything they've told you and of course, if you're face-to-face, you have their reactions. That's not the case in self-readings. You may get various reactive feelings, but it's always tough to know when those are intuitive hits or intrusive thoughts. It's best when reading for yourself this way to let it all go, say or write everything that comes out, and worry about it later. Much of it will not make sense, but that doesn't matter; the things you need to know frequently will. That's the point. Editing yourself can get in the way of an answer, and you don't want that. Everything may have some relevance. Give all the voices the time they need to speak, regardless of whether they "feel" on point or not.

This is why the break between giving the reading and receiving the reading is helpful. It lets your brain switch modes, but it also lets you forget what you've just said. You likely won't retain much of what you said, however you said it. This is good because when you come back to read or listen to it, you're going to be doing so with fresher eyes—eyes un-impacted by whatever natural reactions you may have had during the initial reading. In a way, you become a different person in that space. You can sit in on the reading in a new way.

When you listen or read, recall that some readings are metaphorical and some are literal. A literal reading will describe what's going on without poetry. It means what it says. Otherwise, the cards will speak in riddles, Delphi-like, and require you to draw lines between the myth and the thing you're reading about. It's important in situations where the reading doesn't resonate to pause. Consider the overall tone of the reading and explore whether you're interpreting it in the most appropriate way. There's a possibility that even the most down-to-earth reader may start speaking in poetry when using the freewriting or free-associating technique, because we're literally tapping into different parts of our brain; parts that don't work the same way the logical mind does. And because you're accessing something that I think is more primal, you may discover a different "voice" for your self-readings than you use when you read for others. That's okay. It might even make the experience more powerful.

What's so fascinating about Raff's *Practice of Ally Work,* which inspired this method, is the idea that our imagination isn't some useless distraction. The idea that there are allies in the imagination, what he calls the imaginal realm, fascinates me. Like Claire Goodchild's *Book of Séances,* imaginal ally work takes what has frequently seemed cartoonishly foreign—"contacting" "spirits"—and makes them almost shockingly normal. Goodchild's book made me think of divination in terms of spirituality in a way I'd never been able to before, thanks to my bias against the esotericism of the tarot's early champions. Raff's book made me realize that the imagination can be a magical tool. I don't even recall if he ever uses terms like "magic" in the text; it's a psycho-spiritual book, and the emphasis is really more on the psych part. But I've had moments in my life when my creative mind takes over and I become a channel or a conduit for whatever story wants to be told. It's not as common as I'd like, but it is an especially exciting thing to experience. The ego goes completely away and *something*—inspiration, a muse, a guide—takes over and the creativity pours forth. Magical. So magical, in fact, that it's *exactly* what the Waite-Smith Magician makes me think of. The figure literally channels the spirit through their body and into the earth—which is the feeling of a creator channeling inspiration through their body and into their task.

Tapping into this part of ourselves may mean we have to *listen* differently, too, at least when getting a reading from ourselves. Sometimes you may have to take the story being told and find links between your experience and that story. It's not at all unlike the act of interpreting the reading for someone else. When doing that, you're drawing lines between the metaphor of the card and the experience of the client. "The Devil means this new sex club you're thinking of joining." In the case of reading for yourself, you may need to do the logical part—the interpretation—*after* the reading has been given. It's odd to say, but not hard to do. It's really just reading or listening to the messages and saying, "Oh, that metaphor of the humming honeybees connects to the fight with my sister." It's just about making connections, which we do for our clients. But when we read for ourselves, we may find that we have to make those connections *after* the reading if we didn't do it during. For a client, that would be bad; for ourselves, that's A-okay! Your reading mind may know something your receiving mind doesn't, but it may take a little more creativity to decode.

An Example

I've asked the question, "What advice should I give about reading for ourselves?" I've shuffled and drawn three cards.

Three of Wands (2), The Hanged Man (1), Nine of Wands (3)

Here's how I might work through this, using the freewriting technique:

Threes expand and grow and they also triangulate. Triangulation reminds me of a tryptic mirror—those of the old department stores, where you could see yourself from all angles. Reading does that, too, doesn't it? Especially reading for ourselves, because we need to be reader, receiver, and also some strange integration of both. Fire, of course, suggests energy and in this case the energy I need is divinatory energy—you might call it psychic energy. Whatever you want to call it, you need to be it, be in it, and look at it all at the same time. This validates my concept of separating the "reader mind" from the "client mind." It's worth noting, too, that this particular deck gives a campfire vibe.[43] Sitting around the fire, telling stories; going to spooky places, dark places; sitting in a forest clearing with the darkness kept at bay only as far as the light can reach—and beyond that, dark and unknown. A lot like life. But here it is safe, because here, fire—primitive fire, that major discovery of humans (how can you discover something that always was?)—is keeping us warm and lit. A reading is nothing more than a story we tell ourselves to find "light" (information) in a "dark" (uncertain) world.

Let's move on to The Hanged Man, who is depicted here cocooned, suspended, likely about to break free. He's our psyche, who can't seem to separate the parts of ourselves enough to even see what we look like. He doesn't know that there's such a thing as mirrors. This is the reader trying to free themselves without the knowledge that the constraints they're putting on themselves are actually what's making the reading more difficult. This is the consequence of clinging to certain perceptions, certain dogmas, certain "cans" and "can'ts"—those things we've been told and cling to, even if we don't know we're doing it. Like quicksand, the more we struggle, the more we sink. It's a grim state of being.

The Nine of Wands makes the three threefold, reminding me expansion only happens without constriction. Release constrictions, all of them, everything that we're told to expect and do and think and to simply let the reading twinkle as a candle does. Don't judge the candle; observe the candle. Nines, when they don't embrace their inner three-ness, are constricted because they're tired. The Nine of Wands can signal burnout, but only if we don't make space for the expansiveness of three. In fact, we need more expansion when we read for ourselves, not less. We need literally anything to be possible. One of those old white male writers once said, "Write drunk, edit sober." To read for ourselves, we read freely, gleefully, unconcerned with the accuracy of it—totally unworried about the message. Something we'd never do for a client, but something we have to do for ourselves. We "read drunk," meaning we let go of all inhibitions as a reader and go balls-to-the-wall (an expression that comes from aviation, not anatomy)—and only once that's done can we "sober up"—or "edit" with an eye toward what's really applicable. There may be so much more (three + three + three = a lot!) in there than we expect. But we can only see if we're open and free, and not tightening the ropes around us like The Hanged Man.

I could go on, but better than that let's highlight some things I wouldn't have considered had I not free-written that reading without judgment: First, the idea of the woods—how readings are like a campfire in a dark forest. That's an apt metaphor for reading, absolutely. Also, the cocooned nature of this particular Hanged Man

43 For context, I did not use the Waite-Smith deck for this reading; it was the *Clarity Tarot* by Bel Senlle.

showed me an exciting possibility. (Apologies for switching up the decks on you; I wasn't sure whether or not the Waite-Smith would be what I used and I thought the examples of this reading were too good to throw out.) The way that character can stay in their own awful state simply by fighting too hard against themselves—as well as the inevitable. Death follows The Hanged Man in order, just as freedom only comes from accepting it. Of course, in this case we're talking about a kind of an ego death—a separation from beliefs and interpretations that we cling to, only to our detriment. Further, the "read drunk" concept also came from freewriting—and it's an appropriate context for that card.

My reading seemed to confirm what I said above, which is nice—but I wasn't really that concerned with it proving my thesis. In fact, if it hadn't, that would have been better because it would have shown me something I could consider fixing. It could have shown me something I need to do differently. So often when we're reading for ourselves, it's because whatever is going on in our lives isn't working as hoped or expected and we need or want a change. If the reading doesn't confirm what you'd been thinking, that's great! What's that tell you? Why is it different? Where are your constraints preventing you from seeing what's *really* there? It can help you dig deeper, which is precisely the point. It's when we stay on the surface that we get lame readings for ourselves. And I think a lot of us stay on the surface because we've been told it's difficult and we believe it, so we get lazy, and also because a lot of us value clients' questions more than we value our own/our selves.

You Can, but Should You?

We can read for ourselves, absolutely. There's no reason not to. That said, I tend only to do it for relatively small-stakes things. When I don't know how to get past writer's block, say, or when I don't know how to handle a problem at work. For larger life stuff, I get a reading from someone else. It's really just easier. When I'm upset about something or confused, I'm already constricted and that usually means I'm not being very kind to myself. I have a tendency toward majorly negative self-talk. So taking myself out of the equation is the best thing to do and there's no shame in that.

The added benefit of getting readings from others, if that's something you can do, is seeing other readers' styles. Not so much that you wind up comparing yourself to them, but just to see how readers navigate the cards, how they work with the client, how they interpret, how much talking they do—all of this can act like mirror of your own experience. If, for example, you get a reading from someone who had an annoying habit of interrupting you, it's worth reflecting whether you happen to do that. In the psychological sense, this is projection of a shadow—those parts of ourselves that are there but we can't see. It's not uncommon for things that annoy us in others to be things *we actually do* to others and haven't noticed. It's not unlike the astrological aspect of the square. It's there, but because of the angle it's hard for us to see it. Other people probably can and probably do. And checking with loved ones could be a good way to validate that.

Even when you get a reading from someone else, though, you may need to do a little line-drawing and interpretation of your own. I used to get slightly anxious reading for other readers, because I worried they'd judge me too harshly. What I soon discovered is some of them will just do the reading for you, which I guess is okay but why would you want to pay me to listen to you do what you could have done at home? Ya know? And this is my wonky way of saying, I think that the *interpretations* of the reader doing the reading are the correct ones. But: sometimes the client needs to do a little work on their own connecting the dots between the interpretation and their life. Much like what I described above when reading for yourself. This tends to happen naturally and, again, many readings are fairly literal. But when readers get readings from other readers, it's worth knowing that a different diviner's style may sometimes make it harder for you to connect the dots. If that makes sense. You can't turn off what you know, and what they know may strike you as surprising. And you may have to work a *little* harder to connect the dots for yourself. Much like reading this paragraph for the third time.

When getting readings from other readers, record them if at all possible. This is generally advisable when doing live readings (though I frequently forget to remind clients to do it) but in particular when you're a reader yourself. It may take a little distance and time, not unlike reading for yourself, in order to experience the full meaning of the reading. On the other hand, if you're working with a good reader, this shouldn't be an issue.

That brings up a final point: just because you like a reader personally doesn't necessarily mean they're the right reader for you. It can take time to find readers who "gets" you, particularly when you're a reader. This is partly because we already have a strong sense of the cards and so it's hard to accept someone else's interpretations, but it's also partly because not every reader is well-suited to every client. The reality is that sometimes the reader and client won't gel. Readers tend to view that as a sign the other reader isn't good; it's likely more that they're simply just not for you. If you find yourself getting readings from a specific reader that never make sense, likely it's just not a good pairing. Not everybody who picks up a deck of cards or a set of bones or anything else automatically *can* do it, but in my experience most people can. Having taught classes now for a while, I can tell you that I've never met a student who can't do it. I have met folks who are more disposed to doing it effortlessly than others, but I've never met anyone who couldn't, when pressed, find a logical and effective meaning in a set of cards. The rest of the issue is often whether that person's methods will make sense to you. As readers, we tend to be a little harder to read for because we know so much. But, as always, if you're just going to demand someone else use your interpretations, why pay them? Just do it yourself.

Chapter Fourteen

HOW I READ

I'll confess, I've never been super interested in writing a book where I give my card meanings. There's nothing wrong with it, it's just been done, and it seems like that's the only thing some mass marketers are interested in. How many times can you read what The High Priestess means? Also, we don't learn to divine by reading other readers' meanings. We have to experience what divination tools mean *in real life*, not the summaries of what someone else's lived experience and research has told them. That said, it can be useful to see an *overview* of other readers' foundational meanings. It can open up windows into the methods you haven't seen before. I recognize I'm in the minority in a lot of my divinatory feelings, so I've elected to share my foundational tarot meanings with you and then explore how I typically read.

It's important to know that these "meanings" are where I start and/or what I reach for when a reading isn't springing to life. I don't believe that reading is reciting memorized meanings, and if pressed to answer the question, "What makes a reader a *real* reader (or a 'pro')?" I'd say, someone who can read without reciting memorized meanings; someone who can synthesize the concepts the cards represent with the context of being a living person experiencing the world in a unique and specific way. Beyond that, it's all capitalism.

It's worth noting that I've gone back and forth over the years with what I call the two parts of the deck. I liked "trumps" for a long time, since that connected to the game origins of the deck. I've tried "keys," but it doesn't work for me. Lately, I just call them the "majors" and the "minors," because in music a major or minor key isn't good or bad, it's a matter of notation. Every major key has a corresponding minor in music; they're simply just ways of thinking about which notes get played in a score. A reading is similar. A reading may be major or minor, but that doesn't indicate whether it's good or bad. It just indicates what notes are being sounded.

00. The Fool. Freshness, openness, curiosity (much like the fortune teller's default mode). Foolishness, nonsense, idiocy. Not looking where we're going. For someone accident prone (me!), this can be a warning. For someone who takes themselves too seriously, this represents the mission to loosen up. Getting or being high (altitude-wise or chemically), especially with other mountain top cards like The Hermit and the Waite-Smith version of the Seven of Wands (wands are Fire, fire lights up=pot=high). My Fool meanings depend a lot on pre-Golden Dawn images. In many, the poor dude has his ass hanging out. This can mean, as they say, "showing your whole ass." The Fool has gotten one of the biggest tarot glow-ups, but sometimes it's all about WYSIWIG: "What you see is what you get."

01. The Magician. Pre-Esotericism, this was a street hustler, a gambler, a sideshow act, a con artist, a deceiver, a mountebank. In relationship readings, I don't see this card offering good news. Someone's hiding something. If we're curious about infidelity, The Magician is cheating. If we never had the esotericists who felt they had to rescue this card, we'd never have many of the more positive aspects of this card. It can represent performers, good if you're reading for actors or musicians; bad if you're reading about whether or not someone is sincere in their words or deeds. That said, decks that exist prior to the Waite-Smith weren't in English, and this card was usually called something else, too. The juggler, for example, as well as the mountebank.

Because this card is called The Magician *now,* we can bring in deeper meanings. In such cases, the card represents a conduit for energy or inspiration (don't stand outside during a thunderstorm after getting this card). This is the moment of inspiration or—even better—the act of sustaining inspiration and transforming it into a product. It can also signal sex, particularly with wands, The Tower, and The Devil. Because many depictions of the card today show them with magical tools, this can suggest people who work with tools—carpenters, say, especially with a card like the Eight of Pentacles. It can also signal sex toys, because those are tools, too.

02. The High Priestess/Popess. There's no such thing as a popess, and yet here she is in the deck! As a result, I sometimes see this card representing people demanding to be recognized for who or what they are. This can be anyone who has been dehumanized saying, "No! I am here!" I think of Celie in *The Color Purple.* "Dear God, I'm here! I'm here!" (Cue Fantasia.) Of course, this can represent anyone of any gender expression. No card represents only one gender. In this case, though, the patriarchal history of the world since the dawn of popes does matter. It is from here we get the oppression of anyone who has been told they don't exist, whatever that means to them.

Other times, thanks to the more esoteric traditions, I see this card as a gatekeeper. Anyone in a position to grant or withhold access: bosses, editors, gallery owners or adjudicators, coaches, and recruiters—those sorts of things. When I see this card come up in this gatekeeping way, the client is rarely being granted access by the priestess. If they're the gatekeeper, they tend to be withholding access to others. This *can* suggest the egotistical satisfaction of exclusivity: "You can't sit with us." On the other hand, children should be kept from drinking at the discotheque, right? (I know that sound dated, but I love the world "discotheque" and this was a good chance to use it.) Gatekeeping isn't necessarily a bad thing, but I do find this card typically represents being denied something—access, knowledge, experience, etc. If you're applying for jobs or colleges, say, this card might mean you're facing a battle against "legacy" or nepotism.

03. The Empress. For some reason, so many readers over the years have whittled all the most powerful "female" cards in tarot down to motherhood and nurturing—something that seems at odds with the tarot's feminist foundations of the sixties through the nineties (not to say it's not feminist today, but the concepts of both feminism and divination have broadened in the last twenty-plus years, as has our understanding of gender). It's common to hear The Empress described not unlike a "trad wife": fertility, support, care, feeding, earthiness. Same for the queens. Because I sometimes get scolded by mothers for finding fault with this reduction, I'll say there's nothing wrong with those qualities and they're certainly evident, but I also think there's more to "motherhood" and "womanhood" than that. If The Empress is surrounded by more nurturing cards—cups, for sure, and pentacles/coins—that may be how the card is manifesting in that reading. And it can definitely indicate creativity, which is a fairly traditional meaning for the card, too.

On another note, empresses are historically consorts whose job is creating allyship between nations by marrying well and producing the requisite heir-and-a-spare. We can read the card that way, particularly when looking to it for advice: build bridges, create alliances. This can also represent meditators, therapists, caretakers, or nurses. The card could also indicate people being viewed in terms of their strategic resources rather than their humanity. ("I need to meet her; she's going to be good for my career!")

There are, of course, empresses who had to take the role of head of state. This is the same job as emperors, but the conditions are different. The Empress has to make political moves in a patriarchal world where her intelligence is undervalued, her power limited, and her enemies considerable. She must be clever, agile, intuitive, adept at negotiating, coddling, manipulating. She has to achieve a "man's" job and deliver the results even though all the odds are against her. Remove gender from the equation and we're presented with anyone who has to achieve high standards under long odds. For example, the way white supremacy demands that Black children perform higher than their white peers to be viewed as equal. The Empress is a mover and a shaker in a world that doesn't want them to succeed—a world that, in fact, builds barriers to their success. They succeed anyway. This always makes me think of Queen Elizabeth I. A survivor, a navigator, a clever manipulator of conditions.

While reworking this chapter, I happened to listen to the *Fortune's Wheelhouse* podcast by T. Susan Chang and M.M. Meleen, and they discussed the ways this card can represent the idea of the modern struggle between "wife and mother" and doing everything else. And there are many people, regardless of gender or parenthood, who struggle to meld two parts of themselves, thanks to various conditions. This is also a fitting concept for this card.

04. The Emperor. Everyone seems to hate this card because he's seen as the incarnation of everything evil in modern and historical life: colonialism, misogyny, racism, anti-queerness, etc. He can represent all those things, for sure, and they're alive and well and hurting us. He's also a four, so he's stable, stolid, solid, stoic, maybe even stuck. Lots of reasons to dislike him. Still, nothing is one thing and everything is its own other. That said, he can also be "masculinity" at its most mature and least toxic. Not because of the empirical nature, but because he's the only card in the majors available to do that. So as much as he represents everything toxic about masculinity, he's also a good dad who loves his kids and will play dress-up with them. He's your straight buddy who'll kick a homophobe's ass on your behalf. Context will tell you which version you're getting. If he's surrounded by equally belligerent cards, he's giving colonizer; if he's surrounded by loving, friendly cards, he's a dad or even a hero.

If he's not your *dad,* he could be your *daddy*—which takes us into the world of sexuality and subs, doms, kink, leather, bondage, anything that's giving big top energy. You could read the static nature of four as *bound* (if you're nasty, Miss Jackson). And of course this isn't limited to gender. Anyone can be a "top." The Emperor is that person.[44]

In more daily ways, any boss or leadership role could be represented by this card. I also like the idea of the card representing *strategy.* This comes from a version of the card in the *Japaridze Tarot.* A favorite deck of mine, though I don't love the particular iteration which retitles this card *War.* In order to make that make sense to me (beyond its Aries associations, which aren't that interesting to me generally; I think The Fool should be Aries) is the idea that chess represents a gamified war, and it's known that good chess players are incredibly strategic. Thus, this card frequently represents either strategic people or strategies generally. In a banal vein, this card (as well as The Empress) can represent any leader. This leader is more stoic than the freer-flowing Empress, but again gender isn't implied.

05. The Hierophant/Pope. Even I, who finds The Emperor a frequently sympathetic card, tend to be hard on this one. And to be sure I find it representing dogmatic institutions, outmoded groups or ideas, and systems of rank or systems obsessed with rank. Secret societies could show up here, which means that cults could show

44 Who would be the bottom? Probably the pages—although it's worth noting that I don't view the pages as exclusively young. Simply curious and/or submissive/subservient.

up here, too. Parasocial relationships can be represented, given the power imbalance frequently depicted and the actual power imbalance between the institution and the individual. When we celebritize people, we put them up on pedestals or canonize them, and we might see this card representing that—or even warning us we're doing it. Hero-worship, fetishized power (we can see The Emperor in a negative way when paired with this card), as well as people or institutions who abuse their power. I'd put "law enforcement" and the judiciary here, too, particularly with The Empress, Emperor, or where kings and queens abound in the spread. Boot-licking can be seen here, with those acolytes kneeling before the papal throne. This makes it a short walk between this card and sexuality. I've heard The Hierophant referred to as representing *threesomes*.

This card can—and frequently does—represent faith generally. People of faith, of course, so clergy, ministers, even coven leaders. But also the *idea* of faith, belief, tenets, core values—everything that is positive about "religion" or faith. Again, nothing is one thing, we need cards to play double duty. Context will guide you.

06. The Lovers/The Lover. In French decks prior to esotericism, the card was singular (The Lover), focusing only on one of the characters depicted—of course it was the "man." This makes me think of self-love, masturbation, that sort of thing. It can also suggest selfish lovers or lotharios—those people who want you to want them and once you do, they couldn't care less. That's not a popular interpretation, but it is a thing I've both experienced and done, so....

I don't agree with the general consensus that this card represents *choice.* It's based on the image of Cupid/Eros shooting an arrow. When Cupid shows up, there's *no* choice—and that's frequently the case when falling in love. We can't control who we fall for. If we could, life would be much easier and relationships much more relaxing to navigate. Your heart follows Cupid's arrow for better or worse, that's it. And so, it can also represent passivity or helplessness, general lack of agency. When this card shows up, probably you don't have the options you think you do—or you're choosing not to move. Sometimes that's good, sometimes not.

These are somewhat tangential interpretations, but I centered them mostly to demonstrate the way the card appears *logically.* It can simply represent *love.* Passion, in the sense of enjoying something deeply. It doesn't need to be sexual or relational; I'm loving the device I'm writing this book on, and the card then could suggest that *thing.* It can also be partnerships of any kind, similar to lenormand's ring. I find that this happens more often than mere romantic love. We simply don't live in particularly romantic times.

07. The Chariot. Ninety percent of the time, this represents motion, going places, progress. It's simply a vehicle—though that vehicle could be metaphorical or literal. But let's not forget that a chariot isn't just *any* vehicle: it's a vehicle of status and one of war. If you're riding a chariot, then something is going on: you're either getting lauded or sent to the frontlines. The cards around it can tell you a lot about this. If The Chariot is paired with The Fool, say, we're in trouble. That could suggest things as dramatic as intoxicated driving, or as simple as not knowing where we're going. (If we're stuck in a rut, that could be a good thing!) Partnered with The Emperor, The Devil, or The Tower, we might discover particularly athletic sexual activity (because "driving," ahem). The Empress and The Chariot might suggest a purchase designed for wealth-signaling—like an expensive car or top-tier tech. The Chariot sometimes operates as a carrier, like a vowel sound, bringing one card to the next. Most of the time, though, I find it simply represents movement.

08. Justice. I'm mostly giving Justice the eighth position to tease anyone fundamentally tied to the Waite-Smith system. That said, it's also the original position of the card—*and* I tend not to really care much about the actual number of a major in a reading.

I get annoyed when this is the first card down in a spread because it means I'm going to have to figure out what *kind* of justice we're dealing with. It can suggest social justice, legal issues, or something more ephemeral. There are times when I've honestly wished it wasn't one of the cards, which may be one reason why I see it come up so much. There's probably a lesson in it I'm not yet learning. I've also never bought the idea that the card simply means *balance,* mostly because that just seems too easy. Then again, there's often scales on the card, so it makes sense we would consider the card that way.

Justice is an imagined idea, in many ways. If it were, the world would look very different. People wouldn't be sitting in jail for marijuana possession while I get to comfortably enjoy an edible at home and with the full support of the legal system in my state (which is making money off cannabis sales). As a reader, we need to figure out, then, whether this card is speaking about *real* justice (the kind that *should* be real) or the *justice system,* which is immensely biased. The other cards in the reading can offer guidance. The Hierophant paired with this card, for example, suggests the systems rather than the ideas. Paired with The Fool, perhaps we do get a more "blind" justice. Paired with The Tower, we could get more idealistic Justice—that may seem counter to the way The Tower is often read (negatively), but frequently the destruction (Tower) of the system (Justice) can be a good thing.

In many readings, this card represents "the right thing," as in this is the right thing to do at this moment. If you're asking about a job or a relationship, Justice suggests it's the "right" fit. (The use of the term "right" here implies that there is also a "wrong" fit—which isn't necessarily true. There can be more than one "right" thing in a given situation, or sometimes there aren't any good options and so this suggests the "goodest" option out of the lot.)

When this card represents things happening in the world, the odds favor the house—by which I mean, things will go best for whatever "institution" is being dealt with, or they will go according to the "letter of the law" rather than considering the context or extenuating circumstances. If, for example, you're living in France during the old days and steal a loaf of bread to feed your family and you get caught, the results will favor the law and not your personal circumstances. This is particularly true when in context to other "ruler" cards, like The Emperor, Empress, or Hierophant (though The Empress is more likely to see things in a fluid way than those other two—she's still an agent of the state at the end of the day and she's there to enforce law and order).

Other cards may tell you the opposite. Cards like The Devil, The Tower, Temperance, The Hermit, even The Magician can show us a *morally* just Justice rather than an institutionally just one. Note, though, that The Tower is tricky—it can sometimes simply represent "the house" (an older name of the card was *La Maison Dieu,* The House of God). I tend to view the card more liberally, so it's typically liberation. Context, as always, is the main guide. I'm biased enough to say it is frequently more freedom-centric, because it's blowing up something old.

09. The Hermit. Introversion and shyness. I know we want to go into the gorgeous spiritual landscape with this one, but let's call it what it is: being alone and liking it. Hermits make the choice to close themselves off from the world, and many of us introverts enjoy nothing more ourselves. When you're reading for that poor soul who can't find a relationship, this card is telling you that they either need to go out more or they're more suited to the single life—at least right now. When someone wants to know why they keep getting sick, maybe they've sheltered themselves too much and their resistance is lowered.

Of course, though, we also have wisdom, knowledge, mentorship. This can be external or it can come from within. I'm really not one to resort to "inner knowing" in readings, though, because if people knew the answer inside, they wouldn't need me. If the answer *is* inside, they need to find out where it is and what it's saying. I find too many readers let themselves off the hook with answers like, "You have the power inside you." Okay. What is it? Where? And how do I use it?

If you're thinking of going back to school, this is a good sign—though it does remind us we may need to sacrifice some social parts of our lives to do it.

10. The Wheel of Fortune. Change, cycles, flows, round things. Wheels, especially with The Chariot. It's a clue that we may lack agency; that what's happening will happen with or without our intervention. That's useful to know. The self-empowerment movement is fine, but as we know by this point, frequently centers privilege. You can't positive-think yourself out of a lot of situations, like poverty, abuse, queer-phobic parents, or disabilities. Sure, we can influence life; yes, there are times when we have agency. But not always. Sometimes life is life whether we want it to be or not. At the time I'm writing this, we've just been through a global health crisis. We're experiencing the results of climate change. Maybe these things *could* have been within humanity's control at one point, but we (the people who actually have the power to do something) ceded that responsibility and the wheel is turning as a result. This can also happen at the individual level. It's scary, but, for example, avoidance of getting medical treatment may mean a spin of the wheel with an uncertain outcome. Likewise driving around with unregistered cars or similar. When this card is central in a reading, I know the client will likely have to go through whatever is being gone through; it can't be avoided, no matter what they do. That's just how life works sometimes. But it can also signal that something bad is passing out of our lives, making room for something good. (Of course, if that's true, so is the opposite. The allegory of the wheel often shows us a king at the top who doesn't know he's about to make Humpty Dumpty look lucky.)

11. Strength. I'll give Waite this, when Justice falls in this position, you get a neat trio: Sentencing (Justice), Sentence (The Hanged Man), and Death. Anyway, this card (Strength) is exactly what it says: strength, fortitude, persistence, tenacity, all that jazz. Endurance, energy, output. This can be mental, physical, or spiritual, depending on the context. It also suggests zookeepers, vets, and dentists. Why? Because of the image of a figure typically peering into a lion's mouth. Haven't been flossing? This card suggests a scolding.

12. The Hanged Man. Consequences, consequences, consequences. That fucker ain't up there because he wants to be. He's up there because they strung him up. Now, he might be innocent—which is why Justice is such a difficult card—but he's up there and it doesn't look good for him. When this card shows up, it is either showing us a consequence or warning us that consequences will need to be paid. Sure, that might result in a perception shift, but that's really the realm of The Tower and the suit of swords for me.

It might describe someone who is well-endowed (hung), or you could see it as exercise (discomfort). I don't like it when artists make this card into a bat, only because bats are *supposed* to hang upside down and humans aren't. It's a small thing, but if I were making an animal-themed deck, I'd put a bear or something as The Hanged Man—they generally would not thrive in that position. This card suggests doing things we don't want to do or going places we don't want to go. If, for example, Rihanna asked you to go to the Met Gala with her, this card suggests you'll wish you were home.

The reason that this card has come to be seen as a perception shift has much to do with initiations, which are almost universally suffering experiences. Initiates the world over frequently endure massive hardships in order to experience the kind of ego death that leads to enlightenment. We see this in esoteric traditions, in Indigenous traditions, and even more folk-driven spaces. Zora Neale Hurston describes various initiations she experienced in working with Hoodoo and Voodoo practitioners across the southern US in her famous essay, "Hoodoo in America." It's not so much that The Hanged Man is hanging upside down that changes the point of view; it's the experience of remaining in a state of supreme discomfort. It is the suffering that yields revelations, not unlike Siddhartha under the tree. This card, in my experience, is less likely to signal seeing things in a new way, unless you're seeing them that way because you've been forced to sit in the corner and think about what you've done.

13. Death.[45] This card terrifies many, and indeed sent shivers of anxiety through my spine in my early years reading, and it's because we're afraid to find out we're going to die. Guess what? *We're all going to and we're each currently in the process of doing just that.* Sure, it has represented death for some readers. I haven't had that experience, but it doesn't mean I won't. More often than that, it signals inevitability: the thing going to happen has to happen because it's inevitable. Where it suggests something terminal, it's usually more in the sense of a punctuation mark than a life sentence. It signals stops, endings; fertilizer, decay, rot; compost, gardening, harvesting; spooky things, the unknown; and, of course, orgasms (once called "little deaths"). Don't overthink this card. Chances are if this signaled the physical death of someone, you'd know and there would be *plenty* of other indicators within and without the spread.

I think you have to figure this card out in part based on your cosmology. I'm reminded that there are many traditions in the world where it doesn't mean "finality." I have been rightfully scolded from time to time for assuming that everyone thinks in terms of death as an ending. How you view death itself will influence your reading of Death as a card. This is as it should be, and one reason why I don't actually love sharing my own perspectives on the cards. I don't want anyone looking at my meanings and thinking they're "right." They're not. What they are is the right foundation for me to start from. What happens after that is up to the reading, the context, and the vibes of that day.

14. Temperance. One reason I struggled in my early years with reading was the implication that both Justice and Temperance suggested *balance*. While this card actually has nothing indicating balance in it, the fact that *moderation* is a balanced approach allows me to find this card more typically representing the concept of equality or balance.

Moderation is the key concept for this card, which is what Temperance really means. This can also suggest harmony, because of the card's gentle nature. This can signal cooking, blending, mixing—bar tenders, bakers, chefs. If you're seeing this card for someone who likes a cocktail, it might be a sign they need to cool it. On the other hand, if this card is for someone who tends to be a stick-in-the-mud, then it can suggest living a little. This card seems to deal more with addiction than The Devil does. Because the card is temperate, its own other is *in*temperance. Wands and cups with this card may suggest that level of intemperance. Coins and swords,

45 Note: in many traditions, this card doesn't get a number at all; in others, it doesn't get a name. Either way, we know it when we see it.

which are both metal, may give you a sense of tempering—which is part of what happens when something solid is melted and brought back to a lower temperature for strengthening the object, so metal-working but chocolate goes through this.

The Temperance movement was a unique moment in world history in which a whole bunch of proto-Karens got together to stop people in a "free" country from drinking. This matters because this card can stand in for similarly misguided and problematic movements that say one thing and deep down are actually doing something much crueler. (Refer to my summary of prohibition in Chapter 10.)

15. The Devil. What's amusing to me about this card is the way in which so many tarot readers cling to the shockingly Christian-influenced meaning. I invite you, dear reader, to free yourself from that. The Devil as we understand it in the Christo-Colonial world is based on pre-Abrahamic gods and beings who represented sex, music, indulgence, wine, harvest, magic, chaos, and "good trouble." The Devil is "bad" because organized religion loves (and in fact, *needs*) an enemy. You cannot get people to give you their hard-earned money unless you're protecting them from some dangerous "other." Thus, we can take this card to represent anyone who is othered and villainized for their history, culture, beliefs, or kinks. If this card does depict imprisonment or entrapment, it's only in the way that conservatism attempts to constrain so many parts of who we are naturally. Or, if that's not the issue and we feel the card is strongly depicting servitude, then it's possibly a kink.

What we're looking at in this card is the part of ourselves connected to the Earth, to the gods of fire and the forest, to Pan and Bacchus and Demeter and Hades and Persephone, and all the various kinksters of myth. The Devil reminds us of the pre-civilization parts of ourselves (including those that use divination). This card represents an invitation to be who we *truly* are in our core, our most authentic selves; our naked, unvarnished, un-Photoshopped selves. I have a theory that we are never more our essence than at the moment of orgasm or being startled. In those moments we are totally stripped of the part of ourselves that curates what we look like, what we sound like, and even how much we care about what other people think of us. That's what this card is—that part of who we are that is essential.

Unlike The Hanged Man, the folks shackled to The Devil are *into it.* This is who we are pre-shame, pre-self-censoring, pre-indoctrination. It is the inverse of The Hierophant, and often esoteric decks will mirror The Hierophant or The Lovers in this card. The accepted implication of this being that The Devil perverts or taints what these "purer" cards do. That is nonsense. If anything, The Hierophant perverts The Devil by showing it shame, by making it feel disgusting. The Devil is the queer person, for example; The Hierophant becomes the institutions teaching that queer person shame. When we see this card, it's worth reconnecting to who we are beyond our fears of what people or society will think.

I'm sure it will shock you to know, too, that this is a card associated with sex and sexuality. It's one reason why I think it should be associated with Scorpio, rather than that sign applying to Death. (I understand that Scorpio has been associated with Death long before the tarot, but I still feel strongly that The Devil is a better fit.) In this card we celebrate kinks, desires, and the "darker" parts of being a human.

On the other side of the coin, of course, it can also mean over-indulgence. Most of us need to function to some degree by societal norms, and if we're given to over-indulgence this can put us out of step with the rest of the world. That can sometimes be good, but sometimes not. If you see a lot of cups cards around this one, that's where the more addictive tendencies may come into play—particularly if we see this card's predecessor, Temperance, in the reading, too. We can't give way fully to the feral, no matter how much we'd like to sometimes. At least these days.

16. The Tower. I once heard that this card is potentially mis-labeled and should instead be called *Lightning*. This card can be viewed as the beginning of a series of lights. Each one getting progressively brighter and leading us to the awakening depicted in Judgment, not unlike the Sun coming up in the morning and waking us up.[46] It's sort of a forward-dawning. I like this because this card can often suggest mercurial things, like tech and electricity—both are lightning-like in my mind—as well as ideas, which "strike."

Here too we find perception shifts, and likely more here than in The Hanged Man. These may be massive perception shifts, the kind that happen during societal change or, say, pandemics. But they can be smaller and more "lifey." If you're someone who can't face the idea of privilege, you may find that you're forced one day to come face-to-face with it. That's a Tower moment. Sadly, not everyone who is resistant to understanding the world and how it works experiences these moments. Life would be better for many of us if everyone did. But it does not, and so, in a way, you need to be ready and open for this card to appear. You may not *feel* ready, but likely life has been preparing you for this moment. It's harder on people who haven't been paying attention or who are pretending everything is okay when the reality is far from it. But many of us can sense when a big change is on the way, and I hear so many clients say exactly that when they sit down for a reading. Often times, divination can help us prepare for Tower moments, or at least help us figure out what to do with them after the fact. It's also true that, like an earthquake, Tower moments can have *aftershocks* that will continue for years after—these are the little "ah-ha" moments of revelation that come once you actually start seeing things as they are, rather than through thick layers of bias.

There is, of course, sexual energy here, and though it's typically referred to as masculine, I don't do that. Yes, the image of The Tower is often phallic, but that's just because towers are. It can represent any kind of sexual release, or releases of any kind. If you're curious whether someone will be freed from jail, this card bodes well for them—whether that's good for you, though, is another matter.

46 The actual Sun, in this case. Not the card.

If paired with The Fool, klutzes beware. If paired with wands, certainly sexuality. With cups, we might find wet dreams or similar, as well as sudden realizations of emotion: "I had no idea I loved him that much!" With swords and The Devil, dirty talk (swords, talk; The Devil, "dirty"). We can move between the sacred and profane, here. In fact, this card may be the meeting place of the sacred and the profane.

Like Lenormand, I find that this card sometimes represents any kind of building or an institution known for its buildings, even if they're not falling apart. Older buildings could be suggested because the structure crumbles, but we'd need other cards to get that. If you're trying to buy a house and you get this card, the house should go through a deep inspection before anything is signed. But, really, the building itself or the people in the building can be found here, in which case the drama or destruction isn't really important. Again, other cards and/or the question will guide you—in this case, what's *not* shown in the reading might help you out. If there's nothing else explosive (like the higher numbers in the suit of wands) then you may be looking at something more banal.

17. The Star. This card is frequently associated with hope, but I find that really useless in readings—at least my readings. (As always, this is my experience, not the law.) I tend to view this card as a compass, the way that stars are used for navigation. This is where you're going, what you aspire to, what you dream of. In most readings it tends to represent direction. I think of it as your GPS. This card tells you that you're going *somewhere;* the other cards and the question will tell you what that somewhere is.

Stars are notable and noticeable, and so celebrities and celebrity culture can show up here. If you're going to an audition and get this card, that's an excellent sign. Add The Sun—a big spotlight—and likely you're gonna book the gig, kid. Beyond metaphors, stars are also flaming balls of gas. This, then, could signal stomach issues, heartburn, reflux—or people who are actual gasbags (like those who can't shut up).

18. The Moon. One of the main reasons the astrological associations for tarot are so ineffective to me is that The Moon is syncretized to...*Pisces?* I mean...*look.* I get that there's a "reason" for things; I just think those reasons are bad. As I've said, The Moon should be associated with the moon; Cancer belongs with The High Priestess; The Fool should be Aries. Anyway. Right now, I'm just pointing out why so much of esotericism drives me bonkers: it's almost obsessed with being oblique. I get it. It's worked for a lot of people. Fine. But it don't work for me, kids, and this correspondence is the main reason why. *The moon is The Moon!* Full stop.

This card is all about attraction (the moon pulls both the oceans and us). Cycles, moods. A month. Intuition. Reflection. The cards surrounding it have a lot of influence because this card is so fluid, it needs other cards to contain it—much the way Water works (too much Water in a reading can also require containment). With The Lovers, romance; with The Wheel, cycles; with lots of wand cards, deep attraction; with lots of swords, deeply clear intuition. Meanwhile, if there's a lot of

Earth (coins/pentacles) in a spread, The Moon is going to have a lot of influence over the reading, in the same way that the moon can impact much on Earth—including people's behavior. It can suggest things not seeming real or the inability to tell the difference between fantasy and reality. It might mean fantasies *becoming* reality if there are really active cards (knights and wands). It can suggest animals and animal instinct, and so of course reproduction.

I once had a Facebook argument with a know-it-all straight white dude who was spouting all kinds of stuff about how astrology is for stupid people. I told him people are mostly water and scientists (as well as cops) have long said people act differently under full moons. We are pulled to it like the water. "People are not an ocean," he said.

"Speak for yourself," I said, "I absolutely am." Fundamentalism is fundamentalism, and I don't like it wherever I find it.

19. The Sun. Somehow, we find an astrological correspondence that actually makes sense. It must have been accidental.[47]

This card is all about spotlights and attention—but remember, those aren't always good things. The best disinfectant is sunlight, so what's hidden will be revealed—especially when we find this card with Judgement. Gardening, social spaces, parks, the outdoors. Hot flashes. Friends. Masons (bricklayers) because there's often a brick wall in images of this card. Stoneworkers, then, and other tradespeople. Those who work outside, including lifeguards, swimmers, coaches, and athletes. There's a queerness to this card, too, as it often depicts two naked youths of the same gender presentation. So it can be homoerotic, which I mean both literally and in the way of things that just seem "kinda gay" (in a good way).

Getting burned is going to show up here, too; especially with the Nine or Ten of Wands. Things getting hot, which can be good (sexy!) or bad (things closing in), and so of course hot places: kitchens, say, and anyone who works there. Potters (because of kilns) and brick *makers*, that sort of thing. Sexy people. With The Devil, maybe

47 I'm teasing—mostly. I do understand people find the traditional correspondences useful, and if you do—wonderful. I find them specious. It's the esoteric thing. You have to really *learn* the correspondences, which these societies loved because if you couldn't learn it, you couldn't play. It's exclusive. And while I find reading about all the correspondences fascinating, I also find myself rolling my eyes a lot. I feel strongly that the correspondences should be based not on some half-understood esoteric doctrine, but rather on the behaviors of the cards and the signs and planets associated with them. Also, tarot and astrology are, frankly, not a natural fit, especially because astrology is less fixed than tarot—in the sense that there will never be a new tarot card "discovered," but astronomers do find new entities in the sky. Every time astrology changes, and it should, we don't remake the correspondences. And we should. Good books on astrology highlight the ways in which the more recently "discovered" planets correspond closely with what was happening in the world at the time they were "discovered." Tarot should evolve, too.

this is some really sweaty sex; with The Hermit, maybe it's hot yoga. There could be some narcissism here, particularly with watery cards and The Moon (Narcissus stared at himself in the water, and that's only possible when there's enough light to reflect you). If you have fair skin, make sure you're minding your SPF; if you're in a bad situation, this is going to suggest "hot water" or being under one of those hanging lamps in bad TV cop dramas. For those of us who like attention, this can signal that the attention is getting to be *too much*. Lots of court cards could suggest who the audience is and what they're thinking/feeling about the subject.

20. Judgement. Alarm clocks and wakeup calls. Archeology of any kind, including spiritual/emotional. Grave robbing. Places that are similar to graves, so dank places, small and closed spaces, musty, dark, and deep places—but also, of course, being freed from those places. The cards around it will give you appropriate context. Communities (there's often a lot of people in this card) and cults (secret communities or death-obsessed groups) and other clubs (The High Priestess might suggest how exclusive it is; The Tower how inclusive). Séances. Polyamory, especially with cards like The Lovers, Hierophant, and Devil. Coming out of the closet, spilling tea, revelations of secrets (especially with The Sun—which means that with The Moon, this might mean kept secrets). Dormitories or hotels (places with a lot of beds [coffins]). Jazz clubs and dances and places with live music (the people and the trumpet), including church. This could mean "taking the children to church" in a metaphorical way, or "giving people life, hunty." If you know, you know. (Take that, esotericists. I can say cryptic things, too.)

21. The World. Everything—good things and bad. Having it all! Or having too much shit to carry. Having the whole world on your shoulders. Unclear priorities, as in "if everything is important, nothing is important"; focusing on too many things to the detriment of specifics. Taking on too many projects. Dancing. Nudism. Freedom, self-confidence, lack of ego. Parties, especially with Judgment and The Devil. Maps, atlases, travel and travel plans, as well as things connected to those concepts. When partnered with The Chariot, conveyances for long-distance travel: planes, trains, wagons. It makes anything around it more intense. Big things, round things, rotund things. The bigger picture. The immensity of a situation. The cards around it will tell you whether this is a yay or boo situation.

In exploring how I work with the minors, it's worth knowing the primary tool I work with is element and number. Everything else (artwork, keywords, impulse) comes after I consider the element and the number. This isn't right or wrong, good or bad; it's just how I do it. Here's a summary of how I see the elements and the numbers. These have evolved over time, like my foundational interpretations of the majors, and will continue to do so. At least I hope they will.

Fire/Wands. Passions, sensations, creativity, sexuality, art, things we really care about, our life's work. It can suggest heat in all forms. It can be consuming, it can be dangerous. It needs oxygen (swords/Air) and fuel (pentacles/Earth) in order to sustain, and without them it can burn out. It's fast-moving, temperamental, opinionated, but it's also generous and beautiful and captivating. It's cooking, theatrics, flare. Arguments live here (particularly partnered with a lot of Air), but really exciting adventures also live here (partnered with a lot of Earth, potentially, or cards like The Chariot). Sex lives here, paintings and compositions and stories live here, too. Whatever our art is, find it here—including Excel spreadsheets and teeth cleaning, if that's our calling.

Fire/wands will reflect outdoorsy people and those who work with their hands. Kinesthetic people, people who *do*. Verbs. People who work with gardens and landscaping and woodworking live here. Divas and prima donnas live here, as do celebrities and star-fuckers. Rockstars, groupies, sex workers, and electricians are likely to be represented by this suit. I associate Fire with South and Summer.

The suit of wands obviously takes all that fiery energy, but the tool itself—wands—also suggests things that are important in readings. Wands are of course magical, so magic lives in this suit. But so do weapons. Wands—or batons—are clumsy and used primarily for bashing and bludgeoning. This can represent clumsy fighting or people who are unskilled at something (this of course is the antithesis of how I think of the suit of Fire, but remember that everything is its own opposite). I dislike the term "unskilled labor," as it's a capitalist myth designed to destroy people's humanity—but if you have people who do think in those terms, then they're likely showing up as the suit of wands.

In the old days, this suit (and its mother, the suit of clubs) was associated with the working class, with farmers, and with the trades. So, this suit can represent anything related to similar fields today. From a class perspective, lots of wand cards indicate someone who is dependent on labor to survive—probably hard labor, in the sense of things one really has to put their back into. This is the proletariat, if you want to get into that language, but I think it's easier to think in terms of people who are out in the field (wands/wood grows out there), so this includes anyone who may travel for work or journeyman or the self-employed.

Water/Cups. In a lot of systems, Fire and Water are oppositional. Though I once read that way, I don't much anymore. If you're curious, the elemental dignities as I learned them related to tarot (this is something that comes from astrology but has been adjusted over time) are: Adversarial: Fire/Water, Air/Earth; Complimentary: Fir/Air, Water/Earth; Neutral: Fire/Earth, Air/Water. Obviously, an element with its own element (Water/Water, say) is also complimentary. This was helpful in a spread I used to do for general readings, in which each spoke of a five-pointed star represented one of the elements. If a Fire card fell in a Water position, I knew there was going to be conflict.

These days, I think more in terms of how the elements act in the world rather than in terms of philosophical behavior. Fire and Water are a lot alike: they can both cancel the other out if dominant, they're both heavily creative or destructive, and when they're in full force, we notice them more than the other two elements of Air and Earth. When Fire and Water are combined in balance, they can create steam that pushes engines forward—but when that steam is dammed up, there can be a big explosion. Water and Fire both need release.

Like Water, Fire experiences sensations—but Fire experiences more physical sensations and Water more internal ones. With Fire, for example, you're getting an orgasm; with Water, you're getting the sensations that makes way for the orgasm. This is an example of how these two supposedly adversarial elements can work together: Water gets you the attention of someone you want; Fire makes you both enjoy the interplay.

Water is more ephemeral, and so it represents feelings and things that can be difficult to put into words. (Water is connected to words, Air, because it's made up of oxygen. But while Air can put things into words because it is clear-eyed and ruthless, Water is fluid and wishy-washy and so has a hard time expressing itself in that airy way.) Because Water always takes the path of least resistance, it can suggest "easy" things—or it can suggest taking the easy path. When our way is blocked, Water helps us get around.

Water cleanses, clears, and blesses, but it also floods and damages. Too much of it can be overwhelming; too little, unhealthy. Intuition lives here, along with psychic phenomena. Nostalgia lives here, but nostalgia is a tricky concept. It's often considered lovely, but the past is only lovely if you have something lovely to look back on—or thick enough rose-colored glasses to make it possible to look back on trauma romantically.

If Fire is lust, Water is love. Ideally, a romance or relationship reading will have a good mix of both. In a couple's reading, if one partner is all Fire and one is all Water, they may fight a lot—particularly about sex. The fiery one won't be big on foreplay and will want to get to the money shot ASAP; the watery one will want to be seduced and likely will be hurt by the fiery partner's lack of emotional intimacy prior to physical intimacy. The watery one may be unable to perform sexually if they're not cared for in this way; the fiery one may get bored making out and get frustrated that every encounter needs to be a big production number.

Surrounded by sunny cards, the water is crisp, clear, and blue; surrounded by cloudy cards, the water is gray, dismal, seaweedy. Here we find people in caretaking roles, hospice, massage, spa therapists, healers, even psychics. These are beachy people, surfers, boaters, fishers. These folks are going to be fairly sensitive and probably indecisive—even moody. They're dreamy and idealistic and may have a hard time facing reality.

Cups/hearts were traditionally associated with the clergy, likely because of the chalice's role in the Catholic mass. It's fitting. These jewel-encrusted cups are meant to be vessels for the blood of Jesus—a humble carpenter who loathed ostentatious frippery in religious practice, as well as the merging of faith with capitalism. The clergy represents the dismissal of Jesus's true values and their love affair with wealth and hypocrisy. Thus, these cards can suggest people or communities that are two-faced. It's going to showcase people who have money—probably other people's money. Though Earth is the suit associated with money, if you're looking for someone perpetrating a Ponzi scheme, you would likely see cups and coins together.

Cups can more optimistically represent anyone who works with vessels: bar tenders, submariners, dishwashers, servers, vintners and brewers, bottlers, even pool boys. It can also represent anyone who works with the sea or the ocean: captains, marine biologists, public works employees, sanitation employees, divers, coast guards, swimmers, etc. Those who work in chemistry might be discovered here, particularly with the intellect of swords present. Cups hold, they contain, so it can suggest jailers, too, and people held (again, the influence of wands or swords—as bars—might signal this, but some relevant context would be important, too).

I associate Water with East and Spring. Again, not traditional and frequently annoying to people. Alas, where I sit on planet Earth, water is to my east and we notice water most when it starts to melt, hence spring.

Air/Swords. Where Fire and Water are attention-seeking, Earth and Air are more behind-the-scenes. Air is important and always present, but we're rarely aware of it. The times we do notice are when it's not behaving—like in windstorms and hurricanes. Because weather is influenced so much by temperature, Air can be heavily reliant on Fire for its behavior. From a seasonal perspective, I associate Air with North and Winter.

Air is words, language, communication, thinking. The stuff that comes from our brain. Swords are often full of negative images (which is one reason I typically prefer pip or Marseille-style decks) but they're no more or less negative than the other elements. The negative view of swords/Air comes from old playing card associations that link this suit's predecessor, spades, to difficulty and death. What's funny about this to me is that these older meanings come from the world of fortune telling. The Golden Dawn just accepted that and esotericized them, but they kept the overarching fortune telling themes. Go figure.

The swords are only painful because learning means growing pains. It's not a comfortable suit, but it's not an evil one either. True, when you leave outdated perceptions behind, it can hurt or you can feel the loss—but you're only losing something limiting. The classic Waite-Smith Three of Swords (influenced famously by the Sola Busca deck) is often assumed to represent heartbreak. But if we take the image apart, we see the element of Air (swords) piercing the heart (a pump, and the thing that keeps us alive), delivering oxygen to our blood. That card shows the exact thing that keeps us alive. It also shows the intellectual mind (swords) melding with the emotional (the heart), giving us the union of sensation and rationality—an excellent combo for navigating life. Even when working with Waite-Smith decks, I find it exciting to deconstruct what I think I'm seeing and re-examine it from a new contextual point of view.

The swords will typically show us "indoor cats"—somewhat introverted, as cerebral persons tend to be. (I'm one.) Why go out and be amongst the throngs when being alone is so much easier? We'll find teachers here, along with therapists, philosophers, writers, analysts, neurologists, brain surgeons—but also surgeons generally. Anyone who works with words, education, communication, or the mind. Mediators would show up here, too. Folks represented by this suit are going to be *more* objective than others, but remember that objectivity is mostly mythological because we all operate from bias.

Traditionally, the suit of swords/spades was associated with the military for obvious reasons. Of the four suits, this is the most "refined" of the weapons. Also the most expensive. It requires no training to bludgeon someone with a club, but a sword does require training and skill to use well, depending on the kind of sword. Of course, we may find folks with military careers or backgrounds here, then, but also anyone involved in international relations or diplomacy. We're always going to find the "law" here, so lawyers and cops, judges and magistrates. It's a short walk from there to the politician, whose job is technically "law" (although in the US, the job is more about stroking the emotional cocks of super PAC's and other high-rolling donors). Because of the connection to politics, a partnership of coins/pentacles and swords might suggest political donors and donations. We'll also find journalists (of any kind), editors and editorialists, and pundits here. Want to start a podcast? Swords in a reading are a good sign. The media generally would show up here, too. Other suits can refine it. Wands and swords might suggest entertainment; cups and swords, perhaps talk shows and those weepy dramas; and coins and swords, reality TV.

Because swords are expensive to make and are frequently made from expensive materials, they're definitely the most "elevated" of the suits in terms of class and station. Anyone who has power over anyone else could be repped by this suit. Swords have always been a status symbol, so they can represent someone with status—or someone who wants it. The sciences would show up here, too, thanks to the mental qualities. The other elements or cards could tell you what type. Swords and Judgment might suggest archeological sciences, say; swords and The Empress might suggest gynecology; swords and The Emperor might suggest "hard sciences."

Earth/Coins/Pentacles. For what it's worth, I prefer "coins" as a suit symbol here, just because they're "earthier." But, really, it doesn't much matter. I'll take both over Crowley's "disks." Yikes. (Why didn't he call them "orbs"? That would have been more on brand and another link to astrology—though an astrological orb isn't a disk.)

In Earth, we find everything not listed above—but primarily jobs, family, day-to-day stuff, finances. Here we find people who work in banks or retail, vendors and merchants, folks whose livelihood involves working with money. We'll also find hikers here, and paired with wands, farmers. Anything related to sustenance or health may show up here. We're more likely to see nurses and technicians here than doctors, who are likely to show up in the "bougier" swords suit—but that would also depend somewhat on what kind of doctor and where they choose to practice. With Earth, we're looking at a doctor in a walk-in or community health center, or with an NGO like Doctors Without Borders; in swords, we're going to have surgeons (because of knives), neurologists (because of the brain), and anyone who is considered "elite" (which frequently just means choosing only to see people who can afford to pay exorbitant rates).

I'm often interested in how much Earth shows up in a reading to see how *grounded* a situation is. That's neither good nor bad; it always depends on context. Someone without a lot of Earth in a reading may be in for a good turn if they've been feeling stuck in a rut or weighed down. On the other hand, someone with all cups or swords in a business reading really needs some Earth to ground them. It's conditional. Ideally, I want to see a mix of all elements most of the time, but that's actually not always a good thing either. Context, context, context.

In the olden days, coins (or its predecessor, diamonds) represented the merchant class. This of course connects the suit to money, which Waite didn't like—hence the change to the more esoteric pentacles. It's easy not to want to think about money when you have it, eh? This suit is going to represent "middle class" people, typically—but it could suggest people below the poverty line, particularly with the suit of wands. The interesting thing is that finance isn't particularly "earthy," so there's a little bit of polarity here. Finance takes us away from the earth. But it is also an earthly concern, which is why it applies. The esotericists lived in the land of cups and swords; the rest of us mere mortals live in the world of coins/pentacles.[48] So, while this can represent the financial world generally, it also represents anyone who works—and any work that is a job. Coins/pentacles on their own or with swords are going to suggest things we do for money. If it's with cups or wands, here we'll start to see people's *vocation.* A vocation is a *calling,* in the way of something we're fated to do or something central to who we are. Someone who wants to make divination into a business should be happy to see a nice mix of wands, cups, and coins in a reading. A little swords energy can help them be smart about their plans, but

48 Who lives in wands? We all do. Fire is energy, which every single thing has, feels, and is made of.

too much Air/swords could make them start to question the viability of such an "outlandish" field.

It was learning a numerological system that unlocked tarot for me, at least in the second half of my reading career. *Tarot on Earth,* my first book, is in many ways dedicated to numbers, if only because numerology showed me a way of exploring the minors without worrying too much about what some artist put there. I love artists and I love the art of the decks I work with. But every image on a tarot card is an artistic statement or judgment of a card's potential. A card isn't the image; it's an interpretation of some of the correspondences associated with that card. Pamela Colman Smith's drawings were visual interpretations of the esoteric titles given the cards by the esotericists whose work laid the foundation for the Golden Dawn. They are useful and well-loved. But they aren't the totality of the card's potential.

Generally, odd numbers destabilize. That's not a bad thing, in fact it can be quite good. Context dictates its reality. Even numbers are stabilizing. That can be wonderful after a moment of upheaval, but it can also make them conservative and vain, married to the status quo and the ego which loves the status quo. Five tends to be the most unstable; four, the most stable; six, the most re-stabilizing. As the higher numbers become mixes of lower ones, we also find lots of exciting potential. They have their own meanings but also contain all the meanings of the numbers that make them up. Nine, for example, is three threes. So it can take the three-ness of a suit/element and amp it to the max. It's also six plus three, so that could take the six-ness of a suit/element and maximize it. It's a fun thing to consider. Seven is four (stability) plus three (expansion), setting itself at odds against itself. This tension is exciting, and in many ways tension is where interpretation lives: the space between the question or desired outcome and the cards and their meanings left to answer those.

In other words, numerology is fun.

My system comes from a mix of other systems. You can read about how I developed them in *Tarot on Earth*.

A Digression on Binaries, Polarities, and Dualities

This is as good a time as any to talk about the "twoness" of life. Mystical traditions (which is in my mind, are the broader world of "magical" traditions, including groups like The Hermetic Order of the Golden Dawn and its eventual offshoots) are heavily connected with the binary: male/female, day/night, good/bad, active/passive, etc. Because many people's experiences of humanity have lived in the binary, I can see why this happens. It is the mother/father relationship that has defined much of life. That said, this concept is outmoded. That's an arguably privileged thing to say, not coming from a mystical tradition or cosmology based on this twoness. And yet I'm still going to say it. Our understanding of the world has changed and so must we.

There is a difference between *polarity* and *binary*. I prefer the term *polarity* in the work we do because a pole is *one thing*. The polar opposites are simply *two ends* of *one thing*. They are two points on the same line. They're far apart, but not different. They *are* the pole. The north and south poles are two ends of the same pole, as are the midheaven and IC astrologically—as well as the ascendant and descendant. They are the same line, just different ends of it. In astrology, an *opposition* sounds like it's dealing with things that are against (opposed to) one another in the emotional sense. It's not. They're opposite in the geographic or mathematical sense. In my case, my sun sign (Leo) and my ascendant (Aquarius) are in opposition. What I've learned both from living my life and learning about astrology is that these two points aren't fighting each other as much as see-sawing. There are times where my sunny Leonine nature has helped me cope—particularly in my childhood, when I dreamed of making a life in the arts. That kept me motivated while putting up with the bullies.

In fact, my Aquarian nature was counterproductive in my childhood because it highlighted all the things about me I didn't want anyone to know: that I *was*, in fact, weird and that I didn't fit in. It was my Leo-ness that eventually helped me out of my situation. When I made people laugh, they stopped disliking me. Sure, that also turned me into an asshole—the thing I often made people laugh at was each other. (Hey, I was bullied. I learned from the best.) The older I get, though, the more my weirdness and inability to fit in (Aquarius) becomes not only more important, but the main way in which I get attention (Leo). I don't mean this in a self-effacing way. My individuality is what draws students to my classes and viewers to my videos. It also creates conflict with people, because I'm not interested in boot-licking—not anymore. In Leo mode, I did a lot to fit in. I wanted people to like me. In Aquarian mode, I don't care whether people like me or not. Sometimes that makes me misanthropic. It is a blend of the Leo (who wants to be liked) and the Aquarian (who loves iconoclasm) that shows me at my best.

The opposition isn't about being opposed, per se, but learning how these two polarities can become their best by recognizing that they are *one thing*. Binary suggests something is two things, or really one of two things; polarity suggests the duality, the twoness, of one thing: two points on the pole.

Modern fortune tellers would do well to recall this, particularly when explaining things typically referred to in the binary. I've said elsewhere in this book that "nothing is all one thing." What I really mean, in my sneaky way, is the exact opposite: *everything is one thing*. We are our own opposites. They aren't two parts of us; they *are* us. The ego makes us think we're something, but that's just an impression of ourselves based on our goals and insecurities. Masculine *is* feminine. It has to be. One doesn't exist without the other. We don't know what masculine is if we don't have feminine to contextualize it. Because of that, they cannot exist without each other. So, they both do and do not exist. For us as people, we're points along a spectrum of the masculine/feminine polarity. We are both; we aren't either. Day *is* night, because if there is no night, then day is meaningless. Love *is* ambivalence as much as ambivalence *is* love. We cannot know we love something if we don't have things we don't care about to compare with. You'll note that I didn't say "hate," here. Hate isn't the opposite of love. When you hate something, you feel a great deal for it. That's more like love. Ambivalence is the opposite, because that means not having any particular feeling one way or another. Love and hate are points along a scale of feelings; ambivalence isn't anywhere on that scale (or you could say it's the midpoint between the two, but I don't think so—the midpoint between hate and love is confusion or even loving to hate or hating to love). We can't say something is real unless we know what something unreal is. Everything is one thing, and nothing is one thing.

The binary has become a somewhat lazy way of talking about polarity. It's lazy because it doesn't want to acknowledge the damage binary thinking does to people and to the planet. Perhaps in ancient times, the binary wasn't so dangerous. I think it was, though; because war and enslavement and othering have always been part of humanity's navigation of experience. Good/evil has done more to harm people than any other concept. Nothing is good or evil. What is good or evil depends on context. Poison is evil. Unless it's killing cancer cells. A rival tribe is evil until another, more dangerous enemy forces unexpected alliances. Good/bad is why somehow climate change isn't a Christian issue. How the hell can pouring poison onto the planet your god supposedly made for you *not* be evil? And yet, the binary has made it so "Christianity" is aligned with conservatism and of climate denial. As far as humanity is concerned, the only god that matters is the one we live on and that sustains us. And yet it's not a religious issue?

Binaries are myths but they're powerful enough to keep us warring against each other and often ourselves. And one of many reasons why I'm grateful for the conversation about gender in modern life is the realization that this is so. We are all non-binary because we are not one thing. We are collections of polarities. We may lean to certain sides of certain poles, but we all have poles and we are all somewhere on them.

Because of this, I feel that focusing on divinatory binaries is something we have an opportunity to evolve out of. Not only will it be more inclusive, but it will also yield more accurate readings. Even our obstacles in life are part of us. They wouldn't be obstacles if they weren't in the way of where we're going. Otherwise, they're just *stuff*.

One. Seeds, beginnings, impulses; unity, solitude, individuality; selfishness; primacy; supremacy.

Two. Magnetism, push/pull, attraction/repulsion, polarities of all kinds; coupling, pairing, sexuality (monogamy); splitting, splintering, splicing.

Three. Expansion/expansiveness, birth and children (as in the expansion of a family or even a canon of work), triangulation, stepping outside of something, sexuality (polyamory).

Four. Consistency, stability, security; conservatism, apathy, boredom, blandness.

Five. Shakeups, messes, and mayhem—not always bad. The status quo holds no sway here. Conflicts, but also perception shifts and revelations.

Six. Beauty and loveliness, but also vanity and navel-gazing (particularly when paired with sevens). Repairing and reparations, renovations; healings and reconstructions.

Seven. Luck. Self-reflection and reconsideration. Similar to six, we get a lot of "re" words, which makes sense because we're coming from the midpoint to the final climb. Whereas six "re" words are often used primarily in that construction, seven "re" words often exist without that prefix. Re-evaluation, re-mapping, and re-setting. These are things we often do, but that we have to do again—frequently, that we have to re-learn. It's also a mystical number, for sure. Made up of three (growth) and four (conservatism), suggesting tension.

Eight. Vocation, effort, work, labor. As four plus four, it can be *major* conservatism—or security. But I find it mostly related to work and effort.

Nine. Three times three gives us explosive progress and expansion. The feeling that we'll never get where we're going, despite having put so much work into it. Burnout will live here, as well as other kinds of exhaustion. Anxiety, insomnia, etc., If you're training for a marathon, this can signal stamina—particularly with Strength and/or The Chariot.

Ten. Conclusions. I don't think *marriage;* I think *divorce.* Final curtain. (Incidentally, this is one feature of the Waite-Smith deck that I love: the number of cards in the minors that look like they're showing action on a stage rather than real life. There's a dimension to this that can be really fun.) *Fullness,* other cards can show if it's a culmination or conclusion. Jean-Michel David, author of *Reading the Marseille Tarot* (my favorite book on the topic), explores the way resources diminish as they go from one to ten. With one, you have the fullness of the suit, but it gets split over and over until it's split into ten. So, you can see ten as the diminishment of the energy of a situation or suit.

Reading the minors begins by taking the qualities or vibe of the suit/element and combining that with the qualities or vibe of the number. Hence the idea that the Ten of Cups is more about relationships ending than beginning. The Three of Swords becomes less about heartbreak and more about expansive thinking. Context drives this. If the reading has no need for expansive thinking, that's not what the Three of Swords means this time. This is why I always use *at least* three cards in a reading, and five or nine is even more common.

I don't ignore the pictures or titles/keywords, although I do often prefer to work with decks that have fairly neutral imagery. I like to lay out the cards without igniting any immediate emotional response in myself or the client. This gives me the chance to explore themes and trends without having to race to start explaining away an alarming picture. The image is actually the last thing I tend to look at and when I do, I'm not really interested in what it usually means. I'm more interested in what it might suggest *in that context.* I'm also interested in where people are looking or how the cards seem to flow across the spread. Are there three cards all flowing in the same direction? In a Waite-Smith deck, this might be literal—all the characters are looking to the left, say. In a non-representational deck, like the stunning *Margarete Petersen* (one of my go-tos), the art will tend to offer flows—like lava, pulling you in specific directions. The interrelationship of the cards, the interplay of the figures on them (if there are any) are where I'm focusing my attention. Then, and only then, do I tend to weigh whether the artwork has any meaning in and of itself.

Sometimes specific pieces of information on a card will jump out. Sometimes it's something I've never noticed before. The tiny snail on Smith's Nine of Pentacles is a good example. I recall noticing that in a reading for the first time and it definitely added to the picture of someone who needed to enjoy their time alone (it was a relationship reading for someone who wanted to be coupled and wasn't). In the version of the Waite-Smith that I've been doing the readings for this book with, there isn't a snail.[49] Though it's a replica of the Colman-Smith drawings, the artist painted them herself and didn't include the snail (or the ships in the Three of Wands), and this in a reading could suggest something because I know that those elements are *usually* there, but not in this version of the deck.

While I prefer neutral decks generally, that's not exclusively the case. And I try to mix up the decks I use so that I don't get stale. There are a handful I go to most often, but I'll bring different ones to different events, sometimes to match a theme.

---

49 This is an independently produced and published version of the Waite-Smith called *The Starlight Illuminated* by Carol Herzer. It's a gorgeous deck, full of rich, vibrant color—much more attractive than most mass-produced versions of the same deck.

Sometimes not. I usually just follow my gut. I read at a shop yesterday and had spent the week before considering which I'd bring with me. I wound up bringing three, two of which weren't even under consideration the day prior. I also try to mix up the kinds of decks I use, so I'll work with Marseille-style or pip-style decks for a while, then I'll jump back to more Waite-Smith-based ones. Lately I've been working with Thoth-based decks, not because I'm drawn to anything Crowley stood for, but because there are so many stunning versions of it and I've recently gotten over my annoyance with the keywords or titles.

That's an example, in fact. For much of my life as a reader, I've loathed having keywords on the cards. Don't tell me how to read the damn things! But last year, not long before I began working on this book, I challenged myself to work *only* with decks emblazoned with keywords. I did this for a month, and then it extended into two—and the two decks I chose, I still reach for regularly. I did this because I constantly tell students not to avoid things they feel they don't like when it comes to reading. I say if you don't like Marseille-style decks, spend a week using nothing but that. You may never love it, but you will learn something. So, I did the same, and it changed me again. Where I used to see *only* the keyword, I now see additional context—just like the image. And that opens me up to more potential during a reading. The keyword or title may mean nothing to me, and frequently that's the case; sometimes, though, it changes the whole tone of the reading. I have a modern version of the Thoth deck that styles Justice as *Adjustment.*

Changing up your habits can shock you into new information. Generally, the brain wants to do as little work as possible, which makes sense because it's always working. But when we do the same thing over and over, we get dry. Working with a deck you don't like or a system you're not super comfortable with can open you up to the unexpected. Experimenting with spreads and techniques you usually wouldn't use can reveal ways of working with cards that you'd never expected. Just recently, I returned to my very first book on tarot and found several incredible spreads I'd never taken note of. I'm basing my entire next class on two of the layouts from that book. I came up with a new version of the Celtic Cross many years ago because I don't like the old one, but I liked the drama of the layout. Try new things. Surprise yourself with the unfamiliar. It's not going to be easy all the time, but it can be exciting and revolutionize what you do.

Get uncomfortable. We are so often held back by comfort, because the ego loves it. Growth and learning requires discomfort, as annoying as that is. It's actually been the main theme of this book, and as it winds down it's a good time to mention that again. Fortune tellers are students of the world, which means we're never done growing, never through trying, never finished experimenting. There's always a new technique or tactic that can be played with, altered, and incorporated into our toolkit.

Check My Flow

Here, I offer a kind of high-level summary of how I read, along with some commentary. This is really more for curiosity's sake than anything else. I think each reader needs to find their own way. What I describe below is my typical process as of this writing. Ask me again in a year, and there will likely be many subtle differences—and maybe some major ones, who knows? It's also worth knowing that I deviate from this as often as not. This is just what I've found I tend to do most.

Get Context. Here, the client and I are talking question or theme. I'm getting to know them a little and giving them a sense of what the reading will be like. I'll often remind them that this is their time and I want them to get what they want out of it. I also tell them that the more context they're willing to give me, the more specific I can be. But I also encourage them to share only to their level of comfort. We may do a little work on the question, particularly if the client has a hard time articulating what they want to know. This is where we can make sure we're on the same page. I'll also decide what reading techniques I'll use. Only then will I move on.

Shuffle and Draw. I used to have clients shuffle if we were together, but since the pandemic I don't. I shuffle and ask the client to tell me when to stop. If I'm reading on video and the client isn't there, I shuffle until my hands start feeling hot or if I tend to get two or three messy shuffles in a row (if I get a few messy shuffles, I assume the deck is telling me it's ready). I lay out the cards and move on to phase three.[50]

Scan and Receive. I'm generally quiet for a few moments while I let my eyes experience the cards and combinations. I note how many of each suit there are, how many of each number, what suits or numbers are missing. I'll note any interrelationships between the cards, the balance of elements, and anything that just strikes my eye. I'll also give a look to the images and keywords if there are any. If it's a pip deck, I'll explore whether the shapes of the tools on the cards indicate anything. Marseilles' style swords can often suggest something being trapped (closed) or freed (open) because of their configurations. I'm really just letting the reading wash over me without trying to "know" anything yet. If it's a relationship reading, I'm looking for cups and wands; if it's a business or money reading, I'm looking for pentacles.

Synthesize. Here, I start talking about what I'm seeing. This is the most difficult part to describe, because it's a series of repeated tasks: considering the cards in combination, considering how they relate to the theme or the question, drawing lines

---

50 My general spread is a nine-card box, three rows of three, with no positional meanings. They're just nine cards in a tight square. I put the middle card (second in the second row) down first and the top left (first of the first row) and will look at how they work together. This frequently becomes a bit of a thesis. It'll give me the theme of the reading if it's a general one or connect me to the theme if there is an actual question. But, again, I'm just exploring. This generally takes a couple minutes, not much longer, and sometimes it happens so fast I can leap right in before I've got all the cards out.

between them, and then giving that voice. It sounds really difficult, but it's just the act of interpreting. I don't even think about this part, which is another reason why it's hard to describe. The main point is that I'm bouncing back and forth between the question/theme and the card combos. I'm checking my interpretations against the theme so that I know I'm on the right track.

I'm also asking the client questions, engaging with them, getting their thoughts. I may have had a thesis that turns out not to be sound. I find this happening with the Justice card a lot. I always start by asking if the client is in social work, in some way. Often the answer is no. I bounce back to my other associations. I'm asking questions like, "How does this feel?" "How much does this resonate?" "How on track am I?" I try, but don't always succeed, to keep the questions open-ended. Closed (yes/no) questions tend to lead the client. People want to be agreeable, and so they give you the answer they think you want. Open-ended questions require them to be more honest.

This is the actual reading part of the reading, where I'm trying out translations and seeing if they fit. It's a series of experiments. In the case of my nine-card box, I'm reading the middle and top left cards together, then I'm reading the first row of three, then the second, then the third; after that, I read each column. I may add some lenormand techniques, like mirroring and knighting (usually knighting). This frequently gives me more confidence in what I already know. I've read that you can't learn anything from an astrological chart based on one sign/house/planet combo. If you want to know what someone is like in a relationship, you need to look at the whole chart—not just the "relationship" parts. This is similar. All the combos are more context and will either verify what I think or counter it. If it counters what I think, I bounce back to the question and re-interpret. I'm validating myself based on what I know about the cards, about the client, about the question, and anything else I pick up over the course of the reading. Sometimes—maybe too often—I'm bouncing it against my own worldview. I shouldn't, but I do.

Summarize. People remember the last thing you said, then the first, then whatever came in the middle—if they get that far. It's a good thing, at the end of a reading, to sum up what you've read as succinctly as possible. This makes it more likely the client will remember the important things. In a written reading, I usually put the summary first because that's what they came for. Then I say, "If you want to know how I got there, read on:" and I'll put in my "work." What I call the "math" of the reading—and you've seen me do that a few times herein.

In summarizing, I try to say as little as possible, and when done, to say nothing else. Of course, I still have to ask for the damn money—but that's okay, because most of the time they're already reaching for it.

That's it. That's how I read. If I'm reading lenormand, it's the same process. Same with bones, too. The specifics are different, but the overall method is the same. And what's happened is that in the process of developing that method, I've made it easier for me to read different systems. "All" I need is a foundation for each, and from there, the process is the same. It doesn't matter whether it's lenormand, sibilla, tarot, or charm casting—the process is simply looking at the layout of the pieces, how they work together, and what they "mean."

Meaning

I don't agree with those who say you don't need any training to read anything. I find the folks on social media who have been reading for ten minutes but proclaim to be "pros" cute but specious. It's more than simply describing a picture. It's also more than reciting memorized meanings from a book. That's how we start, that's the foundation, but it has to transcend that. It has to be *reading* and *interpretation,* not reciting. Meaning isn't what someone told you something means; it's what happens in the context of a reading—in the meeting of tool and question.

I learned from Camelia Elias to think of the lenormand cards not in terms of symbology ("the tower is *institutions*") but function ("the tower protects, isolates, imprisons..."). This turns out to be the key to reading just about *everything.* It is fundamental to how I interpret in every system. I know that there are common meanings for the lenormand cards and I know what they are. I know I'm not supposed to tarot-ize them by giving them any elasticity. On the other hand, I know that once I started approaching those cards for function over dogma, my readings started getting way more accurate, way clearer, and way more fun. The heart, say, *can* be love; but what is a heart? It's a pump. Man + Woman + Heart + Moon doesn't signal love; it signals a one-night stand. The heart is pumping, not loving. The moon isn't nobility or recognition, it's night. Sometimes things just are what they are.

My tarot meanings are the same. I'm not so much concerned with what The Tower *means* as what it's *doing*—particularly in this reading, at this moment in time. And this goes for sibilla, although I don't read that much anymore. Honestly, I don't enjoy it as much as other systems; though I appreciate it, because it helped me understand how to work with decks like it. It was the idea of thinking about what a Widower *is* (a partnered thing un-partnered) that helped me begin unlocking this way of thinking. All divination is, all reading is, is simply the act of contextualizing random arrays of detail in terms of life. That's not as hard as it sounds. And it's often really fucking fun.

Chapter Fifteen

In Conclusion

I asked, "How would this book like to conclude?"

I drew:

Eight of Pentacles (2), Three of Wands (1), Page of Wands (3)

Go forth with your passionate eye on the future of this work, do the lifelong work of learning and growing and exploring, and do so always with the deep full-bodied curiosity of the most loving scholar.

That's a pretty good summation of my philosophy about being a student, that's for sure. It's also, in many ways, a good approach to life, and learning how to approach life is one of the great missions of being human. We're always working towards an understanding of how to get through each moment, each day, each relationship, each job, each *everything*. And the truly amazing thing is that we have these tools—tarot, I Ching, astrology, channeling, whatever you like—that can actually help us make sense of things. If there's one thing I'm a zealot about, it's that there's something deeply cool about the fact that divination works—often astonishingly well. When we miss the mark in a reading, I tend to chalk it up more to the fallibility of being human than the potential inefficacy of divination. We're the variable, not it. But *way* more often than not, it's exceptionally effective.

I suppose I'm always somewhat of a zealot about the fortune teller's need to engage in the world around us. I thought for a while about calling this an approach to "engaged fortune telling," but that sounded too fancy, too effete. What I'm after here is humanity and humility. If it's anything, what I'm attempting to offer here is *humane* fortune telling—centered on the humanity of the client, whoever they may be. I'm interested in the fortune teller, in part, as a refuge from the ways so many of us are erased by society at large. Sitting with a good fortune teller, a client should know their humanity is in good hands, that we see their personhood, even if we don't understand it or identify with it. A client should expect that the realities of the world around them will be reflected in the reading, and that they won't face bypassing of any kind—spiritual, philosophical, or emotional. No one seeing any reader worth their salt should face the shame or shade that so many people experience in so many parts of their lives.

The problem is, so many people who I wish could read and understand this book won't do it. Many more may pick it up and say, "Oh, why does he have to be so *political* all the time?" To which I say, "How in hell can you think you're helping people when you think an individual's humanity is up for debate?" I follow up quickly with the answer: "You can't. You're actually hurting them." A healer who operates with hate in their heart can't heal any more than a rock ripped from the earth by impoverished children can heal. I hope to make that message as seductive as I can, but in reality, there's no room for negotiation. If we are reading for others, we hold their humanity in our hands for the duration of the reading—and, in some cases, long after. What we say can and will reverberate. I've experienced it and likely so have you. This is the deal we make. And if we refuse to hold up our end of the bargain, we're failing.

Divination the world over has been wrapped up in the political, if only because it has been used as a tool in the spread of colonialism and Christianity. Those two things, foisted on the world by people who claim enlightenment and the age of reason, have driven a wedge between humans and our contact with the divine. To reconnect at a personal level, and to serve as translator to it, is an incredibly revolutionary act. It is no more activism than posting on social media; on the other hand, the best way to get a choir to sing is to preach to them. By setting an example, we can show others the way. And we may even yield communities in which people never have to consider the politics inside because there won't be any.

I often marvel that I do this work. Everything in my childhood pointed *away* from it, almost to the point that it was designed to force me to swing so far in the other direction that I'd never go back to resisting it again. I don't know that I believe in "destiny," ironically, or that certain things are "meant to be." There are times, though, where I wonder whether this *was* an inevitability; whether I was being called to or pulled to this work. I said this the other day when I marveled at how tricky my entry to tarot was. Suddenly, I started seeing it everywhere, and I couldn't stop thinking about it. Once I bought a deck, well, I was hooked. It feels ordained in some way, but I also recognize that's probably ego. It's just an accident of being alive that I found it and managed to find a way to get good at it.

Finding a way is the main goal. You may agree with much of what I've written here, but that's only important to the extent that it motivates you to create your own path. My hope is that it is an engaged path, a humane path, a path of humility and humanity, and also a path of fun and joy and silliness. I hope that, too, for your clients.

IN CONCLUSION

And I hope you enjoyed this. I hope the Age of Aquarius does dawn and that a world of equity dawns with it. And I hope that, if nothing else, you had fun spending time with me.

As I always say at the end of my videos: take care, be good, and we'll talk soon (I hope)!

—Tom Benjamin
June 2024

RECOMMENDED READING & REFERENCES

Secrets of Romani Fortune-Telling by Jezmina Von Thiele and Paulina Stevens
The Tarot: History, Symbolism, and Divination by Robert M. Place
78 Acts of Liberation: Tarot to Transform Our World by Lane Smith
Sigil Witchery: A Witch's Guide to Crafting Magick Symbols by Laura Tempest Zakroff
Bones, Shells, and Curios: A Contemporary Method of Casting Bones by Michele Jackson
Tarot Reading Explained by James Ricklef
Astrology and the Authentic Self by Demetra George
Big Magic by Elizabeth Gilbert
Tarot for the Hard Work by Maria Minnis
Ego is the Enemy by Ryan Holiday
Bird by Bird by Anne Lamott
Tarot: The Open Reading by Yoav Ben-Dov
Telling Ain't Training by Harold Stolovitch and Erica J. Keeps
The Anti-Racist Writing Workshop: How to Decolonize the Creative Classroom by Felicia Rose Chavez
Thanks for the Feedback: The Science and Art of Receiving Feedback Well by Douglas Stone and Sheila Heen
Professional Tarot: The Business of Reading, Consulting, and Teaching by Christine Jette
The Coaching Habit by Michael Bungay Stanier
The Advice Trap by Michael Bungay Stanier
The Contemporary Astrologer's Handbook by Sue Tompkins
The Tarot Workbook: Understanding and Using Tarot Symbolism by Emily Peach
Hoodoo For Everyone: Modern Approaches to Magic, Conjure, Rootwork, and Liberation by Sherry Shone
The Hoodoo Guide to the Bible: Advice from a Real Hoodoo Worker by Sherry Shone
The Book of Séances: A Guide to Divination and Speaking to Spirits by Claire Goodchild

RECOMMENDED READING & REFERENCES

Tarot for Your Self by Mary K. Greer
The Practice of Ally Work: Meeting and Partnering with Your Spirit Guide in the Imaginal World by Jeffrey Raff
Reading the Marseille Tarot by Jean-Michel David
Hoodoo In America by Zora Neale Hurston, originally published in The Journal of American Folklore, Vol. 44, Dec 1931.

Recommended & Referenced Decks

Voyager Tarot by James Wanless and Ken Knutson
Sun and Moon Tarot by Vanessa Decort
Original Rider Waite Tarot Pack by U.S. Games Systems
The Antique Anatomy Tarot by Claire Goodchild
Clarity Tarot by Bel Senlle
Japaridze Tarot by Nino Japaridze
Margarete Petersen Tarot by Margarete Petersen
Starlight Illuminated by Carol Herzer

RECOMMENDED READINGS

[illegible] of Your Self by Mary K. Greer
The Practice of [illegible] Wellness with [illegible]
[illegible] by John [illegible]
[illegible] by Jean-Michel David
Hoodoo [illegible] by Zora Neale Hurston (originally published in The Journal of American Folklore, Vol. 44, No. 174)

Recommended by Reverend Dr. [illegible]

[illegible] by James [illegible]
[illegible] by [illegible]
[illegible] by [illegible]
[illegible]
[illegible]
[illegible]
[illegible]
[illegible]